OPEN FILES

A Narrative Encyclopedia
of the World's Greatest
Unsolved Crimes

by Jay Robert Nash

McGRAW-HILL BOOK COMPANY

New York   St. Louis   San Francisco   Bogotá   Guatemala
Hamburg   Lisbon   Madrid   Mexico   Montreal
Panama   Paris   San Juan   São Paulo   Tokyo   Toronto

123456789 DOCDOC 876543

ISBN 0-07-045907-X

LIBRARY OF CONGRESS
CATALOGING IN PUBLICATION DATA
Nash, Jay Robert.
Open files.
Includes index.
1. Crime and criminals—Case
studies.   I. Title.
HV6779.N37 1983   364.1   82–22870
ISBN 0–07–045907–X (pbk.)

Book design by Suzanne Haldane

Acknowledgments

I am indebted to many people who aided me in
the research on this book. Deepest gratitude is extended to my conscientious research associate,
Cathy Anetsberger, and my indefatigable typist,
Sandy Horeis.

Those who provided printed material, graphics,
correspondence, and memorabilia include Neil
and Vicky Nash, Jack Jules Klein, Jr., Leonard
Des Jardins, Bill and Edie Kelly, Jerry Goldberg,
Neal and Joan Amidei, Sydney Harris, P. Michael
O'Sullivan, Curt and Betty Johnson, Hank
Oettinger, Jack Conroy, Ray Peekner, Raymond
Friday Locke, Bob and Linda Connelly, Les
Susman,

Arthur von Kluge, Bruce Elliot, Michaela
Tuohy, George Spink, Mark and Lois Jacobs,
Edgar Krebs, Jim and Edie McCormick, Mike and
June Lavelle.

Cinemabilia and The Memory Shop of New
York were particularly helpful in providing certain
graphics, as was the New York Historical Society
and the New York Public Library. Newspaper librarians were of particular help, and my special
thanks go to Lynette Francis, librarian for the San
Francisco Chronicle; Susanna Schuster, editorial research librarian for the Los Angeles Times;

Dorothy Frazier of the Denver Post: the librarians of the Chicago Tribune, Chicago Sun-Times,
and the New York Times.

Librarians and archivists throughout the United
States were also of great help, and these include
Sandra Lynn Medinger, administrative staff assist-
ant of the Nebraska State Archives in Lincoln;
Kevin Carey of the University of Illinois Library;
Melanie Dodson and Ree Dedonato of Northwest-
ern University Library; Jerry Delaney of the Chi-
cago Public Library; Peter Weil, of the microfilm
division, and the staff of the Newberry Library of
Chicago; Pat Wilcoxon, Regenstein Library, Uni-
versity of Chicago, and the staff of the Law Li-
brary of the University of Chicago; the Chicago
Historical Society; the San Francisco Historical
Society.

Many law enforcement officials and officers
were extremely helpful; these include Sergeant
Tony Consieldi of the Chicago Police Department
and the Task Force investigating the Detroit children slayings of 1976–77.

This book is for Norma and Ray

PREFACE

In the past I have written extensively about crime and known criminals throughout the world. It has been an abiding personal passion, however, to delve into those cases that have baffled police around the globe for several centuries. There are thousands of mystifying crimes that could have been included in this volume had there been space. Since there was not, I attempted to include not only the most infamous cases we still retain in memory, but those that made a sensational impact upon the times and society in which they occurred.

The so-called classic cases—the Black Dahlia, Lizzie Borden, Jack the Ripper, William Desmond Taylor, and Julia Wallace—are amply represented, of course, but cases little known today have also received particular attention. These include the inexplicable and devastating mass murder sprees enacted by the Ax Man of New Orleans, the Mad Butcher of Cleveland, the Texas Strangler, and the San Francisco fiend who called himself Zodiac. Moreover, the great unsolved cases of deep history—the killing of Lord Henry Darnley in Scotland, the perplexing slaying of Sir Edmund Barry Godfrey in England, the enigmatic murder of Elma Sands, New York's first classic unsolved killing—necessarily have been included by virtue of their high standing in the annals of crime.

Professional criminals have not been ignored, especially those members of organized crime ostensibly eradicated by killers unknown who came from their own ranks. The strange deaths of Albert Anastasia, Big Jim Colosimo, Sam Giancana, Dion O'Bannion, Bugsy Siegel, still haunt crime historians to this day. There is a phalanx of street people, from gamblers to hustlers, who wink knowingly at the mention of these once dreaded gangsters and mouth the identities of their killers, with a perverse pride of possessing an insider's sacrosanct secret. But they do not know the real culprits, most of them, any more than do the police and the best investigative reporters in the land. (It is close to a certainty that the late Meyer Lansky would have had much to say, if he would have ever talked about the murder of his friend and cohort Benjamin Siegel.

Many of the cases profiled herein are so puzzling as to render the immortal Sherlock helpless and leave the best armchair detective staring into space while pondering these inexplicable events and bizarre personalities.

These studies of the macabre might nag the reader as they did the author, but they should also provide more thought-provoking inquiry than any fictional whodunit. These cases are the real whodunits, the cases that inspired the best detective and mystery writers in the world to pen their books and stories.

In this instance the reader's conclusions are equal, perhaps superior, to that of any master mystery writer, police inspector, or academic criminologist, if conclusions can be reached from the known clues on hand, and often these are miserably scant—sometimes, as in the Julia Wallace case, almost non-existent. All of them are real-life riddles that have challenged the best minds of detection and have triumphed in keeping their sinister secrets. Although I have given my own views in many of these cases, in the final analysis it is for the reader to unlock these forbidding doors and, alone, go down these shadowy halls where notorious phantoms wait.

—Jay Robert Nash
CHICAGO, 1982

Ananda, King of Siam

ASSASSINATION, 1946 THAILAND

Ananda, king of Siam (1926–1946), was an unwilling and unlikely ruler of a fairy-tale kingdom. He was born to Siam's Prince Mahidol and a commoner named Sang-wala. His parents met and married in the United States while Mahidol was study-ing medicine at Harvard and Sangwala attended the Massachusetts Nursing Col-lege. They returned to Siam (now Thai-land), living in the royal palace in Bangkok where, years before, Sangwala had been a maid of honor.

Shortly after Prince Mahidol died of a sudden illness, Sangwala, feeling that court nobles hated her for being a commoner, decided to take her three children to Switzerland. Ananda, oldest of the three boys and heir to the Siamese throne, was raised and educated in Lausanne while his heavy-handed uncle, King Prajahipok, ruled Siam. The king learned of an im-pending uprising in 1935 and fled to Eng-land, abdicating in favor of nine-year-old Ananda. A council of regents ruled in the boy's stead until 1938, when twelve-year-old Ananda was taken to Siam aboard a destroyer which sailed up the Menam River while hundreds of thousands of Siamese lined the banks to cheer their youthful monarch.

Ananda was overwhelmed by the re-ception and was quite confused by the role he was forced to enact, presiding at parades, religious rites, and state affairs and receiving callers from all parts of the world. His mother finally managed to persuade the regents to allow her son to finish his Swiss education, and the boy returned to Lausanne. Upon his arrival in Switzerland the shy youth told newsmen: "I don't think it's much fun to be a king. I would rather stay here and play with my electric trains."

Throughout the years of World War II Ananda did stay in Switzerland, playing with his trains and finishing high school while his country was invaded by Japa-nese troops. The Siamese army, such as it was, put up only token resistance to the invaders, laying down its arms after one day of combat on orders of the country's Quisling, Marshal Phibul Songgram, the pro-Japanese regent who happily entered Siam into Japan's so-called Greater East Asian Co-Prosperity Sphere, and then

Siam's King Ananda (*left*) flanked by his younger brother, Pumipol.

gratuitously declared war on the Allies.

Marshal Phibul ordered his troops to act as guards, showing little mercy, to Allied prisoners captured by the Japanese. For this and other cruel acts, the marshal was placed on trial as a war criminal following the Allied victory in Siam in 1945. He was imprisoned, then released. At that time Nai Pridi, a Siamese patriot who had led the resistance movement against the Japanese throughout the war, took over the government. Pridi invited Ananda to assume his rightful place as king of Siam. A British bomber delivered the nineteen-year-old monarch to Bangkok in December 1945.

Ananda's position was not that of a supreme king, absolutism having been overthrown in a 1932 revolution. Yet he was not a titular monarch either, but shared power with a legislature half elected by the people, half appointed by the court. The new king was a democrat at heart and shocked his advisers when he told them that he planned within a few years to abdicate, turn Siam into a republic, and run for the office of prime minister. He never lived long enough to enact his noble plan.

Late on June 7, 1946, King Ananda was suddenly bed-ridden with a severe stomach ailment. He did not recover until June 9, when he weakly sat up in bed to take some medicine. At about 9 AM on that day a shot rang out from the royal bedchamber. Chat Singhaseni and Butr Pathamasirind, the two royal pages stationed outside the bedchamber door, rushed inside, Sinhaseni later testified, to find the king lying on the floor in a widening pool of blood, a bullet in his head. Sangwala was summoned, and she held her son for some time until physicians arrived to pronounce Ananda dead. The doctors were followed by scores of court officials, department heads, and royal ministers who knelt in obeisance.

Only hours later officials gave out the report that Ananda had died as the result of an accident, that earlier he had been "inspecting an automatic by looking into the muzzle and remarking that its mechanism was very light to handle. . . . It would seem that he had once more inspected this automatic in a similar manner, not checking first whether it was loaded or not, and that while doing so he must have touched the trigger and thereby accidentally shot himself in the forehead."

The official announcement was, of course, preposterous. Ananda, an expert with guns, would never have casually inspected a weapon in that manner when it was loaded. Moreover, he had been violently ill for two days and it was unlikely that, at the moment of his recovery, he would have leaped from his bed and begun to inspect his guns.

Ananda was cleaned up and put on display under a huge gold canopy outside the palace. The bullet wound in his head, however, was quite visible. Tens of thousands of his subjects lined up to pay their respects. As they passed the king's bier, they knelt briefly before their dead king and banged their heads against the ground as if doing penance. The king's younger brother, eighteen-year-old Pumipol,

was promptly named monarch and the matter was officially dropped.

The Siamese people, however, refused to believe the impossible story put out about Ananda's death and demanded an official inquiry. No powder burns had been found on Ananda's head, many said. This proved that the king had not shot himself at the close range described by authorities. To counter this claim, a detective sent by Bangkok's chief of police appeared at the palace leading a pig on a leash. Before officials he held a pistol close to the pig's head and fired. As the animal lay dying in the middle of the grand reception hall, the detective proudly announced: "You see—it is as we have told you. No powder burns!"

Then convened a host of physicians who closely examined Ananda's wound before the king was buried. Fourteen out of eighteen doctors announced that Ananda had been assassinated, not felled by an accidental bullet. Investigations and interrogations continued through 1947. On November 8 of that year Marshal Phibul Songgram, the onetime war criminal, took over Siam in a bloodless military coup. The ex-resistance fighter and Phibul's political foe, Pridi, fled with his followers to Singapore. Phibul announced that his old opponent was a Communist and was probably responsible for the assassination of King Ananda. The reason for his takeover of Siam, said the marshal, was to ferret out the traitors who had slain the king and to keep communism out of the country. To prove to the world that he meant to give his nation a new image,

Phibul, along with the legislature, changed Siam's name to Thailand.

Using Ananda's murder as a reason to purge his political enemies, Phibul ordered the arrest of thousands of suspects who were questioned while chained to dungeon walls in the bowels of the Bangkok palace. Many "suspects" were arrested and shot to death en route to prison, while "attempting to escape." The political pogrom went on for almost nine years until the two royal pages who had been posted outside Ananda's door were arrested in 1955. They were strapped to crosses and then machine-gunned to death.

The real assassin of the king of Siam and the persons from whom he took his orders were never identified.

Anastasia, Albert
SYNDICATE KILLING, 1957   U.S.

The most lethal Mafia killer in the United States, Albert Anastasia, known as the Lord High Executioner and personally responsible for *at least* sixty murders, was himself killed in spectacular gangland style on Friday, October 25, 1957, as he sat in a barber chair in the basement of New York's Park Sheraton Hotel. He was a man no one missed, especially those who had worked their way up the Mafia ladder with him.

Anastasia's beginnings were humble. Born Umberto Anastasio of dirt-poor parents in Tropea, Italy, in 1903, he left school at twelve and later worked his way to the United States aboard a tramp steamer, arriving in 1917. The burly Anastasia—he had changed his name for arcane reasons—found work as a longshoreman on the docks of New York Harbor. He was a brawler and won his fights speedily and brutally, acts that brought him to the attention of local Mafia leaders, who initiated Anastasia into the society in 1919.

He was made a sub-boss of several unions, and within a few years he became rich directing the waterfront smuggling of illegal liquor into New York. Prohibition had just gone into effect, a badly conceived law that employed more than a million people, gleaned revenues exceeding $500 million, and firmly planted the seeds of organized crime.

Anastasia's immediate superior was a snarling psychopathic punk named Salvatore Charles "Lucky" Luciano, to whom he showed slavish submission. It was Luciano who came to Anastasia in 1921 with his first murder assignment. He was to kill George Turello, a longshoreman who had informed authorities about illegal shipments of alcohol. Anastasia strangled the man while an accomplice held the victim. The two men were seen by four witnesses and were promptly arrested and convicted. Anastasia was sentenced to death and spent eighteen months on Death Row in Sing Sing waiting for the electric chair. Expensive criminal lawyers hired by the Mafia, however, managed to get Anastasia a new trial. Before this trial took place the four witnesses against the youthful killer vanished. Over the years this would become the usual procedure in Mafia murders. Albert Anastasia was to commit sixty-three of them by most reliable accounts, but the number of killings he personally handled may have been twice that number.

There were more arrests but few convictions. When authorities could not send Anastasia to prison for murder they arrested him in June 1923 for carrying a concealed weapon. He received a two-year prison sentence and served every day of it. When he emerged he was considered a Mafia hero; the uneducated, brutish Albert moved upward in the hierarchy of the society, taking over the New York longshoremen's union as steward for six locals. Any dock workers who refused to kick back for their jobs were beaten. If they refused more than once they were murdered.

When a left-wing longshoreman named Peter Panto stood up for fellow members against the Mafia goons, Albert ordered him killed. When union business agent Morris Diamond complained that complete cargoes were not being delivered to warehouses, Albert explained that his society always took a percentage of all shipments. Diamond threatened to go to the police and Albert ordered him killed. So proficient at murder was Anastasia that he was asked by a Mafia don to arrange killings outside the organization. Anastasia obligingly stabbed a Brooklyn businessman named Joseph Santoro with an ice pick. Though he was arrested for the murder, Albert was quickly acquitted for lack

Albert Anastasia, the mob's "Lord High Executioner," who was gunned down by unknown killers in 1957.

of evidence. Anastasia's reputation as a man who killed without asking questions soon established him as the Mafia's chief enforcer in New York. To that end he set up the most lethal branch of the society ever to terrorize America—Murder, Inc.

Anastasia made the Brownsville section of Brooklyn his headquarters. He put every cold-eyed killer he could muster on his payroll—Mendy Weiss, "Pittsburgh Phil" Strauss, "Happy" Maione, Louis Capone (no relation to Chicago's Al "Scarface" Capone), Charles "The Bug" Workman (who was responsible for wiping out Dutch Schultz and his mob in a New Jersey restaurant in 1935), Abe "Kid Twist" Reles, and many more. Albert instructed his men either to stab their victims with an ice pick or to strangle them with a scarf. Both were sure weapons and silent. Moreover, knowing that the average gangster was a poor shot and that guns could be easily traced, he outlawed them. Anastasia was also responsible for establishing the chilling code words "contract" (meaning a murder assignment) and "hit" (the actual murder), so that police using wiretaps would be misled.

All of this ritual was approved by Anastasia's nominal boss, Louis "Lepke" Buchalter, a charter member of the newly born national crime syndicate. The syndicate board also heartily approved of the hundreds of expeditious killings performed by Anastasia's "troop," so much so that Albert was ordered to send his "soldiers" out to murder not only rival or truculent gang members but average citizens who stood in the way of Mafia-syn-

dicate profits. Hundreds more died by the ice pick and the scarf.

It was also Anastasia who developed the system of using out-of-town killers as he expanded Murder, Inc. on a nationwide basis. His Brownsville-based killers would fly to Chicago if someone in that city was marked for death. If a New York contract was to be filled, Anastasia's killers in Chicago, Kansas City, or St. Louis would travel to New York to perform the hit. The killers were paid handsomely, earning yearly salaries equal to bank presidents'; Anastasia, coupled to his waterfront rackets, became a millionaire in the murder business.

The police were almost helpless to act against such an organization. Unknown men would suddenly appear, kill a citizen, then disappear, their identities completely unknown in the city where the killing was done, their motives a mystery. The riddle to the mass killings was finally explained when Abe "Kid Twist" Reles and a few of his minions began to inform on Murder, Inc. Reles defected to the law to avoid prosecution for murder and also because he enjoyed the limelight. He talked long and loud, his statements supported by other informants. His testimony was enough to send Maione, Strauss, Capone, Weiss, and even Buchalter to the chair. (Lepke's execution marked the first and last time a board member of the national crime cartel was given capital punishment.) Before Reles could get around to his boss, Anastasia, he fell or was pushed, falling five floors to his death, from a window at the Half Moon Hotel in Coney

Island where he was being held and while he was being guarded by a half-dozen police officers.

Anastasia's name later came up when a small-time hoodlum, Tony Romeo, who had been present when Albert murdered Joseph Santoro, turned state's evidence. Romeo never made it to court. He was abducted from a New York street and driven to Delaware. There, on a lonely road, he was tortured, beaten, then killed. According to Burton B. Turkus, the assistant district attorney prosecuting Murder, Inc. members, Romeo's "head and chest had been blasted by bullets. He had apparently been given a vicious beating first—the treatment the mob ordinarily accords a suspected 'canary,' or one with songbird proclivities. His head was bashed in, the jaw fractured. He was one mass of bruises."

Anastasia was the "one big fish" who escaped the net of lawmen and prosecutors in their dogged pursuit and convictions of Murder, Inc.'s killers. By the late 1940s Albert took over the Vincent Mangano Mafia family. (This was one of the five ruling Mafia families in New York; following Anastasia's murder he was succeeded by Carlo Gambino, the most durable and powerful of all the Mafia dons.) Power, riches, even a gloss of respectability came to the brutish Anastasia. He purchased a luxurious home in New Jersey and began to invest in legitimate businesses. He wanted a new image, and to achieve it he spent money lavishly. To cover these expenditures, Anastasia began to look about at the greenback fields of his fellow syndicate board directors.

Frank Costello at the time controlled all gambling in New York, a lucrative racket that brought the syndicate's "prime minister" untold millions. Anastasia decided to move into this gambling empire. Costello complained to the board, and Anastasia was warned by the family dons to stay with his own waterfront rackets. Not only did Albert ignore the warning but ordered one of his goons, Vincente "the Chin" Gigante, to kill Costello.

The towering killer bushwhacked Costello as he was entering his posh apartment building on Central Park West on the night of May 2, 1957. "This is for you, Frank!" Gigante yelled and fired a shot that creased Costello's skull. Gigante then ran off.

Everyone, including Costello, knew that Anastasia was behind the attack, but no action was taken. A few weeks later Anastasia approached the syndicate's treasurer, Meyer Lansky, who had years earlier financed Fulgencio Batista's military takeover of Cuba. In turn Batista, in the early 1930s, allowed Lansky to set up enormous gambling operations—for a $1 million guaranteed cut of the profits each year—throughout Cuba. Lansky made millions, kicking back a fortune to the national crime cartel which approved and manned Lansky's operations. Now Anastasia wanted to go into Cuba and take over the gambling there. He told Meyer Lansky so.

"Batista doesn't want you on his island, Albert," Lansky calmly told Anastasia. "He told me to tell you to stay out."

Powerful and lethal New York Mafia boss Vito Genovese, the man who may have ordered the murder of Anastasia.

Albert's florid face reddened, and, in front of several witnesses, he roared: "I'm going to Cuba no matter what he says! Now you tell him that from me!"

Albert Anastasia never went to Cuba; neither did any of his killers. The Lord High Executioner was still making plans to invade the island—possibly to depose Batista or to assassinate him if necessary—when he met with Santo Trafficante, a sub-boss of the Vito Genovese family, on October 24, 1957. Albert and Trafficante dined at the Park Sheraton Hotel, where Trafficante was staying at the time. After dinner Trafficante abruptly stood up, leaned over, and kissed Anastasia on the cheek, according to one report. This, of course, was Mafia ritual indicating an execution was at hand. It was the kiss of death, and the execution was scheduled for Albert Anastasia. Whether the power-mad Vito Genovese or Costello or Lansky had planned the killing is not known. But it was planned.

At about 10 AM the following day Anastasia entered the barbershop in the basement of the Park Sheraton on Seventh Avenue. He was alone; Tony Coppola, his bodyguard, oddly enough, was having a cup of coffee across the street. He later explained that he had asked permission to do so and Anastasia had nodded agreement.

No one was in the barbershop except one barber. Anastasia moved his heavy form—he had by now grown fat and jowly—to one of the chairs and snarled: "Make it short!" The barber quickly shaved the Mafia killer, then curled a hot towel around his face and prepared to clip Anastasia's hair.

Two men suddenly walked into the shop. They wore wide-brimmed hats bent low over their faces, sunglasses, and gloves. They pulled out guns and advanced on the chair occupied by Anastasia. The terrified barber leaped away from chair number four.

"Keep your mouth shut if you don't want your head blown off!" yelled one of the gunmen to the barber.

Hearing the words, Anastasia whipped away the towel and tried to struggle out of the chair. He was unarmed. The gunmen opened up only five feet from the deadliest killer in America. Of the ten shots they fired, only five struck their target. Two bullets tore through Anastasia's left arm, one smacked into his right hip, one more plowed into his back, and one crashed through his skull, killing him. Albert fell to the floor, his outstretched arm shooting along a counter and smashing all the hair tonic bottles.

The gunmen fled only after kneeling at Anastasia's prone body to make sure he was dead. They did not take the expensive diamond rings glittering on the don's pudgy fingers nor rifle his pockets to take the $1,900 he was carrying in his wallet.

Police arrived to find the murder weapons, a .38-caliber Colt revolver and a long-barreled Smith & Wesson, near the hotel exit where the killers had casually dropped them. Neither bore fingerprints. They were subsequently traced to Chicago and Indiana, which indicated that the hit men were from out of state, ironically following the procedure that Anastasia himself set up when entering the murder business almost thirty years earlier.

No one ever identified Anastasia's killers, and to this day it is uncertain exactly who ordered the Lord High Executioner executed. Just about everyone who knew him had a reason to want Albert Anastasia dead. He had spent his life seeing to that.

Anderson, Judith Mae
MURDER, 1957 U.S.

On the night of August 15–16, 1957, fifteen-year-old Judith Mae Anderson of Chicago visited a girl friend and then began walking home from 1019 North Central, the address of her friend's house. Judith, described as heavyset but attractive, never arrived home, a mile distant. She was declared missing.

Almost a week later to the day of the girl's disappearance, the chopped-up remains of Judith Anderson surfaced inside fifty-five-gallon drums floating in Montrose Harbor. One drum contained the teenager's head, which had received four .32-caliber bullets.

Investigators learned that Judy Mae had been working in part-time telephone sales for the Patricia Stevens Modeling Agency downtown. A co-worker told police that an unknown man had called Judy Mae in January 1957, asking for a date. When he was refused he shouted over the phone: "You'll be sorry." That day at lunch Judy and her co-workers noticed a tall young man with bushy hair staring at them in the drugstore where they ate. This was the only clue police had to go on.

A short time later Chicago police arrested a tall, muscular youth with bushy hair named Barry Cook, who had had a record of assaults on young women. He was tried for the Anderson killing, along with the murder of middle-aged Margaret Gallagher, who had been dragged into some bushes and strangled on Foster Beach, but was acquitted for lack of evidence. Cook nevertheless was convicted of aggravated assault and attempted rape in other cases and was sent to Statesville Penitentiary, where he served eleven years. He was released in 1967. (At this writing Cook resides in Houston, Texas.)

In all, more than ten thousand persons were questioned in the Anderson case, and more than two thousand suspects were investigated. Scores of possible killers were put through lie detector tests. Yet the identity of the killer of Judith Mae Anderson was never determined.

Anderson, Thomas Weldon
MURDER, 1910 ENGLAND

One of the strangest and most perplexing unsolved murders in modern England was that of Thomas Weldon Anderson, a middle-aged actor found shot to death in the backyard of his mistress's home in a London suburb on June 16, 1910. Anderson, who acted under the name of Atherstone, had been separated from his wife for ten years and lived with a mistress at 17 Clifton Gardens on Prince of Wales Road in Battersea Park. The couple at first dwelled in a basement apartment at this address, then moved to the flat above.

Anderson's mistress proved to be a kind, understanding woman who acted as a mother to the actor's two teenage sons. Yet she and Anderson often quarreled violently and this led to the actor's decision to leave in early June 1910, taking up a new residence at King's Cross. He met with his seventeen-year-old son and learned that the youth was to have dinner with the mistress on the night of June 16—strictly a mother-son type of meeting. Anderson gave his approval but told his son he would not attend the dinner.

On the night of June 16, 1910, the mistress and Anderson's son were dining in the Clifton Gardens flat when they heard two shots in the backyard. They ran outside to see a small, powerfully built man scrambling over a high brick wall that adjoined the house next door. Not until police arrived a half hour later was Thomas Anderson found crumpled beneath the back staircase next to the door of the empty basement apartment. He was dead, shot twice.

Anderson's assailant had not altogether disappeared. He had been seen by several people as he scaled the wall, dropped to the other side, and raced pell-mell down several streets toward the Thames River. He was described as young, well-built but extremely small, no more than five feet three inches. The man utterly vanished down the dark streets near the river.

The actor had been shot twice after what appeared to Scotland Yard detectives to be a violent struggle with the little man. Oddly, Anderson was found wearing slippers. His boots, wrapped in brown paper, were found on the mantelpiece of the empty basement apartment. Even more odd was a package found in the actor's hip pocket, one wrapped in paper, tied with a string, and containing an eighteen-inch-long strip of cable, one which armchair detectives later thought to be a possible murder weapon, but intended for whom?

There were more questions than answers in the Anderson killing, and they kept coming over the years until the case assumed the legendary proportions of the classic murder mystery. It was speculated that Anderson had crept into the empty basement apartment beneath that occupied by his mistress, removed his boots, and donned slippers so that his movements could not be heard as he prepared to murder the woman he had lived with. Yet this seemed more than improbable in that he had encouraged his son to dine with his mistress. He loved the boy so much that he would never had done him harm and would have had to deal with him if he had attacked the mistress.

The appearance of the little man was even more baffling. Were Anderson and the assailant in league together, many asked, falling out at the last moment before committing murder? It was also

thought that the two met by mere chance that night, Anderson on his way to perform some other crime, the little man merely a burglar who thought to break into the basement apartment and who bumped into the actor, struggled with him, then, in panic shot him to death. Then again, why would any experienced burglar want to break into an obviously empty apartment?

None of these questions has been answered in the eight decades since Thomas Weldon Anderson went to his death.

Ann Arbor Murders
HOSPITAL SLAYINGS, 1975 U.S.

Panic seized the staff of the Veterans Administration Hospital in Ann Arbor, Michigan, in the summer of 1975. Patients were dying of respiratory arrests at an alarming rate and no one could initially explain the causes. Rumors flew to print that as many as forty men had perished and that their deaths were not only inexplicable, but that someone was undoubtedly behind the cardiac failures resulting from simple loss of breath. Since the hospital was federal property and under jurisdiction of the federal government, FBI agents were called in to investigate. In late August officials reluctantly declared that eight men had died from unnatural causes and that it was obvious that a killer was loose in the hospital wards.

In mid-August twenty-three of the hospital's patients suffered heart failure or stoppage of breathing. The crisis reached its peak on August 15 when seven patients suffered lung and heart failure and during one hour the entire staff of physicians was frantically trying to save three men. Four of the seven died. There were others, FBI agents later stated: eleven out of fifty-six patients who had been stricken with breathing failures died in a six-week period, from July 1 to August 15, 1975, six times the usual number.

Bureau experts analyzed the urine of the afflicted patients and discovered that a drug, deadly and exotic, had been added to the dextrose and water solutions being administered to these patients. The drug was determined to be Pavulon, a muscle relaxant and derivative of curare, a vegetable poison South American Indians ritualistically used on blow-gun darts to paralyze enemies and animals.

Pavulon, kept under lock and key in the hospital and used only in certain surgical cases where artificial lungs were involved, was available only to staff members. Someone had gained access to the drug and had either injected the victims directly or had dosed the intravenous medication that fed the patients. Although several of the patients who died were elderly, many were in their forties and, in the case of the younger men, it was concluded that it required heavy doses of Pavulon to kill them.

A careful FBI hunt for the culprit ensued. Authorities refused to comment on the investigation for almost a year. Then, in mid-June 1976, two nurses, Leonora M. Perez, thirty-one, and Filipina B.

12

Narcisco, thirty, were indicted on several counts of murder. Natives of the Philippines, the nurses, it was reported, were the only ones on duty and in the immediate area of the patients when they were stricken. Both nurses were imprisoned pending trial and insisted from the onset that they were innocent.

At their trial, the prosecution hammered away at the nurses' exclusive access to the victims at the times they were stricken. Family members of the deceased recalled seeing the two Filipinos in and out of the victims' rooms at the times of the seizures. Yet no one actually saw Perez or Narcisco administer the drug Pavulon—or any drug, for that matter—before the respiratory failures. This point was made repeatedly by the defense.

Worse for the prosecution, no real motive for the mass killings could be established. It was hinted that euthanasia—the mercy killing of hopeless cases—had been put into practice by the nurses, but this could apply only to a few of the victims, most of whom had been expected to recover from minor ailments. One young victim was suffering only from a smashed elbow. Rumors outside the courtroom had it that the Filipinos simply hated Americans or that they sought revenge for their poorly paid, overworked medical positions. (Filipinos dominate many U.S. hospital nursing staffs, a work force that has proven to be cheap and manageable in that it has little or no citizen status, and its members are on special work visas and cannot resort to union activity to improve their status and treatment.)

Lack of evidence against the Filipinos

compelled the court in June 1977 to drop all the murder charges against Perez and Narcisco. Three months later the nurses were put under psychiatric observation and studied. Their behavioral patterns appeared normal. (There was nothing in the nurses' background to suggest criminal tendencies.) They underwent a new trial in December 1977 and indictments against them were dismissed in February 1978. They were set free.

The mass killings in Ann Arbor remain a mystery, one that has hospital directors shuddering with apprehension to this day.

Avery, William H.
MURDER, 1890 U.S.

A wealthy businessman, William H. Avery of Fort Collins, Colorado, contracted a strange illness in early May 1890. Despite the attentions of several doctors, the banker's intestinal pains grew more and more acute. Physicians were also at a loss to explain his incredible thirst. The thirty-six-year-old Avery died in screaming agony on June 2, 1890, and was promptly buried, a victim of an inexplicable malady, decreed the coroner.

Suspicion among the local inhabitants arose, however, when Avery's young and attractive wife, Mary, ran off with the banker's junior partner, one Frank Millington. Avery was only two weeks in his grave when Millington married the ungrieving widow. The couple returned to Fort Collins on the Fourth of July, and their open display of carefree love soon

William H. Avery, wealthy businessman who was mysteriously poisoned in Fort Collins, Colorado, in 1890. (*Courtesy Denver Public Library*)

Mary Avery, who stood accused of murdering her abusive husband. (*Courtesy Denver Public Library*)

caused residents to state above a whisper that the pair had murdered the hapless Mr. Avery. One man, Avery's brother, also a wealthy banker, thundered his suspicions, telling all who would listen that Mary and Millington had poisoned his brother to obtain his $100,000 estate. He demanded the exhumation of Avery's body. The corpse was dug up and examined, and a coroner's jury convened shortly thereafter.

To capacitate an overflow throng, authorities held the hearings in the Fort Collins Opera House. Spectators heard Mrs. Avery-Millington state that there had been no discord in her marriage to Avery and that Avery had amiably agreed to a quiet divorce so that she could marry his junior partner. Further, she added that her departed spouse had generously offered to give her a $30,000 settlement. The idea that she and Millington would murder Avery was preposterous, snorted Mrs. Avery-Millington.

Other witnesses came forward, however, to testify that the Avery marriage had been anything but blissful. One of the family servants stated that Avery was in the habit of kicking his wife. She burned up a dinner once and the banker kicked his wife in the behind. On another occasion, Avery, his wife, and their fourteen-year-old daughter, Pearl, were returning home via train from an eastern vacation. The banker, typical of his selfish nature, had reserved a sleeping berth only for himself, leaving his wife and child to sit up several nights in the coach. Mrs. Avery protested and Avery kicked her again, so hard that she went flying down a train aisle in full view of guffawing passengers.

Defense attorneys for the Millingtons produced doctors who insisted that they had examined the corpse and found no poison, that the stricken man had died of "intense gastritis," from which he had suffered since childhood. Arsenic was at hand, they said, but only externally as a result of sulphuric acid sprinkled about the viscera to suppress the death odor when the body was briefly put on display before mourners.

The prosecution produced an equal number of physicians to claim that arsenic had been found in Avery's system. Moreover, one of Avery's maids stated that Millington was present in Avery's home on many occasions when the banker was at work and spent a good deal of time in Mrs. Avery's bedroom. She had witnessed Millington actually helping Mrs. Avery to dress one evening. Even more shocking was the maid's description of how Millington's eighteen-year-old sister, Dillie, appeared one night at the Avery house, thinly disguised as an old woman and delivered a mysterious package to Mrs. Avery. Only hours later the banker grew agonizingly ill. The package, thundered the prosecution, certainly contained the arsenic that killed Avery.

This story moved the coroner's jury to indict the Millingtons, including Dillie, on a charge of murder. The citizens of Fort Collins grew so menacing toward the Millingtons that the resulting trial was moved to Denver. But, again, the hear-

Spectators, eager to witness the scandal-ridden Avery trial, rush for seats in the makeshift courtroom. (*Courtesy Denver Public Library*)

Jury members were put to sleep at the Avery trial by long-winded testimony. (*Courtesy Denver Public Library*)

ings were dominated by enormous crowds, which were somewhat appeased when the trial was held in the huge Chamber of Commerce building. The crowds were raucous and often violent, men and women struggling for a place to stand in the makeshift courtroom.

The sensation created by the trial was used to good advantage by defense attorneys, who argued that the Millingtons were not really standing trial for murder but for their sexual indiscretions. The prosecution kept hammering away at the poison angle, although it discarded the notion that Dillie Millington had delivered the lethal stuff to Mrs. Avery. A pharmacist testified that Mrs. Avery's daughter had purchased poison from him, buying a large quantity of a product called Rough On Rats.

Pearl Avery then took the stand to deny innocently and convincingly that she had ever bought Rough On Rats. "I don't even know what that stuff is," she pleaded.

The prosecution countered with its top forensic expert, Dr. Walter S. Haines, who traveled from Chicago to testify, at a fee of $7,000, that he had removed enough arsenic from Avery's body "to kill more than two dozen people."

More medical experts were brought in by the defense to attack Haines's findings. The trial dragged on for weeks, with more than three million words entered into the trial transcript. The jury and the spectators were ground into torpor by the droning testimony of witnesses and long-winded speeches by lawyers. The once sensational trial lapsed into tedious hours of endless boredom.

At the end the jury yawned a not guilty verdict. Members felt that there was a reasonable doubt that the Millingtons had dosed the wife-kicking William Avery with arsenic. The defendants were released, but they did not enter a life of luxury. They had spent more than $25,000 on their defense, draining the Avery fortune. About three years later Mary and Frank Millington broke up, with Mary dying a few years later.

The poisonous death of William H. Avery was never solved.

Ax Man of New Orleans, The
MURDERS, 1911–19 U.S.

In 1911 New Orleans suffered three terrible murders after an unknown assailant attacked and killed three Italian grocers with an ax, chopping to death first Tony Schiambras, then two others, named Cruti and Rosetti. The killings by this lethal fiend abruptly ceased and nothing more was heard from him until May 23, 1918, when someone chiseled out the back door panel leading to the home and grocery of Joseph Maggio, crept through the darkened interior to a bedroom, and using a small handax, began chopping at the sleeping forms of Maggio and his wife.

Maggio's brothers, Jake and Andrew, were awakened by a gurgling sound and rushed into the couple's bedroom to find Mrs. Maggio on the floor, her head caved in and her throat slit from ear to ear. She was dead, almost decapitated. Their brother Joseph lay on the bed, his head split and a wide gap cut into his throat; he was still alive, trying to speak, his words running together in the loud gurgle that had awakened the brothers.

By the time police arrived, Joseph Maggio had died. Officers found a bloody ax on the back steps of the house and a razor dripping gore on the floor of the murder bedroom. In front of the grocery on the sidewalk police discovered the following message scrawled in chalk: "Mrs. Maggio is going to sit up tonight just like Mrs. Tony."

Detectives suddenly remembered the 1911 ax killings, recalling that the first murder victim then was named Tony. It was concluded that the same fiend was again at work in New Orleans. Jake and Andrew Maggio, who had been arrested for the double murders, were released as investigators began to search for an ax-wielding psychopath.

No new suspects were arrested, and the police were obviously stymied. The investigation was further bogged down when Detective Theodore Obitz, who was in charge of the case, was murdered while apprehending a burglary suspect.

The axman struck again in late June 1918. A delivery man arrived at the back door of a grocery owned by Louis Besumer early on June 28. He noticed that the back panel of the door had been chiseled away. Remembering the Maggio killing, the delivery man cautiously called for Besumer. Besumer threw open the door and staggered outside, a deep gash in his head and blood streaming over his face. Police, a short time later, found Besumer's common-law wife, Mrs. Harriet Lowe, inside the bedroom, badly wounded by a gash in the skull. They also found the ax used on the couple in a bathroom, their blood coating the razor-sharp edge. The Besumers survived the attack and police quickly and wrongly began to suspect the grocer himself of being the axman.

Neighbors had pointed out that Besumer was a foreigner who had migrated from South America and spoke many languages. He received mysterious mail from abroad. He was most likely a German spy who had gone crazy, many whispered. Such preposterous suspicions were normal at the time, with America fully committed to World War I; spies were reported lurking around every corner by war-fevered citizens.

Besumer's common-law wife didn't help matters. Mrs. Lowe, still recovering from her terrible wound, dazedly regained consciousness in early July to blurt to police: "I've long suspected that Mr. Besumer was a German spy." The grocer was arrested, protesting his guilt and telling officers that he was Polish, not German. The following day, July 6, Mrs. Lowe told detectives: "I never said Mr. Besumer was a German spy. That's ridiculous." Besumer was released.

Mrs. Lowe went on babbling suspicions for a month, describing her attacker as having the appearance of none other than Besumer. She underwent surgery a month later and, before her death in August, whispered that Besumer had probably been her killer. Again the grocer was arrested, but he was not held long.

Only hours after Besumer was placed

behind bars on August 5, 1918, the axman entered the bedroom of Mrs. Edward Scheider—her husband was also a grocer—and struck the pregnant woman's head repeatedly with an ax. Miraculously, Mrs. Scheider not only survived the bestial attack but delivered a healthy baby. She told police that the intruder was a tall, heavyset white man but could not fully describe him. She had only had a moment to glimpse his form after opening her eyes to the sounds of floorboards creaking in the bedroom before he brought the ax down on her head in a glancing blow.

The attacks caused the citizens of New Orleans to burn their lights late into the night. Neighbors formed block patrols to help police look for the mass killer. The *Times-Picayune* blared a headline: IS AN AXMAN AT LARGE IN NEW ORLEANS?

The answer to that question came on the night of August 10, when Joseph Romano's two young nieces rushed into their uncle's bedroom after hearing sounds of a struggle. They found Romano, a barber, mortally wounded on the floor, his head caved in by an ax. Romano's assailant, whom the nieces glimpsed briefly as he slipped out a first-floor window, was a tall, heavyset white man. The barber could add nothing to the description; he remained unconscious and died hours later.

Police found the same modus operandi in the Romano case as had been employed in the other ax killings. A panel to the back door had been chiseled out at he rear of the Romano home.

The same method of entry was used by

the axman to slip into the grocery-home of Charles Cortimiglia on March 10, 1919. The killer, who had baffled police for a year, had become emboldened, abandoning stealth. He had broken into the Cortimiglia home at the rear of the grocery and attacked the wide-awake grocer in his bedroom. Mrs. Rose Cortimiglia, hearing her husband's screams, rushed into the bedroom. A large white man was brutally crashing an ax down upon her husband's head. Cortimiglia fell to the floor, his wife rushing to a crib nearby to scoop up her two-year-old daughter. She turned to flee, but the axman caught her and threw her to the floor.

Holding her child close to her, Mrs. Cortimiglia screamed: "Not my baby! Not my baby!"

Ignoring her pleas, the axman swung his weapon twice, once wounding Rose Cortimiglia, the second blow squarely hitting the child on the head, killing her instantly. He then fled. The adult Cortimiglias survived the attack. Then Rose suddenly accused members of the Jordano family, who lived across the street and ran a competing grocery, of having made the attack. Her husband told the press that his wife was hysterical, that several members of the Jordano family had actually run to their rescue after hearing their cries, causing the killer to flee. The Jordanos, father and son, were nevertheless arrested and held for trial.

Three days later the editor of the *Times-Picayune* printed a letter dated "from Hell" and signed "The AXMAN." It stated that its author was a devil and would visit New Orleans on March 19, 1919, but that he would not enter any home or establishment where jazz was being played, since he was a lover of jazz.

The entire city prepared for the lethal visit on March 19, and that evening almost every home blared with jazz as terrified citizens desperately wound up their gramophones and wore out jazz records. Those who did not own a gramophone crowded into the jazz joints in the French Quarter as a way of seeking safety. The axman, however, failed to appear.

Frank Jordano, who had been pinpointed by the hysterical Rose Cortimiglia as the axman, was placed on trial on May 21, 1919, and was convicted five days later, surprising even the prosecution, which knew its evidence to be almost nonexistent. Jordano was sentenced to be hanged.

But the axman kept striking. Frank Genusa, a grocer, heard a knock at his door on the night of August 10 and opened it to catch his friend Steve Boca, who fell forward into his arms, an ugly gash from an ax in his head. Boca survived. Incredibly, his benefactor, Genusa, was arrested. Boca pleaded with police, telling them that Genusa was his friend, not his attacker, and, only after prolonged testimony on his part, was the badly injured Boca able to convince investigators that Genusa was innocent.

On the night of September 2, a pharmacist named William Carlson heard odd noises at the rear of his house and went to investigate. He saw a chisel being thrust through a door panel. Quickly he retrieved his pistol and fired at the man on the other side of the door. The intruder

19

dropped the chisel and ran off. On the following night a nineteen-year-old girl, Sarah Laumann, was struck repeatedly by an ax as she lay sleeping in her bed. She survived but could not identify her assailant.

The next and final victim of the axman was Michele Pepitone, who was sleeping in the back room of his father's store on the night of October 27, 1919. Mrs. Pepitone, sleeping next to her husband, was awakened when Michele's hot blood splashed on her face. She rose screaming to see the shadowy form of a large man escape through the back door, where a panel had been chiseled out. Michele Pepitone's head was unrecognizable. The killer had chopped it to pieces, striking Pepitone's skull at least eighteen times, splattering the walls and ceiling with blood. Police thoroughly investigated but again drew a blank.

A few days later Rose Cortimiglia raced into the editorial offices of the *Times-Picayune*. The distraught woman told the editors that she had wrongly accused the Jordano family of killing her child and attacking her and her husband. "It was spite that made me do it and God has punished me," she wailed. "I have lost all. My baby is dead. My husband has left me. I have had smallpox. . . . I lied . . . I lied." Her confession saved Frank Jordano, who was scheduled to hang within days.

The ax killings suddenly ceased, and the mass murderer vanished from New Orleans. His bloody scourge of the city led many to believe that he had been a latter-day Jack the Ripper [see entry] and, perhaps, had been inspired by the Ripper's activities, widely publicized in London in 1888. He had, like the Ripper, sent a letter to the press, and, just like the Ripper, dated his letter "from Hell." And the axman's victims, like the Ripper's, had all been a special type of person. Where the Ripper had murdered only prostitutes, the axman for the most part slew grocers.

Others speculated that the axman was a Mafia hit man, a killer-for-hire who had been carrying out executions against grocers who refused to make kickbacks to Mafia bosses. It was also said that the mass killings were part of a Mafia vendetta, which trailed back to 1909 when Pietro Pepitone, father of the murdered Michele, shot and killed Paul Di Cristina. A top Mafioso in New Orleans, Di Cristina had hastily emigrated from Palermo, Sicily, after having arranged for the death of New York Police Lieutenant Joseph Petrosino, who was shot in Palermo's town square in 1909 while investigating Mafia operations.

Di Cristina had been attempting to extort money from the elder Pepitone and when he boldly rode up to the front of the grocer's establishment in a wagon to demand his tribute, Pietro stepped from his store with a shotgun and blew away Di Cristina's head. Pepitone was convicted of manslaughter and, sent to prison for twenty years, was pardoned six years later. The rash of ax killings was said to be in retribution for Pepitone's killing of Di Cristina, although few believed in the vendetta, especially since it was never proved that any of the axman's victims was related to Pepitone, other than his oldest son, Michele.

The only person who harbored the vendetta theory was Mrs. Michele Pepitone. She believed that the killer of her husband, if not all the axman's victims, was a mysterious figure named Joseph "Doc" Mumfre, a blackmailer and terrorist who worked inside the shadows of the Mafia. Little is known of Mumfre's background, except that he had served a prison sentence for dynamiting a grocery store and had operated with blackmail gangs in eastern cities before moving to New Orleans. Ed Reid was later to state in *Mafia* that "the advent of Mumfre in New Orleans coincided with the first ax murder, and the date of his departure, shortly after [Michele Pepitone's] murder, marked the end of the gruesome killings."

Only a few months after her husband had been axed to death, Mrs. Pepitone married one Angelo Albano, who had kept company with Mumfre. Two years later the Albanos moved to Los Angeles, where Mumfre was living under the name of Leone, busying himself with blackmailing schemes.

Mumfre came to Albano's house to renew his friendship. At that time he demanded money from his old friend, and Albano threw him out. Weeks later, in October 1921, Angelo Albano disappeared. Shortly thereafter Mrs. Pepitone-Albano went to the chief of police in Los Angeles and accused Mumfre of killing her second husband and hiding his body. Since there was no evidence that Albano was dead, no arrest was made.

A short time later a veiled Mrs. Pepitone-Albano, dressed all in black, stepped from the shadows of an alleyway just as Joseph Mumfre was walking by. She fired several shots into him from a small revolver, and Mumfre fell to the sidewalk, dead.

The widow was sent to prison for ten years but was released after serving only three. She insisted that Mumfre had been the axman, but no evidence supporting her statements could be produced.

The identity of the mass killer who terrorized New Orleans on and off for many years remains as much a mystery today as when he stalked and murdered those who slept in rooms silent of jazz.

B

Bailes, Marie Ellen
MURDER, 1908 ENGLAND

Six-year-old Marie Ellen Bailes was en route to her home at Islington in North London, returning from St. John's Catholic School on May 30, 1908, when she vanished. The following morning a man entered a public restroom on St. George's Road carrying a large package. To the attendant on duty the man appeared extremely nervous. When the man left empty-handed, the attendant opened the cubicle and saw that the package had been left behind. He opened it to discover the body of the Bailes girl, her throat slit.

Police searched desperately for the man described by the attendant but the homicidal maniac was never found.

Bayer, The Widow
MURDER, 1879 FRANCE

An egg and butter merchant, the Widow Bayer was found dead in her shop on May 30, 1879. Paris detectives found that the woman had been strangled and her shop robbed. Further, they were baffled by the fact that the Widow Bayer's body bore the marks of kicks rendered by someone wearing shoes without heels. Suspected in this case were a man and wife named Ka; the man was known to wear heelless shoes. Both knew the Widow Bayer and had been seen at one time or another talking to the shopkeeper only hours before the merchant was murdered. Yet no concrete evidence could be established that would convict the pair, let alone cause their arrest.

The Bayer murder remains unsolved in the murder files of the Paris police. Alfred Morain, onetime chief of police in Paris, was convinced the man named Ka was responsible for the killing and that his wife had aided him in murdering the Widow Bayer. "Both were incorrigible drunkards," Morain later stated. "The woman died of congestion of the brain in a gutter at Les Halles. The man was later shut up in a lunatic asylum."

Bingham Poisonings
MURDERS, 1911 ENGLAND

The Bingham family members were the official custodians of historic Lancaster Castle in England. William Hodgson Bingham, who had been caretaker at the castle for more than thirty years, died in January 1911. His son, James Henry Bingham, was appointed to the caretaker position. A short time later James asked his sister Margaret to accept the position of housekeeper in the castle. Only a few weeks after Margaret undertook these duties, she, too, died, and was replaced by her half-sister, Edith Agnes Bingham.

Bingham found his sister a quarrelsome nag. He made plans for a new housekeeper to move into the castle on August 14, 1911. Two days before this date, however, Bingham died after eating a steak which had been prepared by his sister Edith. Authorities grew suspicious after noting three deaths in the Bingham family inside of nine months. They investigated and found arsenic in all three of the deceased Binghams. Edith was promptly arrested, charged with murder and was tried, ironically, in the very castle where she had been the housekeeper.

The prosecution maintained that Edith poisoned her relatives to gain a small inheritance and that this was easily accomplished in that she had access to white arsenic which was used about the castle to kill weeds. The defense countered that there was not a shred of evidence to prove that Edith either possessed or dosed any of her family members with poison, a tell-ing point with the jury, which acquitted Edith Bingham after a twenty-minute deliberation. The Bingham poisonings are still a mystery.

Black Dahlia Case, The
MURDER, 1947 U.S.

One of the most sensational and baffling killings in twentieth-century-America was the murder of the beautiful dark-haired young woman who, following her appalling murder in Los Angeles in 1947, became known to the world as the Black Dahlia. Her real name was Elizabeth Ann Short. Nothing in her poverty-stricken background ever suggested that she would attain the status of international fame, albeit posthumously. Her sobriquet is now synonymous with sadistic sex murder. After more than three decades, the murder of the Black Dahlia continues to mystify the Los Angeles Police Department, where her swollen red-inked file still taunts investigators, who wearily shake their heads at the mere mention of Elizabeth Short's name.

"It was that name 'Black Dahlia,'" commented Harry Leslie Hansen, one of the detectives who worked on the case from the beginning, "that set this one off . . . just those words strung together in that order turned Elizabeth Short's murder into a coast-to-coast sensation. 'Black' is night, mysterious, forbidding even; the Dahlia is an exotic and mysterious flower. There could not have been a more intriguing title. Any other name and it wouldn't have been anywhere near the same."

Abject horror, not intrigue, however, was the scene that confronted a young mother walking with her child along a vacant lot in the early morning of January 15, 1947. The woman suddenly saw something partially blocking the sidewalk. As she approached her curious expression changed to terror. There, in front of her, was the naked body—or pieces of it—of a woman, half the torso on the sidewalk and the other half in the weeds of the vacant lot. The woman scooped up her child and ran to a phone where, hysterical, she called the police.

At that moment detectives Harry Hansen, called Red by his friends, and Finis Arthur Brown were investigating the death of a man who had died of apparently natural causes. They were waiting for the coroner when the police radio in their unmarked Chevrolet crackled to life with the voice of Los Angeles Homicide Captain Jack Donahoe, who said to Hansen: "Red, we've got a rough one. Drop what you're doing, have a uniformed officer stand by there for the coroner, and you and Brown get over to an empty lot on Norton, between Thirty-ninth and Coliseum Street. It's a block east of Crenshaw, in the Leimert Park section."

Hansen and Brown sped to the location. Several uniformed policemen were already present to keep passersby back. Hansen and Brown ran from their car to the vacant lot, then halted in horror. Seasoned detectives as they were, both men

grew sick to their stomach. Looking down, they saw the dismembered body of a woman. She had been bisected at the waist, cut neatly in half by some fiendish killer who, experts later agreed, possessed surgical skill.

The girl's face was hardly recognizable; it had been savagely slashed and battered. The mouth had been cut at the edges so that it extended from ear to ear in a gaping, obscene grin. Circle and cross cuts mutilated the breasts, thighs, and arms. Cigarette burns pockmarked the flesh, and at the wrists and ankles there were noticeable rope burns. It was apparent that the victim had been bound hand and foot and great and painful punishment administered to her long hours before death gave her release. Lee Jones of the L.A. Crime Laboratory arrived and minutely inspected the corpse. It had been drained of all blood and then meticulously cleaned before the body had been dumped in two pieces in the lot. "Tortured," Jones told Hansen and Brown. "Then scrubbed clean with a brush. Bristles still embedded in the flesh." Jones also noted that the initials "B.D." had been carved into one thigh.

It was quickly determined that the girl was in her early twenties, had been tall and willowy, and that her hair was natural raven black, although it had been recently hennaed, along with her eyebrows. She possessed even in death great beauty. She had been dead no more than six or eight hours before her body was discovered.

Fingerprints were taken and sent by

sound photo to FBI headquarters in Washington. In a matter of hours, the card-selector system pulled forth, from the millions of sets of prints, a card identifying the victim as Elizabeth Ann Short, born in Hyde Park, Massachusetts, July 29, 1924; last known address, Santa Barbara, California.

The twenty-two-year-old girl, learned the Los Angeles *Herald-Express*, had recently lived in Long Beach, and reporter Bevo Means was sent out to interview her former landlady. It was during this interview that Means learned of Elizabeth's fanatical quirk of constantly dressing in black—black shoes, black skin-tight dresses and evening gowns. She had worn a jet-black jade ring. Even her lace undergarments, it was later learned when her trunk was located, were all black.

The landlady sent Means to a Long Beach drugstore which Elizabeth had visited regularly, so that she could meet men at the soda fountain. The druggist vividly recalled the raven-haired beauty with pert nose, gray-green eyes, and skin the color of cream who had dressed all in black; many men had flocked about her in his store. "Elizabeth? Sure, I remember her. Who could forget a beautiful girl like that? Always in black. The fellows coming in here called her the Black Dahlia."

Hours later Bevo Means's story broke, and it was in this report that the sobriquet of the Black Dahlia—the B.D. of the hideous initials in her thigh—was first mentioned. The name was so sensational that wire services and newspapers across the country picked up the story.

Elizabeth Short, an unknown and aspiring Hollywood actress whose 1947 mutilation murder electrified the world as the Black Dahlia case. (*Wide World*)

Elizabeth Short was suddenly known to millions of Americans, elusive fame embracing her in death when it had shunned her during life.

Bit by bit, Hansen, who had been permanently assigned to the case, pieced together the short life of the Black Dahlia. (He was to stay with the Short case until his retirement in 1971.) Hansen learned that Elizabeth, one of five sisters, had quit school and left her poverty-ridden home in Medford, Massachusetts, in 1942. The seventeen-year-old, loved-starved and with the single ambition to enter show business, headed for America's glamour capital, Hollywood.

Instead she landed in Santa Barbara, finding work as a canteen girl at Camp Cooke. Elizabeth worked through 1944 at the post exchange as a sort of hostess, handing out coffee and doughnuts to lonely GIs. She was once elected "Cutie of the Week." At the time Elizabeth met and became engaged to a handsome Army Air Corps officer, Major Matt Gordon, Jr. He was assigned to a post in India and was killed some months later.

Soon after Elizabeth was picked up by juvenile authorities in a Santa Barbara lounge and arrested for drinking with soldiers. The underage girl was shipped back to Massachusetts but got off the bus when halfway home and stubbornly returned to California; arriving in Hollywood, she befriended and moved in with a fifteen-year-old girl who convinced her that the best way to break into movies was to accommodate rich, draft-exempt Hollywood playboys. Elizabeth Short became a call girl. She was soon living high, if not lux-

uriously, her rent paid by film producers and her wardrobe purchased from the better shops. She had cash and promises that her beautiful face would soon grace the motion picture screen. It was at this time she developed the penchant for wearing all black clothes. Some unknown assistant producer dubbed her the Black Dahlia, a sobriquet in which Elizabeth Short reveled.

The movie contract, however, never came. Elizabeth went on with her nightlife spree until 1946, when, disillusioned, she returned briefly to see her mother in New England. From there she drifted to Florida and Chicago, where she worked as a cocktail waitress. Then it was back to California. She lived for a while with an elderly theater owner in Los Angeles, then joined six women who were working the street around North Cherokee Avenue. Elizabeth made extra money posing for nude photos, the closest thing she ever achieved to a picture career.

By December of 1946, Elizabeth was a tired twenty-two-year-old drifter, only a few steps up from the meanest streetwalker. She abstained from men briefly after moving in with a mannish woman who introduced her to Hollywood's lesbian community. That life obviously repelled her. Elizabeth moved to San Diego, where a kindly woman took her in after listening to her convincing lie that she was a destitute war widow. She had worked that routine successfully from Long Beach to Santa Barbara. In early January 1947, Elizabeth told friends that she intended to reform, then find a regular job and try to find a man who would not

26

consider her a piece of sexual merchandise; that she wanted to settle down, perhaps have children. The Black Dahlia would be no more, she promised, adding that she had met the love of her life, a man she called only Red. (Coincidentally, this was the same nickname applied to Detective Hansen.)

All of these facts were unearthed by Hansen within the first week of his investigation following the savage slaying of Elizabeth Short. The final week of her life was almost a blank to police. From January 9 to 15, the day her mutilated body was discovered, details of the Dahlia's whereabouts were sketchy, almost nonexistent, and police theorized that it was at this time that Elizabeth may have been abducted, held captive somewhere, and slowly tortured to death.

Detectives did have clues, many of them. Tire tracks near the site where the corpse was found were checked out but led nowhere. Cars seen and described in the area of the vacant lot in the early hours of January 15, 1947, were hunted, but nothing concrete turned up. The first real break in the case was as bizarre as the method Elizabeth's killer had employed to destroy her.

The killer, much like Jack the Ripper and the Axman of New Orleans [see entries], chose to contact the press anonymously, incapable for reasons of ego or madness to keep out of the limelight. Six days after the savage slaying, Jimmy Richardson, city editor of the Los Angeles *Herald Examiner*, received a call. The voice at the other end of the line was "soft and silky," according to Richardson. The editor's stomach tightened as he listened to the smooth voice rattle off exact details of Elizabeth Short's murder, minutiae concerning the butchery inflicted that only the killer would know. "I killed her," the sinister voice said. "I'm going to turn myself in, but I want to have a little more fun. I want to watch the cops chase me some more."

Richardson felt that the caller possessed a tremendous ego. He was not necessarily proud of murdering the Dahlia, but he did take vain pleasure in eluding police. The man ended the call with the words: "You can expect some souvenirs of Beth Short in the mail."

Postal inspectors next delivered a strange letter to L.A. detectives, addressed with letters clipped from newspaper advertisements. It was addressed to the "Los Angeles *Examiner* and other Los Angeles papers," and read on the front "Here is Dahlia's Belongings. Letter to Follow."

The envelope contained Elizabeth's birth certificate and her small black address book. The book yielded the names of seventy-some men whom Elizabeth had known in her California travels. A force of fifty detectives was assigned to track them all down and interrogate them. While this manhunt proceeded, Hansen and Brown found the Dahlia's trunk and suitcase in a storage locker in the Greyhound Bus Terminal. The trunk contained a packet of love letters from Elizabeth's male friends. A hunt for these admirers was also begun.

The killer, after calling the *Herald Examiner* and sending the packet to police, made one more contact with authorities,

27

Message from the killer of the Black Dahlia which yielded no fingerprints; the envelope contained Elizabeth Short's birth certificate, address book, and personal papers. (*Wide World*)

mailing a postcard, again made up of letters clipped from newspapers, which read: "I've changed my mind. You would not give me a square deal. Dahlia killing justified." There were no more mailings from the sender.

Detectives did have what appeared to be a strong lead on one suspect, the man Elizabeth had called Red. Hansen and Brown unearthed a telegram sent to Elizabeth when she was staying in San Diego only a week before her death. It read: BE THERE TOMORROW AFTERNOON LATE. WOULD LIKE TO SEE YOU. RED.

The wire had been sent by one Robert "Red" Manley, a twenty-four-year-old hardware salesman who had recently been married and lived in Huntington Park,

California. When first picked up, Manley adamantly denied having known Elizabeth Short. "I don't know her!" Manley yelled at Hansen when he was picked up. "I never met the woman!" After being brought in for questioning, Manley's statements changed radically. He admitted that Elizabeth Short had met him at a San Diego bus stop. "She had bad scratches on both her arms and above the elbows," he said. "She told me she had a friend who was intensely jealous of her . . . an Italian with black hair." Manley said the boyfriend lived somewhere in San Diego, but he did not know his name.

Manley went on to state that he took Elizabeth from the bus station to the place where she was staying with friends to get her bags. They went on to a motel and spent the night. He stressed that there was no sexual liaison with the Dahlia and then said that he had lied about knowing Elizabeth because he had been having arguments with his wife and didn't want to aggravate the situation by admitting to his escapade with the Dahlia.

Manley was one of the last persons known to have seen Elizabeth alive. He had spent a terrible night with the Dahlia, Manley reported. She had gotten sick after drinking too much. On the afternoon of the following day, January 9, he drove her to Los Angeles and dropped her off at the Biltmore Hotel. That was the last he saw of her.

Police went over Manley's story inch by inch and checked his whereabouts at the time of the murder. He was finally released after detectives were convinced of his innocence. (Robert Manley, however, was not free of the Black Dahlia. In 1954 his wife committed him to an insane asylum, claiming that "he hears noises, writes foolish notes, and has a guilt complex." Manley was again grilled by police but was again cleared after taking truth serum.)

Other men, dozens of them, were thoroughly investigated as possible suspects, but all were cleared of having been with Elizabeth at the time of the murder. A bus driver reported that he had picked up Elizabeth in Santa Barbara and dropped her off in Los Angeles on January 14, early in the morning. Two waitresses and a gas station attendant who knew Elizabeth

Prime suspect in the Dahlia case, Robert Manley—shown here with his wife, Harriett, just before being booked on January 20, 1947—was later released as innocent; he wound up in an insane asylum.

swore that they saw her at about 5:30 PM on that same day in San Diego; these three witnesses insisted that they saw the Dahlia driving on Balboa Street with a red-haired man at the wheel. He was wearing some sort of green uniform, perhaps that of a marine. These were the last people, if their stories were correct, who saw the Dahlia alive. The following morning her bisected corpse was in the vacant Los Angeles lot.

Robert Manley was only one of more than four hundred suspects questioned and investigated by dogged detectives. And there were also confessions that came into police for years, setting a record of thirty-five such phony confessions. Shortly after the Dahlia slaying, Dr. J. Paul de River, staff psychiatrist for the Los Angeles police, told officers that the case would spark a bevy of guilt-laden souls. By then several individuals had come forward. "The confessors will keep coming," de River predicted. He was right.

Army corporal Joseph Dumais told police that he might have murdered Elizabeth. Police had found Dumais's clothing blotched with blood and clippings about the Dahlia killing in his room. "It is possible that I could have committed the murder," the corporal told detectives. "When I get drunk I get rough with women." His story did not hold up, however, and he failed to answer what Harry Hansen and Finis Brown called the key question, which dealt with the state of Dahlia's carved-up corpse when she was found, an aspect of the torture slaying known only to the killer and few lawmen.

All of the many who came forward to

confess failed to answer the key question and were cleared of the murder in the years to come. John N. Andry, a chief pharmacist's mate in the navy, was picked up after bragging in a Long Beach bar that he had great skill in cutting up bodies. Said Andry: "Well, I'm capable of doing it." He then said that he "was only kidding."

About a week after the slaying, Captain Donahoe of Homicide received a phone call from a thirty-three-year-old unemployed waiter named Daniel S. Voorhees. The waiter screamed over the phone: "I can't stand it any longer! I want to confess to the murder of the Black Dahlia!" While being driven to headquarters Voorhees mumbled over and over, "I killed her, I killed her." He signed a confession to that effect at headquarters but said he never mailed the letter and postcard. Days later Voorhees tired of the game, snarling to detectives: "I'm not gonna talk to you anymore. I've talked too much already. I want to see my attorney." He was sent on for study as a mental case.

A tall, dark-haired woman who had been a WAC during the war walked into a San Diego police station, yelling that she had murdered the Dahlia. "Elizabeth Short stole my man, so I killed her and cut her up!" Hansen, Brown, and other officers grew exhausted handling the confessions. "Most of them were exhibitionists and publicity seekers," Hansen later stated. One man confessed because his wife was missing and he thought she would contact him if she saw his picture in the newspapers.

And there were crackpots who begged

for a piece of the Dahlia's clothing so that they could feel it and then name the killer. An old woman called Detective Hansen and told him: "Bury the girl with an egg in her right hand. The killer will then be found within a week. That's the way it works in Alabama!" A photographer tried to convince the coroner to give him Elizabeth's eyeballs so that he could photograph them and record the last image seen by the girl, her killer, this being an old crime myth in tracking down murderers.

Reports, thousands of them, were made to police over the months following the killing. All of them were empty, malicious, or downright absurd. A waitress overheard two men discussing the Dahlia case at her lunch counter. "They looked sinister," she said over the phone to a detective.

"How?" asked the detective.

"They looked like they had guns under their coats and one of them had an apprehensive look and ordered only a half cup of coffee."

"What's the name of your restaurant?" asked the detective.

The waitress told him.

"That was us! My partner and I ate there today," the detective said, hanging up in disgust.

The ridiculous reports and phony confessions were relatively harmless compared with the brutal slayings that followed the death of the Black Dahlia. In the months that followed, six women in the Los Angeles area were murdered in similar fashion. Three days after the Dahlia killing, Mary Tate was sexually attacked (the Dahlia case showed no forced entry) and then strangled with a silk stocking. Mrs. Jeanne French was found in February, her body mutilated, obscenities written on her stomach in lipstick. Mrs. Evelyn Winters was cut to pieces on March 11, 1947. Also strangled with a silk stocking, her body left naked, was Rosenda Mondragon. Mrs. Dorothy Montgomery was next; she was horribly mutilated after being stripped naked. Mrs. Laura Trelstad was strangled after having been mercilessly beaten. All these slayings bore striking similarities to the method of the Dahlia killer, and police speculated that at least two or more of these brutal slayings may have been the work of Elizabeth Short's killer. These murders, along with the Dahlia bloodletting, remained unsolved.

A curious but not implausible assumption on the part of Captain Jack Donahoe was that the killer of Elizabeth Short was not a man at all but a *woman.* Donahoe contended that the types of wounds made on the Dahlia's body were similar to those found in other mutilation killings in which women were proved to be the murderers. "They are the deadlier of the species," Donahoe often repeated. And the wounds on the chopped-up corpse of Elizabeth Short, he believed, were those of spite, ones inspired, perhaps, by the kind of hatred only a female rival would manifest.

But most of those who confessed or were arrested on suspicion of the killing were males, more of them each passing year. In December 1947 Donald Graeff was arrested for cutting his initials in the hip of one Mrs. Helen Miller, a poverty-stricken woman to whom Graeff had offered shelter. He claimed that he had been drunk at the time of the mutilation of Mrs. Miller. After a strenuous grilling, Graeff was cleared of the Dahlia slaying.

Nine years after the Short murder a New York dishwasher, forty-four-year-old Ralph von Hiltz, said that he had witnessed the Dahlia slaying, that a friend of his had mutilated and killed Elizabeth Short. He had had no part in the murder, von Hiltz insisted, but he did help his friend cut the body in half. He was later released as a tongue-wagging crank.

Detective Harry Hansen, by the time he retired in 1971, was convinced that the Dahlia killer had never been picked up. "I know for certain I never met the killer face to face," he stated. "I know he didn't manage to slip through with the other subjects. We considered the possibility of his coming right in, making a confession, then cleverly sidestepping the key question. We watched for that, had taken measures to expose him in that event. We never underestimated this guy. You'd never believe the amount of checking we did on this case. We followed everything as far as it would go, then we'd turn right around and walk through it all again."

For Hansen, Elizabeth Short may have contributed to her own terrible end. "From all accounts, Elizabeth Short liked to tease men. She probably went too far this time and just set some guy off into a blind berserk rage."

Whatever the motive, the fiend who killed the Black Dahlia is still at large today or has gone to the grave without uttering a word of the gruesome nightmare he (or she) visited upon the lonely and confused Elizabeth Short more than three decades ago.

Borden Case, The
MURDERS, 1892 U.S.

No murder case in nineteenth-century America stirred more controversy and aroused the public at large more than the Borden case. As a result of the hatchet slayings of Andrew Jackson Borden, sixty-nine, and his wife, Abby (Durfee Gray), sixty-four, on the morning of August 4, 1892, their daughter, Lizzie, thirty-two, was branded a murderer until the day she died on June 1, 1927. The branding was applied by some newspaper wag who made up a bit of doggerel that convicted her out-of-hand long before she faced trial. It read:

Lizzie Borden took an ax,
And gave her mother forty whacks;
And when she saw what she had done,
She gave her father forty-one.

The fact that a jury found Lizzie innocent of parricide and the good possibility that someone else, either a member of the Borden household or an intruder, had ample opportunity to kill the Bordens have been largely ignored over the decades. There has been much made of the rumors that Lizzie had every motive to murder her father and stepmother, that she grew to hate her father because he was stingy with her and threatened to cut her and her sister Emma, forty-one, out of his considerable will in favor of his second wife, that she hated her stepmother Abby because she had replaced her own mother and stolen the affections of her father. But the facts indicate otherwise.

Andrew Borden was a stern father, yes, and one who penny-pinched, even though he was the president of three banks and owned most of the valuable property in Fall River. Yet he had purchased land for his daughters and settled considerable cash on them. They had handsome allowances with which to purchase their clothes and such luxuries as an average New England family of the day thought proper.

Lizzie's attitude toward the second Mrs. Borden was cordial, often close. Lizzie's mother, Sarah Morse, had died when Lizzie was a mere baby; Borden married again in 1865 to Abby Gray, when Lizzie was less than five years old—hardly at an age when Lizzie would have developed a bond for her real mother that would prompt her to hate a woman who acted as a kindly and understanding stepmother. (As an adult, Lizzie normally called Abby "mother" but did admit that, on rare occasions when she was upset with her stepmother, she did call her "Mrs. Borden," which was no more than a matter of pique.) She knew she had nothing to fear from the woman, least of all losing her father's fortune to her. Borden's will was fixed and had not been altered for a decade, and this, too, Lizzie and Emma Borden knew. Abby Borden was a retiring, almost shy, person who waited al-

Lizzie Borden, shortly before the ax murders of her parents in 1892. (*Courtesy Fall River, Mass., Library*)

most slavishly on her husband and step-daughters, incurring no one's wrath. She was anything but a threat to either of the Borden daughters.

The family maid, Bridget Sullivan, made up the fifth member of the household—a hardworking, closed-mouth person who labored from dawn to dusk in and about the large three-story Borden house at 92 Second Street. Not until recent years was any serious suspicion cast upon the maid in the matter of the Borden slayings. Her actions after the killings, however, indicate that she could have been the killer.

Much conspired to implicate Lizzie in the murders of her parents before the bloody morning of August 4, 1892. Her father and stepmother had been taken ill after eating dinner the night before. Lizzie and the maid, however, ate the same dinner and were also slightly sick. It was later said that Lizzie had attempted to purchase prussic acid (to clean a sealskin coat) from a local druggist that day and had been refused, and that somehow she had managed to poison the food the family ate that night. Yet it was Bridget Sullivan who had prepared the meal; furthermore, it would have been idiotic, if Lizzie was truly the calculating fiend that many later attempted to portray, for the daughter to poison her own food: the meal was not served on separate plates by the maid but on common platters from which they all helped themselves.

On August 3, John Vinnicum Morse, a man of about sixty, visited the Bordens. He was the brother of Borden's first wife and was a close family member. He oc-

cupied a guest room that night. Emma Borden, Lizzie's older sister, left that day to stay with friends in Fairhaven. When Lizzie's Uncle John awoke on August 4, he left early to visit friends in Swansea. (He was nowhere near the Borden house at the time of the murders, it was later proved.) That left Lizzie, Abby, and Andrew Borden in the house with the maid, Bridget.

Andrew Borden left the house on Second Street about 9 AM to make a stop at the Union Savings Bank, of which he was president. He was to make a few other business calls, collecting money on loans or rents from his many properties. Those who dealt with Borden considered him a hard man with a dollar. He was respected but not liked. Some even hated him. One unknown man dealing with Borden had, within a week before the murders, come to the Borden house and argued so hotly with Andrew that he was asked to leave. It was also a known fact that the Bordens had suffered several night burglaries of their barn and even a daylight burglary in the house in recent months.

The bank president had enemies, enough to give Lizzie nightmares. She confided to a neighbor, Alice Russell, that her father's enemies might "burn the house down over us," and that "I feel as if something was hanging over me that I cannot throw off." Some later interpreted these statements as Cassandra-like prophecies that would be thought to be the work of invading enemies but that were designed to prepare others for the impending murders Lizzie herself was planning. However, Andrew Borden's enemies were real, not imaginary, as had been the burglaries, events that brought fright and no little trauma to the much-protected Lizzie Borden, whose entire life had been of a sheltered, almost hot-house nature.

At 9:30 AM, so far as anyone could later determine, three women—Abby and Lizzie Borden and the maid, Bridget—were alone in the house. Mrs. Borden went upstairs to make up the bed in the guest room that was being occupied by John Morse. Bridget went to the barn in back of the house to retrieve a pail and brush to wash the windows. The maid, according to her own report, remained outside the house washing the ground-floor windows in the heat of an intensifying August sun. She was seen to do so for a few minutes by the servant girl who worked for the next-door neighbors, the Kellys, whose house was south of the Borden home. Lizzie was somewhere in the house at the time.

At approximately 10:30 PM Andrew Borden returned home. He tried the front door and found it locked. Bridget heard the rattling of the door, dropped her brush, went into the house by the side door, which was unlocked, and went to the front door to let Borden in. Just as she did so she saw Lizzie Borden on the lower steps leading upstairs, as if she had come downstairs in response to her father's knocking.

Borden went into the dining room, asking for his wife.

"She's gone out," said Lizzie. "She had a note from somebody who was sick."

The Borden house, showing the barn at back, as it appeared at the time of the murders. (*Courtesy Fall River, Mass., Library*)

Borden shrugged, then went to his bedroom, going up the back stairs. He returned to the main floor in a matter of minutes and sat, resting, in the sitting room. Bridget was now inside the house, going from room to room, washing the insides of the windows. Lizzie began to iron some handkerchiefs in the dining room. When Bridget came in to wash the dining-room windows Lizzie looked up from her ironing and asked: "Maggie, are you going out this afternoon?" (Lizzie always called Bridget Maggie, after a former family servant.)

" I don't know," replied the maid. "I might and I might not. I don't feel very well." (The family had eaten a heavy breakfast of mutton-broth soup, mutton, johnny cakes, coffee, and cookies; consuming mutton-broth soup on such a blistering August day would have upset anyone's stomach.)

Lizzie then added: "If you go out, be sure and lock the door, for Mrs. Borden has gone out on a sick call and I might go out, too."

"Miss Lizzie, who is sick?"

"I don't know. She had a note this morning. It must be in the town." Lizzie then reminded the maid that there was a cheap sale of dress goods at a local store.

The maid told her that she intended to buy some of the dress cloth. She then went up the back stairs, a few minutes before eleven, to rest in her third-floor attic room. This was her custom after working from 6 AM—an hour of rest before preparing the family lunch.

Bridget later testified that she did not

The body of Lizzie Borden's stepmother in the upstairs guest room.

sleep, only rested on her bed and could hear every creak of the old house. She heard the City Hall clock strike eleven. Ten or fifteen minutes passed before she heard Lizzie calling out in a frantic voice: "Maggie! Come down!"

Bridget went to the stairs and called out: "What is the matter?"

"Come down, quick! Father's dead! Somebody came in and killed him!"

The maid raced downstairs and went to the door of the sitting room where Lizzie was standing.

"Oh, Maggie, don't go in," Lizzie told the maid. "I have to have a doctor quick. Go over [to the home of Dr. Bowen, the family physician who lived diagonally across the street]. I have to have the doctor."

Bridget ran to the doctor's home but learned that the physician was making a house call. She returned to tell Lizzie that Dr. Bowen was gone, then asked the Borden daughter: "Miss Lizzie, where were you when this thing happened?"

"I was out in the yard," replied Lizzie, "and heard a groan, and came in and the screen door was wide open." She next told the maid to fetch her friend and neighbor, Alice Russell. The maid again raced off.

Mrs. Churchill, the neighbor just to the north of the Borden home, looked from a window to see Lizzie standing at the screen door at the side of the house. She appeared greatly upset; her hands trembled as she held on to the door. "Is there anything the matter?" Mrs. Churchill asked.

Andrew Jackson Borden, dead on the couch in the family sitting room.

"Oh, Mrs. Churchill," Lizzie begged, "do come over. Someone has killed Father."

Mrs. Churchill ran to Lizzie and entered the side door, holding the Borden daughter by the arm as if to steady her. "Oh, Lizzie! Where is your father?"

Lizzie spoke in a dazed voice; she was obviously in shock. "In the sitting room," she answered.

"Where were you when it happened?"

"I went to the barn to get a piece of iron." (By "iron," Lizzie later clarified, she meant a fishing sinker which she intended to use for fishing when she visited the Borden farm outside of town; the trip had been planned for a week and Lizzie always went fishing when at the farm.)

Mrs. Churchill then asked: "Where is your mother?"

"I don't know. She had a note to go see someone who is sick, but I don't know but she is killed, too, for I thought I heard her come in. Father must have an enemy, for we have all been sick, and we think the milk has been poisoned."

Mrs. Churchill then went off to search for a doctor. En route she asked some neighbors to phone the police. Bridget reappeared just as police officer George W. Allen entered the house. He was followed quickly by Dr. Bowen. The physician, with officer Allen at his side, entered the sitting room to find his friend Andrew Borden lying on the couch, his face a bloody pulp. He had been attacked while taking his customary nap, it appeared. There was no sign of struggle; the victim's hands were not clenched. No furniture

had been upset. The couch and the wall behind it, however, were splattered with blood.

Dr. Bowen thought that the first blow certainly must have killed Borden while the victim was asleep. He shook his head at the gory sight and murmured: "Physician that I am, and accustomed to all kinds of horrible sights, it sickens me to look upon the dead man's face."

Lizzie was sitting in the kitchen at this time with Mrs. Russell and Mrs. Churchill, who comforted her. She sat as if in a stupor, one of the natural reactions for someone in shock after having found a loved one dead, especially brutally murdered. Lizzie mentioned that someone should find Mrs. Borden to inform her of the tragedy. Mrs. Churchill and Bridget began a room-to-room search of the sprawling house. They fearfully climbed the stairs to the second floor.

Mrs. Churchill was almost at the top of the stairs when a chilling sight met her gaze. "As I went upstairs," she later reported, "I turned my head to the left, and as I got up so that my eyes were on the level with the front hall, I could see across the front hall and across the floor of the spare room. At the far side of the north side of the room I saw something that looked like the form of a person." Bridget went into the room for a few moments, then rejoined Mrs. Churchill on the stairs; they both retreated downstairs to the kitchen in great haste. Mrs. Churchill sat down on a kitchen chair, a look of horror frozen on her face.

"Is there another?" asked Mrs. Russell.

"Yes," replied Mrs. Churchill in a near moan. "She is up there."

Dr. Bowen and officer Allen raced to the guest room that had been occupied by Uncle John Morse. Mrs. Borden was on the floor, her buttocks hiked into the air in an awkward position as she lay on her knees, her head to the floor face forward. A pool of blood surrounded her, and blood was splattered on the wall and bed covers near her body.

Dr. Bowen and a medical examiner who had just arrived detailed the woman's many vicious head wounds and concurred that she, as well as her husband, had been chopped to death with a hatchet or a small hand ax. Mrs. Borden's skull had been crushed by the blows of the killer who, in the frenzy of the killing, had hacked off several locks of hair which were lying on the floor next to the body. (The medical examiner was to count nineteen head wounds on Mrs. Borden. Her husband had been struck ten times. This was a total of twenty-nine wounds, not the eighty-one "whacks" claimed in the doggerel that was to haunt Lizzie Borden for the next thirty-five years.)

In the next few days, relatives, friends, police, physicians, and various city officials grilled Lizzie as to her whereabouts at the time of the murders. Her answers varied. She said she was in the backyard, in the barn, in the loft of the barn looking for sinkers, she was under the pear tree picking pears and took these into the barn to eat. Her seemingly confused and different answers caused her to be put under house detention by Mayor Coughlin.

An inquest was convened, and Lizzie, never an outgoing person, was terse if not hostile in her answers. She was unable to prove that she had been outside of the house at the time of the murders, but then neither could Bridget Sullivan, who, from the start, volunteered herself as a witness for the prosecution.

Lizzie was arrested and held for trial, which did not begin until June 5, 1893. District Attorney Hosea Knowlton made much of Lizzie's confusing answers as to her whereabouts at the time her father and stepmother were killed. He insisted that she hated her stepmother and her father, whom she thought had arranged her disinheritance. This was the motive for her brutal slaying of the couple. Knowlton inadvertently implicated the older sister Emma by stating that *both* the daughters hated Abby and Andrew Borden for this reason. (A later theory had it that Emma Borden, who staunchly defended her sister throughout the trial, could have returned from Fairhaven, slipped into the house and murdered both Bordens, then returned to her out-of-town friends to establish her alibi.)

Knowlton also ridiculed Lizzie's story about someone sending Mrs. Borden a note asking her to attend a sick friend, that Mrs. Borden suddenly appeared holding the note and showed it to Lizzie. Where was the note? It could not be found. Why did not the sick person come forward? There was no note and no sick person, the prosecutor claimed. It was all an invention of an iron-willed and calculating daughter to cover her own murderous trail that led upstairs to the body of her stepmother.

The defense of Lizzie Borden was strong. Defense counsel George D. Robinson, a former Massachusetts governor, pointed out that the murder weapon, a hatchet, had not been found by police. A hatchet of sorts, with the handle broken off, had been put on exhibit, but it was easily discredited as having been the murder weapon. The blade had been found in the Borden basement covered with ashes and cobwebs, its edge rusted out and with not a trace of blood on it. Blood was also another telling point for the defense.

Robinson convincingly illustrated how the killer of the Bordens, chopping away at the victims, would have been coated with gore, and no blood was found on Lizzie in the hour and a half in which the murders were discovered. And she had not changed her dress from early morning to the time when the bodies were found. This, even Bridget Sullivan, who had testified against Lizzie in hostile fashion, was forced to admit. (A recent TV movie on the case showed Lizzie stripping naked and killing the Bordens, flitting from one room to another to wash off the gore before donning the same dress again; but there was no convenient place other than the sink room where this could have been accomplished, and at the estimated time of Mrs. Borden's murder, Bridget was washing windows at the back of the house where this room was located and would have heard the noise of the running water. This room was also thoroughly inspected a half hour after Dr. Bowen arrived at the Borden home and no traces of blood were found. The floor of the sink room was not even damp.)

The possibility of a stranger's entering the Borden house—and it was pointed out that the house had been recently burglarized in broad daylight—was a very real one. The side door was open. Lizzie was in the barn and Bridget, before Andrew Borden was killed, was outside washing windows, then later in her attic room, or so she said. Bridget had much to hate the Bordens for—she was a virtual slave to them and Andrew paid her meager wages. He and Abby made it quite clear that she worked for the family but was not part of it; she was not permitted to enter any of the bed chambers on the second floor and had been given a room in the sweltering attic in spite of the fact that there were *three* guest bedrooms. Actually she, given her whereabouts in the Borden house at the times of the murders, had a better opportunity to murder than Lizzie. And she had a better motive—revenge for the miserable servitude of which she had complained long and loud to friends.

Bridget Sullivan, in the opinion of this author, had a clearer motive to murder the Bordens than a daughter who lived comfortably and knew she would inherit with her sister the bulk of her father's estate. The homicidal history of house servants killing their employers, from Helen Jagado to Kate Webster, is long and convincing. And in almost all these scores of killings the reasons have proved minor, even petty. A sharp command, a degrading comment could be enough to set off a blind rage, stored for years, in a normally tranquil servant, resulting in murder. It should be kept in mind that Bridget Sullivan abruptly went to prosecutors at the beginning of the investigation in an attempt to convict Lizzie, the one person in the Borden household who had treated her in a kindly manner.

The prosecution thundered that Lizzie had burned a dress some days after the killings, implying that this dress had been covered with the blood of her victims. The defense quickly countered by informing the court that Emma Borden had found an old dress of Lizzie's in a closet, one she had worn months earlier and that was covered with paint, not blood. It was Emma who suggested Lizzie burn the dress, which she did. Bridget reluctantly confirmed Emma's story.

As each day of the trial passed, the reporters representing forty newspapers churned out reams of copy that sensationalized the Borden case across the nation. The mere fact that the thirty-two-year-old spinster was on trial for murder riveted the attention of the American public. She was an heiress of a great fortune from an old New England family that represented a virtuous past. Lizzie was a secretary of the Christian Endeavor Society, a member of a Fruit and Flower mission and the Woman's Christian Temperance Union, and, most of all, a Sunday school teacher. It was unthinkable that such a woman was capable of murdering Abby and Andrew Borden.

It was also unprovable. On June 20, 1893,

Lizzie Borden pensive at her trial, with her sister Emma (*hand over face*).

Lizzie Borden, attentive, as she listens to her lawyer in closing arguments.

Lizzie Borden was asked to stand in the New Bedford courtroom to face a jury of her peers. She stared at the jury without emotion, typical of her phlegmatic character.

The foreman of the jury rose and, responding to the clerk, pronounced her "not guilty." The courtroom burst into applause, most of the spectators being from Lizzie's church congregation and social clubs. Lizzie sank into her seat slowly, as if in a dream.

She and her sister were left approximately $350,000, a sum that was almost doubled through shrewd investments by the time Lizzie died in 1927. She moved to a large, comfortable estate called Maplecroft, busying herself through the rest of her life with social club functions and aiding helpless animals (she left $30,000 to a society to prevent cruelty to animals at her death).

Though possible guilt is debated to this day, this writer believes her an innocent and much-maligned historical creature, concurring with a writers' group organized in 1961 as the Friends of Lizzie Borden. The group at the time included Rex Stout, Ellery Queen (the pseudonym for Frederic Dannay and Manfred Lee), Erle Stanley Gardner, and Clifton Fadiman. The group dedicated itself to the "rehabilitation of Fall River's most famous woman."

The Borden case officially, and logically, remains open.

Bowers, Dr. J. Milton
MURDERS, 1865–85 U.S.

Dr. Milton J. Bowers was a marrying man. Unfortunately none of his wives seemed to last. Three of the doctor's spouses died after marrying him, all under mysterious circumstances. Born in Baltimore in 1843, Bowers had a shadowy background. He claimed to have been orphaned at age five and raised by an uncle. In 1859, he later told friends, he was able to collect $20,000 from his father's estate; he promptly traveled to Germany where he briefly studied medicine. He returned to the U.S. shortly before the Civil War and worked on the staff of the Patterson Hospital in Washington, D.C. He had no diploma at the time and it is a wonder that he was allowed to practice. Bowers finally managed to become a certified physician after graduating from Bennett Eclectic Medical College in Chicago in 1873.

The doctor's first wife, Fannie Hammond, whom he had married in the middle 1860s, died about the time a mysterious fire consumed Bowers's Chicago home in 1874. Leaving Chicago, Bowers set up a short-lived practice in New York some weeks later, marrying Teresa Sherek, a seventeen-year-old actress he had met in Chicago. They were wed in late 1874 and moved to San Francisco the following year. There, on January 28, 1881, the second Mrs. Bowers died following a short and unspecified illness.

Only six months following the death of the second Mrs. Bowers, the doctor proposed to Mrs. Cecilia Benhayon-Levy. She accepted over the objections of her family, chiefly Cecilia's brother, Henry Benhayon, who voiced loud suspicions of Bowers relating to the mysterious death of his second wife. In the summer of 1885 the third Mrs. Bowers took to her sickbed with what her husband diagnosed as a liver ailment. The twenty-nine-year-old woman lingered for two months, then died.

Henry Benhayon openly accused Bowers of killing his sister; when, at his insistence, Cecilia's body was exhumed, it was soon learned that the third Mrs. Bowers had been killed by phosphorus poison. Bowers was promptly convicted of murdering his wife (his nurse and housekeeper were labeled accessories after the fact), and he was sent to prison to await execution while he filed his appeals.

While Bowers was in prison an extraordinary event took place—Henry Benhayon, his chief accuser, was found dead in a boardinghouse room on October 23, 1887, a bottle of potassium cyanide on the bed table, along with three suicide notes. One of the notes, addressed to the coroner of the Bowers case, contained Benhayon's confession that he, not Dr. Bowers, had poisoned his own sister to death.

Bowers appeared to be vindicated and officials made plans for his release from prison. Detectives, however, complicated matters when they discovered that Benhayon was not the person who had rented the room in which he died, an apparent suicide. The man responsible for the rental was none other than John Dimming, husband of Bowers's housekeeper. Further checking on Dimming re-

vealed that he had visited Bowers in his prison cell and, according to the statements of a San Francisco druggist, had purchased a bottle of potassium cyanide.

Dimming was now put on trial. The prosecution claimed that Bowers had somehow blackmailed Dimming into killing Benhayon and forging the suicide note that cleared Bowers. In December 1897 Dimming was tried but a deadlocked jury forced a new trial. (It was at this time that Dr. Bowers demanded a new trial, which was refused pending the outcome of the Dimming trial.) Dimming was tried again in 1888 and acquitted. The acquittal meant that, under the law, the Benhayon suicide note was genuine and, as such, cleared Bowers of murder.

The physician was released after serving four years in prison. Bowers quickly married a young woman he had been seeing while still married to the hapless third Mrs. Bowers. He continued practicing, growing rich, it was said, by performing illegal abortions. Bowers died in bed in 1904, his fourth wife living beyond him by a decade—a fate not shared by his three previous wives, whose deaths, especially Cecilia's murder, remain a permanent mystery.

Bradley, James
MURDER, 1982 U.S.

One of the most promising basketball players in recent years, six-foot-ten-inch James Bradley was shot and killed by a single bullet fired by an unknown assailant in downtown Portland, Oregon, on February 20, 1982. The reasons for Bradley's murder, Portland police admit, are obscure at this writing but might have had something to do with drugs. Bradley had been arrested two days before his death for peddling cocaine. He was free on bond pending trial when he was killed.

Bradley had shown himself to be a spectacular basketball player while in high school and college. Later, while playing for the Kentucky Colonels, he was heralded as another Magic Johnson or Larry Bird. Bradley first made a name for himself at Roosevelt High in East Chicago, Indiana (he was then a six-foot-four-inch forward), leading his team to the state championship in his senior year.

Sports Illustrated predicted that Bradley would be one of the nation's leading college basketball players, which he proved to be in 1971 at Northern Illinois University, where he led the squad to a national ranking. He later signed—for $750,000 for a five-and-half-year period—with the Kentucky Colonels, an American Basketball Association team which subsequently moved to the National Basketball Association and which won the league championship in 1975–76. Bradley contributed much to the win, but in years to follow his discipline broke down. He began to miss practice, make mistakes, and receive fines that mounted into the thousands of dollars. He was motivated only for brief periods of playing time.

The once promising player moved to the Baltimore Claws in 1976, but the newly created team died stillborn. Then it was

on to the ABA Denver team, where, after missing practices, he was let go, having played in only seven games.

Bradley next traveled about the globe, playing with foreign teams in France and the Philippines. On returning to the U.S., he managed to secure a place with the Rochester Zeniths of the Continental League, being paid $350 a week for fifteen weeks. If Bradley had made good with the Zeniths, an NBA farm club, he might have had another chance at the big leagues. He played hard for four years and greatly aided his team in winning two championships. Again he tried the big time, trying out for the NBA team in Portland. He failed to make the squad but stayed on in Portland, drifting about, investing a little money in business ventures, living a seemingly purposeless life.

Trouble came on February 18, 1982, when Bradley was arrested by Portland undercover detectives after he attempted to deliver cocaine to them. Two days later, Bradley was leaving a disco bar called the Copper Penny II in downtown Portland. It was 3 AM as he walked to his 1977 Cadillac parked near Salmon and Park streets. When Bradley was about sixty feet from the car, someone fired a single shot at him, the bullet striking him in the back and killing him.

Some insist that the killing was drug-related, that Bradley, who was out on bond pending his trial for drug peddling, might implicate higher-ups in Portland's drug racket and that he was murdered to silence a dangerous tongue. Others claimed that he was shot by a jealous husband angered over Bradley's advances to his wife. The speculations are still being made and the killer or killers are sought to this day.

Branson, Edith May Olive
MURDER, 1929 FRANCE

Edith Branson was a liberated woman, an artist who had lived many a harrowing adventure and one who enjoyed a number of tempestuous affairs. She was also the centerpiece in one of the strangest homicides involving an expatriate living in France at the end of the Jazz Age.

Branson was born in England to a well-to-do middle-class family. An early-day suffragette, she joined the Women's Army Corps during World War I and was sent to France. While serving near the front lines, Edith came under bombardment and her life was saved by a quick-acting colonel who spirited her to safety. Branson promptly married the colonel, but the union ended in separation a few years later. By then Edith had begun to paint seriously—she had dabbled in the art for years—and soon her works were exhibited in Paris salons and such distinguished galleries as the Royal Academy of London.

With success, Edith moved to Paris and indulged in numerous affairs among the colony of expatriates; but she preferred the natives, writing glowingly to one friend: "Frenchmen make the best lovers in the world." Tiring of the Paris scene toward the end of the 1920s, Branson, at age forty-three, moved to the South of France, settling in Les Baux, where she purchased a small inn, the Hôtel de Monte Carlo. She lived in a nearby cottage, continuing to paint while she oversaw the operation of the hotel.

This idyllic life exploded with the sound of gunfire on the night of April 28, 1929, when neighbors heard a loud shot ring out from Branson's property at about 9 in the evening. Police investigated the following morning and, after an exhaustive search, found the painter at the bottom of a cistern beneath several feet of water. The corpse was pulled out and examined. The dead woman wore only a nightgown and socks. A bullet had been fired into her head. At first detectives theorized that she had committed suicide, yet there was no motive for such an act. Further discrediting the suicide theory was the fact that there was no water found in the dead woman's lungs, proving that she had been shot and then put into the cistern. Police found the rooms of Edith's cottage flecked with her blood. Moreover, the large and rather savage watchdogs she kept had not made a sound on the night of the murder, indicating that the dogs were familiar with the killer.

Suspects narrowed down to François Pinet, who managed Edith's hotel, and Joseph Girard, a housekeeper. Pinet had been seen near Branson's cottage on the night of the murder by an eccentric artist named Vernon Bernard Blake, who lived nearby but had not spoken to Edith for several months after a testy debate over

45

aesthetics. Girard, who had helped police find the body, was held as a material witness but was soon cleared of any complicity; he lived off the grounds with his wife and proved he could not have been near the murder site at the time Edith was shot. That left Pinet.

A search of the manager's rooms revealed two wills signed by Edith Branson, one leaving everything she owned to him and a second with a later date bequeathing everything to her niece, who lived in Paris. Pinet admitted that he had seen the victim on the night she was killed, but it was an innocent house call; he had merely stopped by to deliver some petrol as Edith had requested. He was nevertheless arrested and held for trial on a charge of murder, the while protesting to police: "She was worth more to me alive than dead!"

Pinet's trial began in January 1930. Though much was made of the twenty-six-year-old manager's tempestuous trysting with Miss Branson, a woman nearly twice his age, no concrete evidence was put forward to convict Pinet. He was acquitted and returned to Les Baux, where he was given a hero's welcome.

The murder of Edith Branson was never solved. Several fiction writers over the years used the case as an inspiration for novels. One journalist penned a fact-fiction account wherein he portrayed Edith Branson and Vernon Blake as international spies who only pretended to be artists and whose evil intrigues brought about her murder, a story that caused a libel action by Blake's relatives (he had by then died) and an out-of-court settlement.

46

Bravo, Charles
MURDER, 1876 ENGLAND

One of the most alarming murders of Victorian England was that of a successful lawyer, Charles Delauny Turner Bravo, who, after an illness of three days, died on April 21, 1876. It was an agonizing death as witnessed by his wife, Florence, and her maid-companion, Mrs. Jane Cannon Cox. Several distinguished physicians, called to attend Bravo by Florence, labored to save the barrister's life. The doctors, noting the victim's symptoms, immediately suspected poison. The famous physician Sir William Gull inquired: "Mr. Bravo, what have you taken?"

"I rubbed my gums with laudanum," he replied. (This was a common home remedy to relieve toothaches and neuralgia.)

"Laudanum won't explain your symptoms, Mr. Bravo."

Following the lawyer's death, an autopsy was performed at Gull's suggestion. He had flatly stated that Bravo, during his illness, was dying of "irritant poison." (It was this same Sir William Gull who was Queen Victoria's personal physician and was later accused of covering up the identity of a prime suspect for the Jack the Ripper murders of 1888 [see entry]).

The pathologists found that Charles Bravo had died of antimony poisoning, receiving twenty to thirty grains in a single dose. An informal inquest was held on April 25, 1876, at the Bravo home, a luxurious mansion called the Priory on Bedford Hill Road in Balham. The affair was so informal that Florence Bravo served refreshments to jury members who smilingly decided that it could not fix blame for her husband's death, leaving the verdict open. Most familiar with the case at that time believed Bravo had committed suicide, a notion his wife and Mrs. Cox did little to dispel.

When reviewing the findings of the lighthearted inquest into the Bravo death, the Lord Chief Justice quashed the jury's findings and convened another inquest on July 11, 1876, an inquiry that took on the form of a trial, with Florence Bravo and Mrs. Cox—without being officially named as such—standing forth as the accused.

Florence Bravo's scarlet past came to light during this inquest. She had been the widow of a Captain Alexander Ricardo of the Grenadier Guards. Ricardo, an alcoholic, had died in 1871 in a drunken stupor, leaving £40,000 to his attractive twenty-five-year-old wife. The rich widow for several years thereafter was mistress to Dr. James Manby Gully, sixty-four years old. Gully was famous as a phrenologist (practitioner of a discredited science by which criminals were supposedly identifiable through the shape of their cranium and other physical characteristics). Gully was also a noteworthy playwright, and physician to such literary lights as Charles Dickens, Thomas Carlyle, and Alfred Tennyson, as well as Benjamin Disraeli, the British prime minister.

Florence met the handsome Charles Bravo in late 1875, marrying him on December 7 of that year. She had already broken with Gully and was eager to begin a relationship with a man more her own age. Charles's motives for marrying Florence, however, were less than honorable. She soon discovered, it was declared at the second inquest, that he was after her sizable bank account. Bravo had been congratulated by an acquaintance upon becoming engaged, a witness stated, and he replied: "Damn your congratulations. I only want the money."

Others stated, including Mrs. Cox, that Bravo badly mistreated his new wife, displaying childish fits of jealousy whenever she spoke to another man and even striking her in anger over imagined flirtations.

There was also talk about Charles's insatiable sexual appetite and how he attempted repeatedly to impregnate Florence. She had three miscarriages in several months and took to drink, another report had it. The case against Florence Bravo mounted, making it appear that she had good cause to murder a jealous, greedy, sex-craved, and physically abusive man who had married her for her money. One theory had it that Florence longed to return to the arms of the elderly Dr. Gully and, to that end, with the help of Mrs. Cox, put poison into the decanter of Burgundy from which Bravo drank copiously on the night he took violently ill.

At this juncture, however, her devoted maid and companion of long standing, Jane Cox, came to her rescue. (She herself was thought by some to be Bravo's murderer in that she feared he would fire her.)

"Mrs. Cox," the maid recalled Charles Bravo telling her on his deathbed, "I have taken poison. . . . Don't tell Florence."

47

Mrs. Cox went on to imply that the elderly Dr. Gully, Florence's benefactor, may have arranged for Charles's demise out of jealousy.

This caused Gully to testify, a degrading experience that ruined his medical practice and his reputation. Gully denied having anything to do with the Bravos following his breakup with Florence. He was cleared of any wrongdoing.

The jury in the second inquest could not deny that Bravo had been killed; the autopsy proved that. It declared that he had been murdered but emphatically added that "there is insufficient evidence to fix the guilt upon any person or persons." Florence Bravo was dismissed, along with Mrs. Cox.

The twice-widowed woman drifted into oblivion, comforted by her riches. It was long rumored after the second inquest that Florence had not only murdered Charles but her first husband as well. Ironically, she died like her first husband of acute alcoholism, at Southsea on September 13, 1878. Jane Cox, who had certainly swayed the jury from indicting her mistress, sailed off to Jamaica to live out her days in relative comfort, reportedly given a large sum of money by Florence Bravo.

No one was ever certain who poisoned the pernicious Charles Bravo, but a popular parody of the day, much like that applied to Lizzie Borden [see entry], condemned Florence Bravo out of hand. It read:

When lovely woman stoops to folly
And finds her husband in the way,
What charm can soothe her melancholy
What art can turn him into clay?

The only means her aim to cover,
And save herself from prison locks,
And repossess her ancient lover
Are Burgundy and Mrs. Cox!

Brink's Robbery, The
ARMORED CAR ROBBERY,
1976   CANADA

Using several cars to block the path of a Brink's armored car making deliveries, five men ambushed the vehicle on a Montreal side street, stopping it on March 30, 1976. The robbers surrounded the armored car and one of them pointed an antiaircraft gun at the vehicle, threatening to fire and "blow it up" unless guards inside opened the doors.

Reluctantly the Brink's guards opened the rear doors of the armored car and the robbers looted the money sacks inside, transferring these to their cars. All the while the man with the antiaircraft gun continued to train his weapon on the truck. In a matter of minutes the thieves emptied the Brink's vehicle and sped off in their cars, which were later found abandoned at a nearby golf course.

The thieves made off with more than $2.8 million in cash, the largest theft suffered by Brink's in its history. To date, the robbers are still at large.

British Bank of the Middle East

BANK ROBBERY, 1976 LEBANON

A band of unknown men thought to be guerrillas entered the British Bank of the Middle East in Bab Idriss, a suburb of Beirut, Lebanon, on January 22, 1976. They quickly blew open the huge vaults and emptied their contents, mostly safe deposit boxes, in the space of fifteen minutes.

The theft was enormous, one of the largest on record. According to former Lebanese Finance Minister Lucien Dahadah, the thieves took an estimated $50 million. Other sources claim that at least $20 million was taken. Though this loot—most of it in cash and jewels—was reportedly taken by minions of Yasir Arafat to finance his Palestine Liberation Organization operations, the identity of the thieves has never been determined.

C

Carey, Estelle
MURDER, 1943 U.S.

The butcherous murder of Chicago showgirl Estelle Carey was one of the Windy City's most spectacular unsolved killings, one, police later claimed, that was directly linked to the crime syndicate. In fact, it was this killing, said police, that led to the unveiling of the crime cartel's nationwide operations in the early 1940s.

A little after 3 PM on February 2, 1943, firemen, responding to an alarm, rushed into a handsomely decorated apartment at 512 West Addison Street. What they found made them reel back in shock. Before them lay a dead woman who had been hacked and chopped to pieces. Her feet and legs were literally burned off. She had been butchered savagely. Matted hair was found next to the body by detectives who were soon on the scene, but exactly whose hair it was could not be determined at the police lab. It was apparent that Estelle had fought viciously for her life. Signs of a violent struggle were everywhere. As police later reconstructed the crime, Miss Carey was apparently sitting in a chair reading Wilkie Collins's mystery *The Moonstone*, a copy of which was found nearby. There were bloodstains all over the apartment—on the stove, on the rear door, through which the killer had obviously fled (the front door was bolted and locked), and on the cupboard doors.

A variety of weapons had been used on Estelle. Found scattered about the apartment were a bloody butcher knife, an electric iron coated with blood, a blackjack, and a smashed whiskey bottle, its edges covered with gore. Though there were bloody smudge prints everywhere, not one fingerprint could be found, other than Estelle's and those of her roommate, Maxine Buturff (who proved to be elsewhere at the time of the killing).

In interviewing Estelle's neighbors, police turned up Mrs. Jessie Lovrein, who lived in the same apartment building and said that from her back window she saw a man going down the rear stairs of the building at approximately 2:30 PM, about the time of the murder. She gave a hazy description of this man, stating that after leaving the back porch of the apartment building he walked across the snow-swept lot toward Lake Shore Drive. She added that he was carrying two fur coats. A check of Estelle's wardrobe revealed that a mink and a sable coat were missing.

Oddly enough, more than $2,500 in jewelry Estelle kept in a shoebox was untouched, along with a key to her safe deposit box. The safe deposit box yielded about $2,000 in cash, jewelry, and bonds, but no clue as to the identity of Carey's maniacal killer.

When investigators began to look into Estelle's background they discovered that she, for years, had had strong contacts with the underworld. Earlier she had made more than $500 a week, then a whopping salary, as the leading " '26 girl" at a posh Rush Street nightery called the Colony Club. A "26 girl," at that time, was one who operated a "26" game, in which dice are thrown for low bets, usually ranging from 50¢ to $1; but at the Colony Club the stakes were much higher, so lucrative that Estelle had made a great deal of money overseeing a half-dozen other young women and games. This illegal operation, along with more sophisticated gambling, flourished up and down Rush Street, sanctioned by police who were on the payroll of, among others, Nick Circella, alias Nick Dean, who owned the Colony.

Not only had Dean been Estelle Carey's employer, he had been her lover as well. Dean, however, could not have killed Carey inasmuch as he was out of town when she was murdered. He was in hiding at the time, wanted for income tax evasion. So, too, was his partner, George Browne, who owned a piece of the Colony Club. Browne was chiefly involved

Chicago nightclub hostess and mob girl Estelle Evelyn Carey, whose brutal murder in 1943 vexes police to this day. (*Wide World*)

with labor racketeering and had, with Willie Bioff, moved into the high-level extortion of motion picture studio moguls, threatening to have various unions vital to that industry strike unless they received enormous payoffs.

Bioff and Browne held out on their syndicate chieftains, pocketing the Hollywood extortion moneys. When threatened by crime cartel members, they decided to cooperate as informers to the government, telling all they knew about nationwide crime operations. Nick Dean also informed and it was speculated that his girl friend, Estelle Carey, who knew what Nick Dean knew, was killed by a syndicate goon to keep her mouth shut.

The presence of the blackjack in the apartment where she was murdered gave some detectives the idea that the beautiful blond woman was a mob victim. Yet others argued that syndicate hits were not performed in such a gruesome manner. A mob victim was invariably strangled and the body placed in a car in a lot to decompose. Some thought that the syndicate hit man had purposely done a clumsy job in killing Estelle to make it appear to be anything but a syndicate killing.

Police routinely went through Carey's address book, checking and rechecking her male friends. One, businessman Earl M. Weymer, had had dinner with Estelle only two nights before her murder, but Weymer proved to have an airtight alibi. No other male acquaintances came under suspicion.

The police went back to their syndicate theory, discovering that, even after Estelle

had left the Colony Club (later raided and permanently closed) and had no visible means of support, she continued to buy expensive clothes and jewelry, and had traveled in style to Florida a few weeks before she was murdered. Apparently she attempted to disguise herself at the time, by dying her hair red and donning glasses. She had also used aliases when registering at Florida hotels.

Detectives also believed that Carey knew where Nick Dean's syndicate fortune was hidden and may have put her hands on it and hidden it herself. Her death had involved torture, police concluded, her killer perhaps putting the victim through an ordeal to discover where she had stashed her gangster-lover's loot. The killer, if this motive was valid, was undoubtedly a syndicate minion working for higher-ups who wanted the money they felt Dean had withheld from them, as had Bioff and Browne (both later killed for their greedy holdouts).

In the end it remained speculation. The demoniac killer of Estelle Carey was never found.

Chevis, Lt. Hubert George
MURDER, 1931 ENGLAND

Bizarre and inexplicable was the murder of British Army Lieutenant Hubert George Chevis, who died of poison on June 21, 1931. Chevis was dining with his wife in his Aldershot, England, billet when, after taking only a few mouthfuls of partridge,

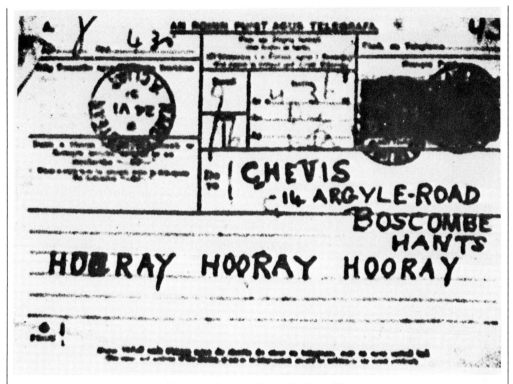

The mysterious telegram cheering the murder of Hubert Chevis.

he suddenly pushed away from the table, telling Mrs. Chevis that the food tasted bad. Within hours Lieutenant Chevis died in writhing agony; he had been murdered by strychnine. His wife was also ill from the poisoned partridge but survived.

An inquest left the verdict open and the murderer was never found. The killer gloated over the crime in that he or she sent a telegram to Chevis's father, Sir William, at the time of the officer's funeral, which simply read HOORAY, HOORAY, HOORAY. It was signed by a "J. Hartigan" and wired from Dublin. A sec-

ond prophetic telegram sent weeks later to Sir William boasted: "It is a mystery they will never solve."

"Charlie Chopoff" Slayings
MURDERS, 1972 U.S.

Manhattan police were shocked and baffled by the maniac who went on a murder rampage throughout 1972, selecting as his victims four young boys whom he strangled and stabbed to death. The killer then mutilated the victims, severing their limbs and leaving them in alleyways. Because of the killer's murder methods, he was named "Charlie Chopoff" by police, who have never managed to identify him to the time of this writing.

Collins, Shirley
MURDER, 1953 AUSTRALIA

Fourteen-year-old Shirley Collins left by inter-urban train for her first date on the evening of September 12, 1953, traveling to Richmond Station in Melbourne to meet Ronald Holmes, twenty-one. She never arrived there, and her mutilated body was found two days later at Mount Martha, thirty-eight miles outside of Melbourne.

Holmes's alibi was firmly established; porters testified that he was in Richmond Station for several hours waiting for Shirley to show up, this at the time doctors fixed for her death. The condition of the girl's body first suggested a rape killing. Her underclothes had been stripped from her body and scattered about. But medical examiners later reported that she had not been violated. Her killer, however, had slain her as would a beast. He had literally battered her to death with beer bottles, crushing her skull repeatedly. He had then ripped up two huge paving blocks from a walkway and viciously dropped these on her head, thoroughly reducing the girl's face to a bloody pulp.

Though Melbourne police worked for

months to track down the nameless killer, they came up empty-handed.

Colosimo, James
GANGLAND MURDER, 1920 U.S.

"Big Jim" Colosimo was Chicago's third great crime czar, following in the footsteps of Roger Plant (1860s–1880s) and "Big Mike" McDonald (1880s–1912). Where Plant had concentrated on robbery and McDonald on confidence games, Colosimo was the lord of the First Ward, the center of vice—chiefly prostitution—and gambling. His financial backers and political protectors were Michael "Hinky Dink" Kenna and "Bathhouse John" Coughlin.

In the space of a few years Colosimo was the virtual crime boss of Chicago, controlling all the rackets, his strong-arm squads directed by his nephew Johnny Torrio. A millionaire many times over, Colosimo indulged his whims by adorning his body with diamonds, much the same way Diamond Jim Brady did. He also opened up a posh nightclub and restaurant, Colosimo's Cafe, at 2126 South Wabash Avenue, where high society wined and dined with reporters, the city's industrial captains, impresarios like Florenz Ziegfeld, boxers such as Gentleman Jim Corbett, and the worst elements of the underworld.

Big Jim's penchant for opera soon had the world's greatest singers accepting his invitation to dine in his cafe. Enrico Caruso graced the cafe with his ravenous appetite and, on other occasions, customers could gawk at the likes of Amelita Galli-Curci and Luisa Tetrazzini. Another who drew Colosimo's attentions was Dale Winter, a beautiful brunette singer who had appeared in several frothy musicals. Big Jim insisted that Miss Winter had serious operatic talents and began to act as her agent. He also divorced his wife, Victoria Moresco, who had once been one of the leading madams in the red light district and had gotten Big Jim his start in crime.

In 1919 Colosimo was approached by his nephew, Torrio, who implored him to widen his empire into bootlegging, arguing that the newly established Prohibition Amendment would provide millions in illegal alcohol traffic. Colosimo, an old-fashioned gangster, told his nephew that he was happy with what he had and that no one in his organization was to bother with booze. Torrio, later credited as being the "father of modern American gangsterdom," merely shrugged.

Torrio, on the morning of May 11, 1920, called Colosimo on the phone to tell him that a shipment of whiskey for his cafe would be delivered around 4 PM. At about that time Colosimo was summoned to the vestibule of his club to sign for the shipment and was promptly shot to death. His killer fled down the street without taking Big Jim's sparkling diamonds or rifling his pockets, which contained thousands of dollars. Cafe employees attempted to pursue the killer but lost him in the heavy crowds on Wabash Avenue.

No one ever discovered the identity of

Chicago crime czar Big Jim Colosimo, shown with his showgirl sweetheart Dale Winter shortly before his murder.

Colosimo's body sprawled in the vestibule of his nightclub on the afternoon of May 11, 1920.

Al Capone, the primary suspect in the killing of Big Jim Colosimo.

Big Jim's killer. Some said that the heart-injured Victoria Moresco had sent an agent to avenge her wounded pride. Others claimed that police, frustrated at not being able to indict Colosimo for the many gang murders he had ordered, sent their own emissary. Gang experts shook their heads and pointed to Torrio and his personal enforcer, Al Capone, as the real culprits; these two took over Colosimo's empire an hour after he crashed to the floor of his club.

Big Jim was given a lavish funeral with tens of thousands of dollars' worth of flowers carted with him to the cemetery. The fifty-year-old crime czar's funeral set the style of gangster send-offs in Chicago for the next fifteen years. His protégée, nineteen-year-old Dale Winter, whom he had recently married, went on to make a name for herself on Broadway, appearing in such smash musicals as Jerome Kern's *Irene*.

Years later, Louis "Little New York" Campagna, one of Capone's many thugs, was asked who really killed Big Jim. "Aww, that don't matter none," snarled the thug. "The bozo was bumped because he wouldn't peddle beer! Imagine?"

Comeans, William
MURDER, 1980 U.S.

Strange threats in the form of notes were delivered to William Comeans, fourteen, a native of New Rome, Ohio. Comeans, a newsboy, had complained to his parents that two men had tried to strangle him while he was delivering papers but he managed to escape. His descriptions of the men were incomplete and, on January 7, 1980, Comeans was abducted from the front lawn of his home. His body was found hours later. The boy had been strangled with his own scarf.

Following the boy's death, the killer or killers began sending notes to others in New Rome, telling them to guard their children closely. "Time is short," said one note. "All have been warned," read another. The third chilling missive read: "It's time." Though the killer caused the small community to be turned into an armed camp, he has not struck again to the time of this writing.

Connecticut Mutual Life Insurance
ROBBERY, 1889 U.S.

The Manhattan offices of the Connecticut Mutual Life Insurance Company were burglarized on September 4, 1889, the vaults looted completely by at least three cracksmen, police later guessed. Taken in the gigantic haul was more than $500,000, one of the largest robberies in American history to that time.

The burglars had picked their way through several locked doors, then drilled through the vault doors to spring the huge locks. The job, most agreed, had the earmarks of Max Shinborn, then one of the most notorious burglars in America, a man

who gleaned millions from scores of bank burglaries and finally retired to the French Riviera to live out his life in luxury, purchasing, along with a fancy villa, the title of "Baron M. Shindell."

Croydon Killings
MURDERS, 1928–29 ENGLAND

When Edmund Duff died on April 26, 1928, after eating a chicken dinner, Dr. Robert Bronte of Croydon, England, found nothing unusual in his autopsy, and a coroner's jury returned a verdict of "Death from natural causes." A second member of the family, Vera Sydney, Duff's sister-in-law, along with the family cook and her aunt, grew ill after eating lunch on February 14, 1929. Miss Sydney died two days later. Though she manifested all the signs of poisoning—stomach cramps, writhing, vomiting—her death was attributed to gastric influenza.

Vera's mother, Violet Emelia Sydney, had a relapse at her daughter's death. A local physician, a Dr. Binning, prescribed a mild medicine, which Mrs. Sydney took and then grew ill. Before the sixty-nine-year-old woman died on March 15, 1929, she insisted that the medicine was "gritty," and that someone (other than the physician, who was later cleared) had poisoned the prescription. Arsenic was found in the medicine, which led to the exhumation of Duff and Vera Sydney. Both of the bodies contained arsenic. Inquests were again held. Edmund's widow, Grace

Croydon Killings

Duff, was suspected of poisoning all three family members, since the victims had been dosed with meals and medicine inside the Croydon home, yet there was insufficient evidence to indict her.

Grace Duff died in 1973 of natural causes at age eighty-seven. Two years later an English journalist attempted once again to prove her guilty, declaring that Grace had been in love with a local doctor who provided her with the poison to rid herself of an unwanted husband and to murder her sister and mother to gain the family inheritance. The Croydon killings, however, remain officially unsolved.

D

Darnley, Lord Henry Stewart
ASSASSINATION, 1567 ENGLAND

Mary Queen of Scots, at sixteen, married Francis, the Dauphin and son of Henry II of France, on April 24, 1558. When Henry died, Francis became king of France and Mary, queen. Two years later, on December 5, 1560, Francis died, leaving Mary to fend for herself. She returned to Scotland even though her sister, Queen Elizabeth I of England, had sent warships to intercept her; the two queens had been bitter enemies since Mary had denounced Elizabeth as illegitimate, claiming the English throne for herself.

After many intrigues Mary, mostly to spite Elizabeth, took a second husband, Lord Henry Stewart Darnley, eldest son of the Earl of Lennox, a staunch Catholic. Elizabeth, fearing that Mary would raise an army against her and attempt to re-establish the Catholic faith as dominant in England, reportedly intrigued with certain Scottish nobles to end Darnley's life. It is not certain, however, just how Elizabeth I was implicated in this plot. Many historians insist that she was not.

On the night of February 9–10, 1567, Mary visited Darnley in his rooms at a mansion at Kirk o'Field outside of Edinburgh. The new king of Scotland was recovering from smallpox and Mary ministered to him for a few hours before going to a wedding ceremony. Some time later, unknown assassins crept into Darnley's room and strangled him. They thought to cover their crime by placing several kegs of gunpowder in Mary's room, which was below Darnley's, and exploding it.

When several Scottish nobles turned on Mary, the queen fled to England, where, for eight years, Elizabeth kept her under house arrest. During this time several official inquisitions into Mary's possible involvement with Darnley's murder were convened. Letters the Scottish queen had written and had kept in a small jewelry box, later to be termed the infamous "casket letters," were held up as evidence against Mary that she had conspired to kill her husband, in order to take up with another, more powerful noble. The letters, however, brought no conclusive proof against Mary.

Elizabeth, vexed at not getting an indictment against the troublesome Mary, then ordered her execution on the pretext that the Queen of Scots had conspired to restore the Roman Catholic religion to England. Mary, certainly innocent, was executed by the headsman in the Great Hall of Fotheringhay Castle on February 8, 1587. The murder of her second husband, Darnley, remains a mystery to this day.

Detroit Children Killings
MURDERS, 1976–77 U.S.

The opulent bedroom communities of Detroit had never seen anything like it. Children were being abducted, kept a few days to a few weeks, and then deposited dead along stretches of lonely roadways. A homicidal maniac was loose, one who killed ritually and often with a sardonic touch. The killings, four to seven murders, occurred in the comfortable townships of Oakland County, Michigan, northwest of Detroit.

Police were powerless, it seemed, as they reeled from one horrible murder to the next, unable to find a single substantial clue leading to the killer's identity. Detectives—there would be an enormous task force assembled before the killings subsided—did know that they were dealing with a man who slew by ritual (and that he was most probably a white-collar murderer). The condition of the bodies told them that.

Two teenage girls seem to have been the first victims of this methodical killer.

Cynthia Cadieux, age sixteen, who lived with her mother and stepfather in Roseville, vanished on January 15, 1976, after leaving a girl friend's house at 8:30 PM in Roseville. Her naked body was found the following morning at two o'clock on Franklin Road. Cynthia's clothes were piled fifteen feet away from her corpse, which had been dragged some distance on a snow-covered pavement. A powerful blow to the head with a blunt instrument had fractured her skull. Four days later Sheila Srock, age fourteen, was murdered by an intruder at about 8 PM in her sister's home in Birmingham. Her body was found partially clothed; the girl had been shot three times. Another teenage girl, thirteen-year-old Jane Louise Allan, who was a habitual runaway, was killed later in the year, in August 1976, after getting a ride in Pontiac Township. The Allan girl was later discovered dead on a road near Miamisburg, Ohio. A coroner's report revealed that she had been found fully clothed, bound hand and foot, and that her body had been in water for more than two days. Her death was attributed to carbon monoxide poisoning.

None of these teenage murders seemed related to police, but four deaths following that of Sheila Srock were all the work of one man, detectives believe to this day. The first of these was Mark Stebbins, age twelve, who lived with his divorced mother in Ferndale. Mark had been playing games at the American Legion Hall in Ferndale on February 13, 1976, and left the hall shortly after noon, telling friends he was going to watch TV. He was found

Four of the seven victims attributed to the killer who murdered children in the Detroit area in 1976–77 (*left to right*): Timothy King, Kristine Mihelich, Mark Stebbins, and Jill Robinson. (*Courtesy Oakland County Task Force*)

dead in Southfield on February 19, at noon, when someone stumbled over his body in an office building parking lot.

The Stebbins boy was fully clothed, but his hands bore the marks of rope burns. Police noted that the body had been thoroughly cleaned and laid out in a funeral position. He had been sexually assaulted and then suffocated.

Next came Jill Robinson, age twelve, who left a hobby store on Woodward Avenue in Royal Oak on December 22, 1976, at 7:30 PM. Her fully clothed body was found on December 26 along I-75 Roadway in Troy. A shotgun blast to the girl's head had ended her life. Police theorized that the killer took the girl to the roadway when she was still alive, dragged her out of his vehicle, and then inexplicably shot Jill to death before fleeing. He did, however, as in the case of the Stebbins boy, take time to lay out the child in a funeral

position. And, as in the case of the Stebbins child, Jill Robinson's body had been thoroughly cleaned.

The child killer struck again by abducting ten-year-old Kristine Mihelich of Berkley, who vanished three blocks from her suburban home when she went to buy a magazine on January 2, 1977. She was found alongside a lonely road in Franklin Village on January 21, 1977. She had been suffocated but not sexually assaulted. Like Stebbins and Robinson, Kristine's body had been cleaned and laid out in a funeral position.

A little more than two months later, on March 16, 1977, eleven-year-old Timothy King of Birmingham went to a drugstore to buy some candy. He vanished for seven days. This time, however, witnesses caught a glimpse of a man talking to Timothy. The boy was seen with a white male, twenty-five to thirty-five years old, a man with a shag haircut and bushy sideburns who was driving a blue Gremlin compact car.

Frantic, Mrs. Marian King, the boy's mother, made a tearful appeal to the abductor on TV, begging him to return her child safely to her, that she would have a chicken dinner waiting for Timothy. On March 23, 1977, next to a lonely road in Livonia, Timothy King's body was found. The boy had been sexually assaulted, then suffocated. His corpse had been thoroughly cleaned (even his clothes had been cleaned and pressed), and he had been laid out neatly in a funeral position.

Near the body was found a skateboard which Timothy had been carrying when he vanished. A close examination of the body revealed that the boy had, like the three others before him, been bound before being killed. An autopsy revealed that the killer had watched Mrs. King's TV appeal; the remains of a chicken dinner were found in the boy's stomach, a gruesomely sardonic gesture on the part of the murderer. Though the police were able to publish a sketch of the possible killer, based on information about the man Timothy had talked to outside the drugstore, no concrete clues to his identity were uncovered.

There were striking patterns in the killer's modus operandi, however. The killer had sexually abused his male captives but not the females. He had thoroughly cleaned all the bodies as part of his ritual before depositing them along roadways, careful to put their bodies in tidy positions on their back, hands over chest. The cleaning of the bodies was meticulous, according to Medical Examiner Werner Spitz, who examined the King boy: "He was scrubbed. His fingernails and toenails were immaculate. Even his clothes had been cleaned." The police reasoned that this was done to eliminate any particles of hair, rugs, or any other matter that might be traced to the killer. Others, from occultists to psychiatrists, felt that the killer cleaned his victims as a sign of self-admitted guilt, after the fashion of killers who compulsively wash their hands.

There were striking similarities in the victims themselves. All were from middle- to upper-middle-class families in Detroit's bedroom communities. All were white with fair complexions and freckles. All were Roman Catholics. Most were shy, quiet children, loners (except for Timothy King, an outgoing, friendly boy).

Their killer had chosen to suffocate all the children. The Robinson girl may have been suffocated but recovered while being placed on the roadway, which caused the murderer to shotgun her to death. He was also referred to as the "snow killer," a maniac who murdered only when snow was on the ground, at least in the four homicides that police definitely linked together.

The nationwide press reports on the killings and the public outcry in Detroit's affluent communities soon caused more than two hundred of the best detectives from fifty police departments to join in a task force to hunt down the killer. At first police thought their prey to be a blue-collar worker. Then their attitude changed.

Three police composite sketches of the suspected abductor-murderer of the Detroit-area children, the last believed to be the most accurate. (*Courtesy Oakland County Task Force*)

Birmingham police chief Jerry Tobin stated: "We think he is a white-collar-class person or a professional man—somebody who is trusted, like a doctor, a policeman, a member of the clergy."

The strange rituals practiced by the killer led some authorities to believe, however, that the killer may have been a foreigner, perhaps a native of the Middle East, where burials are accompanied by extreme fastidiousness, where bodies are methodically scrubbed after death. Moreover, a local psychiatrist was reportedly in touch with a friend of the killer's, a man with a decidedly Middle Eastern dialect who phoned him, speaking in a high-pitched, hysterical voice. (The author has heard a tape of this phone call.) The informer told the psychiatrist that he could meet the killer in one of the many gay bars on Detroit's Woodward Avenue, but no one contacted the psychiatrist when he went to the bar at the appointed time.

Doggedly, the police task force began to assemble information, reports of any and every suspect in the county, reports by the tens of thousands that were all carefully categorized through a massive computer system. Scores of detectives, as the months went on, answered even the most ridiculous of reports. If someone saw an old man pat a child on the head, the old man was interviewed within hours. (The author accompanied detectives on several interviews which resulted in dead ends.) On one occasion, a parishioner reported her local priest as having been "too friendly to Sunday school children." The priest, after questioning, was exonerated.

The massive investigation went on for

many months following the King boy's death, but without results. Every owner of a blue Gremlin in the Detroit area was grilled, but all were found to be innocent. The man who had been seen talking with Timothy King was never found. And the Detroit child killer has not struck again to the time of this writing.

It was felt later that the killer realized that to continue his rampage of child murdering might mean his capture. There were simply too many police on the street looking for him. The killing stopped, and a member of the police task force later stated that "the madman probably left the area, going to another state."

Such lone killers, police know, are the most difficult to track down. They do not operate in the known underworld and therefore cannot be turned in by police informers. They usually catch themselves, turning themselves in after being plagued by guilt, if ever. Sometimes, as was the case of Peter Kurten, the mass child-killer of Düsseldorf, Germany, they tell a loved one of their atrocities and are subsequently arrested and punished. Kurten, a white-collar worker who led a respectable life during the day, casually told his wife over breakfast one morning that he had been slipping out of the house late at night to murder for thirteen years; his wife turned him in. He was beheaded.

So far, the Detroit children slayer has not been overwhelmed by his own conscience.

Dimmock, Emily Elizabeth ("Phyllis")

MURDER, 1907 ENGLAND

A London prostitute who called herself Phyllis to her trade, twenty-three-year-old Emily Dimmock enamored a dining car chief, Bertram Shaw, into supporting her as his mistress. Shaw rented rooms for Phyllis at 29 St. Paul's Road in Camden Town, but refused to marry her. This did not upset Phyllis, who took full advantage of Shaw's absence on his overnight train runs to bring other men to her apartment.

Returning from his usual trip from Sheffield to St. Pancras on the Midland Railway line, Shaw arrived at Dimmock's apartment on September 12, 1907. He found the folding doors separating the sitting room from Phyllis's bedroom locked and had to force them open. Inside, sprawled naked on the bed, was his mistress, her throat slit wide open.

Police investigating the murder quickly exonerated Shaw, who easily proved that he was aboard a train at the time of the killing. Another man, Robert Percival Roberts, a ship's cook who had dated Phyllis, was pulled in for questioning. He, too, had a concrete alibi. Roberts was able, however, to furnish detectives with information. He remembered seeing a letter, he said, that Phyllis had shown him, on which he described certain drawings like a rising sun winking. Portions of this letter were discovered in the effects of the murdered woman and these bits of paper led to the arrest of a commercial artist named

Robert William Thomas Cavers Wood.

Wood was tried after he was identified as the man leaving Dimmock's apartment building on the morning of her murder. The man who said he saw Wood leave the building at a little after ten o'clock that morning was carman Robert Henry MacCowan. The carman explained that the man was wearing a bowler hat and a dark overcoat. He picked Wood out of a lineup of men wearing this apparel. Once in court, however, MacCowan's identification was shaken by Wood's brilliant defense attorney, Edward Marshall Hall.

The attorney had MacCowan describe the morning of the murder as "drizzly, thick, foggy and muggy," then proved the carman's memory faulty by pointing out from official records that there had been no rain that day. MacCowan had also repeatedly insisted that the man emerging from Phyllis's building was "broad-shouldered." Hall ordered his client to stand in the dock and the gallery gasped as they inspected Wood's extremely narrow shoulders.

MacCowan countered by stating: "He would look broader in an overcoat."

Hall then had his client put on an overcoat. "Now," demanded the attorney, "would you describe that man as broad-shouldered?"

"He has broader shoulders than I have," snapped back MacCowan.

Marshall Hall snickered. "Would you describe a bluebottle as an elephant because it is bigger than a fly?" The remark totally unhinged the witness and destroyed his credibility.

A sketch made by artist Robert Wood while in court standing trial for the murder of Emily Dimmock, a woman he casually knew and herein depicted as a man-manipulating monster.

Dimmock, Emily Elizabeth ("Phyllis")

Ruby Young, a discarded girl friend, testified for Robert Wood and almost got him convicted.

Justice Grantham, as drawn in court by the accused, Robert Wood, during his sensational trial for the murder of Emily Dimmock.

Yet there was the matter of the alibi that Wood could not produce as to his whereabouts at the time of the murder. He had told his friends and constables arresting him that he had been walking alone at the time. A former lover, Ruby Young, produced an unsolicited alibi for Wood, first stating that she was with him at the time of the murder, then withdrawing the alibi, as if to say that she had been coerced into lying for Wood. All of this was shown by Hall to be the vicious underplayings of an abandoned woman bent on vengeance. So hostile did crowds in and out of the courtroom become toward Ruby Young that she had to be smuggled out of the Old Bailey disguised as a cleaning woman.

Before the jury returned a "not guilty" verdict, Wood's trial had become a cause célèbre, with all of London avidly devouring every courtroom dispatch. "A scandal in low life," is how one newspaper described the trial. Yet Wood, an engaging young man with a considerable talent as an artist (he spent his time in the dock coolly sketching the judge and battling attorneys), had won the sympathy of the public long before his peers discarded the flimsy circumstantial case against him.

When he was set free, he shrugged and smiled and stepped from the courtroom amidst wild cheers from the gallery. Women wept and men thumped him on the back. West End theater productions were halted in mid-sentence so that stage managers could announce Wood's innocence. Cheering, singing throngs marched up and down London's streets all night long, celebrating the release of the defendant.

Possibly in those throngs marched Emily Dimmock's anonymous killer.

Doze, Grace
MURDER, 1927 U.S.

A most unusual unsolved murder was not discovered by the son of the victim until fifty years after the killing. Clifford C. Doze of Buffalo, New York, happened to be glancing at his hometown newspaper, the *Evening News*, which carried a reproduction of its May 21, 1927, front page, a fiftieth anniversary issue which announced LINDBERGH IN FRANCE. A small inset story from the same 1927 edition declared in smaller letters: "Murdered Woman is Mrs. C. G. Doze."

Doze, fifty-three when he discovered this story in 1977, had been told by his father, grandmother, and later, his stepmother, that his mother Grace Doze had merely left the family, walked out, and never returned. Through microfilm of the local newspaper, Doze discovered that his thirty-year-old mother, her hair bobbed, wearing a blue dress and two-toned shoes, left her Buffalo house on May 17, 1927. Her body was found four days later—the day Lindbergh landed in Paris—and her story landed on the front page next to the banner headline announcing the majestic feat of the American aviator. This news story was never shown to three-year-old Doze.

In his research, Doze also discovered that his mother had been apparently abducted, beaten, and then strangled before her body was tossed into Ellicott Creek outside the small town of Tonawanda which neighbors Buffalo and that more than two hundred persons inspected the corpse before it was identified as Mrs. Doze.

Doze's father, who had often quarreled with his mother—she had once stabbed the elder Doze in the arm and repeatedly threatened to leave him—was questioned in the case but released. The killer is still unknown to Doze and authorities today.

E

Elwell, Joseph Browne
MURDER, 1920 U.S.

On the morning of June 11, 1920, Mrs. Marie Larsen, a housekeeper, let herself into her employer's elegant New York mansion at 244 West 70th Street. It was exactly eight o'clock, the usual time for the punctual Mrs. Larsen to appear. Upon entering the living room, the housekeeper let out a scream and then ran for help. Minutes later she was babbling about a stranger slumped dead in Joseph Elwell's home.

Closer investigation revealed that the dead man was no stranger but Elwell himself, as he truly was, and not the dapper, youthful-looking man known to his housekeeper and his friends. He was found with a bullet hole in his bald head, his slack jaw revealing a toothless mouth. Elwell, who was one of the world's greatest authorities on bridge, had kept a youthful appearance by wearing expensive wigs and dentures, with regular trips to cosmetic surgeons.

In addition to becoming a millionaire through his expertise on cards—his book *Elwell on Bridge* was the definitive work on the game—the onetime hardware salesman was a popular lady's man. In fact, there were so many ladies in his life that police were long convinced that his killer was a female. His wife, whom he had married in 1904 and from whom he had recently been divorced, had financed his early career, taught him manners, and given him polish while introducing him into high society. She was a prime suspect but soon proved to have an iron-clad alibi.

More than seventy women were interrogated by police, who found their names in Elwell's personal address book. None of them proved to be serious contenders for the role of his murderer, including the last person known to see him alive, Viola Kraus. Miss Kraus, who had recently been divorced herself, had been telling one and all that she was about to be the new Mrs. Elwell. She had dined with Elwell at the Ritz the night before the murder and had then gone on with him to the New Amsterdam Roof to see a musical called *Midnight Frolic*.

Elwell took a taxi home alone, stopping only for a morning newspaper, the driver letting him off at his mansion at about 2 AM. Four hours later a milkman left two

68

bottles. An hour later the mailman arrived, and, police later learned, the bottles were gone. In reconstructing the last hours of the rakish Elwell, detectives concluded that he had stayed up all night. He had taken in the milk bottles and had picked up his mail at 7 AM. Inside of the next hour someone never known to the police killed him before Mrs. Larsen arrived at 8 AM.

Elwell was found with letters from the day's mail in his hands, but they gave no clue to his killer's identity. The fact that the victim was dressed in his pajamas caused investigators to believe that he was murdered by someone, a lady, with whom he was having personal relations. Oddly enough, the windows of the living room in which Elwell was killed were open and the drapes and shades pulled away so that any casual passerby could have glanced into the mansion and undoubtedly seen Elwell's killer stand close to him and drill a .45-caliber slug into his head. Yet no one in the moving crowd outside reported anything.

The fact that a .45-caliber army revolver was used to kill Elwell gave police pause; it was not a weapon a woman was likely to use—too cumbersome and unwieldy. Further confounding detectives was the fact that none of the card master's money was touched, hundreds of dollars being available in desk and bureau drawers. His jewelry and valuable antiques were also untouched. All of this ruled out robbery and left as a motive only jealousy. At first it was thought that one of Elwell's many female friends had shot him, incensed at

Dapper Joseph Elwell, super bridge expert, whose mysterious death in New York in 1922 still baffles police.

being discarded. Then a detective suggested that perhaps a bridge player who had lost at cards might have shot him. Knowing the passion of some bridge players, the police seriously considered this theory. It mattered little. No one ever really knew for sure why or who put a bullet into the late authority on high society's foremost game.

Evangelista Slayings
MURDERS, 1929 U.S.

Benjamino Evangelista, who liked to be called Benny, was most probably insane; nevertheless, he cleverly preyed upon the superstitions of his fellow Italians with a business acumen that might rival Henry Ford's. Where Ford, a citizen of Detroit, as was Benny, sold cars to millions, Evangelista sold hexes and herbs and spiritual remedies to the hundreds of Italians who lived in his Detroit community.

Although he was a churchgoing Roman Catholic, as were his wife and four children, Evangelista set up his own temple in his basement, a sort of occult room with a crude altar featuring a large, single eye—the "Evil Eye," if you will—and from the ceiling of this basement temple he hung all manner of papier-mâché and wax figures of sinister and foreign images—lesser occult gods, Benny said, who worked their separate magic. The slightest breeze set the grimacing figures in motion, which is what Evangelista had ordained when he

ordered the figures made by a local craftsman for $100.

In addition to this weird temple, Evangelista worked out of main floor offices in his home at 3587 St. Aubin Avenue, functioning as a real estate broker. He owned considerable property in the area, and scores of renters who came to pay their bills also brought wives and children suffering from various maladies. After collecting the rent, Benny would mumble occult chants, perform some brief cabalistic rites with dolls (with or without pins), and end the show with a joint-jolting dance of his own invention. He would then pat the patient on the head and pronounce him or her cured.

Evangelista, however, took no chances with his own health; he had a highly paid physician to care for his family.

Outwardly, Benny Evangelista appeared to be a successful, contented man—one who never displayed anger, let alone violence. Yet the violence that entered the Evangelista household on the night of July 2–3, 1929, left Detroit's police and public alike with nightmares for decades afterwards.

At ten thirty on the morning of July 3, 1929, Vincent Elias, another real estate broker having business with Benny, arrived at the three-story Evangelista home. He knocked on the unlocked door, and, when no one answered, he entered the small office at the front. Elias was instantly petrified at the sight that greeted him. Slumped in his desk chair was Benny Evangelista, or most of him. Benny's head had been neatly decapitated and was sitting on the floor, eyes staring upward in death, next to the body to which it had once been joined. Elias let out a yelp and ran for the law.

Squads of police, plus newsmen who had been tipped off to the gruesome slaying, stormed into the Evangelista home to view Benny's beheaded corpse and, to their shock, found the real estate broker's family in a similar state of dismemberment.

Mrs. Evangelista lay in her bed, her head almost severed, hanging by strands on her arm. The four Evangelista children, from eighteen months to eight years of age, were in other beds, chopped to pieces, their limbs hacked fiendishly from their torsos. Detroit had never seen a bloodbath such as this or a mass murder that commanded, in weeks, months, and years to come, as much press.

Detectives were hampered from the start in their investigation. In addition to a horde of newsmen, a stomping, pawing army of police raged through the Evangelista home, destroying what evidence might have been uncovered. In their eagerness to track down the maniac who slew this entire family, police and reporters handled every object in the home. All investigators came up with was a somewhat smudged and bloody thumbprint on the latch to the back door of the building. And this print was a source of irritation to the homicide department in Detroit for years to come.

Sixty officers were assigned to the case, interviewing hundreds of people, even citizens who never met the bizarre Benny Evangelista. (The local parish priest told reporters that the Evangelistas were "illiterate" and that Mrs. Evangelista was the true occult fanatic: her husband was merely a shrewd huckster who made money on ignorant and superstitious Italian immigrants.)

In the weeks that followed, only one slim suspect was plucked from the phalanxes herded into police stations for questioning. His name was Umberto Tecchio, one of Evangelista's tenants who had been paying off a house on time. It was learned that Tecchio had visited Benny on the night of the murder, July 2, 1929, to make a final payment on his house. Camillo Tress had gone to the Evangelista house that night with Tecchio but adamantly insisted that his friend Umberto had left Benny's premises no later than 11 PM and that Evangelista was alive at the time.

Tecchio was excused and the case bogged down in a swamp of rumors, hearsay, and conjecture. Tecchio died peacefully of natural causes in his bed on November 26, 1934. A few weeks later, his former wife, who had remarried twice after leaving Tecchio, came to the police and told them that the murder weapons used in the Evangelista case were two machetes Benny had employed in his cult rituals (to slay chickens, etc.) and that these two machetes she later found in a bag kept by her ex-husband. The police, by that late date, searched in vain among Tecchio's effects for the machetes. Then another person stepped forth now that Tecchio was safely dead, a onetime newsboy named Frank Constanzo. He told police that he had been delivering news-papers at five o'clock on the morning of the Evangelista murders and witnessed Umberto Tecchio standing on Benny's front porch, as if he were leaving the home. He had said hello to Tecchio, said Constanzo, but the heavyset Tecchio merely snarled a grunt back to him.

After hearing about the Evangelista slayings the boy was so terrified that he kept silent about seeing Umberto until the man died. Many people had been frightened of Tecchio. He was suspected of practicing Black Hand extortion (some Black Hand notes were found in Evangelista's papers, but were not traceable). Moreover, Tecchio had once killed a man, his brother-in-law, Bartolomeo Maffio. He had been arguing with Maffio over a debt and wound up plunging a dagger into Maffio's heart on April 19, 1929, this being only three months before the Evangelista clan was wiped out. Tecchio was exonerated in this killing; it was decreed that he had acted in self-defense.

Tecchio's wife, who later was to go to the police with the machete story, divorced Umberto following the Evangelista slayings and married a man named Louis Peruzzi. The Peruzzis continued to live in the house Tecchio lost in the divorce, the house Umberto had desperately purchased from Evangelista. Umberto in early 1932 had threatened to blow up the house unless it was returned to him. It was not. On November 9, 1932, Louis Peruzzi was shot to death as he sat smoking a pipe on the front porch of his house. Police at the time, even though they had been asked

for protection by Peruzzi against Tecchio some weeks earlier, ruled Peruzzi's death a suicide.

The suicide theory utterly captivated Detroit detectives in those days. Back in the summer of 1929, when Tecchio's thumbprints failed to match that of the bloody print taken from the Evangelista home, investigators had got the bright idea to try to match the victim's own print to their find. A squad of detectives went to the cemetery where Benny Evangelista had been buried a month earlier. In the dead of night these rather ghoulish sleuths dug up Benny's corpse and took a thumb-print. A few were even surprised when it did not match that found in the cultist's home, thinking Benny to be the real culprit. These amazed detectives never did explain how Benny managed to chop up his family, behead himself, *and then* hide the murder weapons.

What ruled Tecchio out as a real suspect, police finally said—despite the confessions of Umberto's ex-wife and a newsboy speeding along on a bike—was the fact that none of his clothes had been stained with blood, and the killer, following such an orgy of bloodletting, would have been drenched with human gore. Constanzo, the newsboy, had to admit that no bloodstains appeared to be on Tecchio's clothes when he saw (or thought he saw) Tecchio standing on Benny's porch.

For years detectives were at cross-purposes on the case. At one point in 1935 two senior Detroit detectives began to debate the use or misuse of the bloody thumbprint to the point where they actually struck each other. Had they probed deeper into Evangelista's background, the Detroit police might have come closer to the killer than shouting speculations in squad rooms. Information about Benny's beginnings dribbled out over the years, and, perhaps, much of this man's strange history shed the strongest light upon the exotic killings.

Benny Evangelista had immigrated to America from Italy at the turn of the century. He first settled in Philadelphia, where he went to work as a member of a railroad repair gang. In the same crew was another immigrant from Italy, one Aurelius Angelino. The men became fast friends, sharing a fanatic belief in cult mysticism. They came to believe that they could put spells on their enemies and work magic.

Evangelista later wrote a weird, unpublished volume which he entitled *The Oldest History of the World, Discovered by Occult Science in Detroit Michigan*. In the volume Benny jotted down his feverish notions of the worldwide cult he would begin, calling it the Great Union Federation of America. He likened himself in this rambling manuscript to an ancient king, whom he dubbed Itol. King Itol had an errant, deranged son, whom Benny called Trampol. The son was a murderous creature, Benny related: "He had no remorse, for he was a magician. He had a great power of magnetism. He pardoned

no one. He had not but murder in his heart, and the people were frightened of him."

Trampol, as events later indicated, could well have been Evangelista's close occult associate in Pennsylvania, Aurelius Angelino, always a moody, truculent type. In 1919, Angelino grabbed an ax and went on a murder spree, chopping up two of his four children before being subdued. He was sent to an insane asylum. Evangelista suddenly moved his family to Detroit. Angelino escaped the asylum twice but was recaptured. In 1923 Angelino made good a permanent escape and was never seen again, except, perhaps, by the newsboy Constanzo. Aurelius Angelino was a large, hulking man, similar in size to Umberto Tecchio, and it may have been Angelino, his warped mind driving him to fulfill some enigmatic and awful mission to the Evangelista home in 1929, who was standing on that porch in the dim light of dawn on July 3, not Tecchio.

Some detectives thought long and hard about that possibility and strengthened their suspicions by checking once more that bloody thumbprint. There were no prints of Angelino to match it against. However, detectives were sure that the bloody thumbprint was that of a left-handed man. Tecchio had been right-handed. Angelino had been left-handed.

F

Faithfull, Starr

MURDER, 1931 U.S.

Daniel Moriarity was looking for nothing in particular, just anything he might use or sell that day, June 8, 1931, as he leisurely made his way down the sandy beaches of Long Beach, twenty miles from the throbbing city of New York. Moriarity moved slowly under the hot morning sun, scanning the tide and shoreline for salable debris that might be delivered into his beachcomber's hands. Suddenly he stopped, gaping at the form of a woman lying half in the surf, half on the sands. Then he turned and ran to inform police of the strange flotsam he had discovered.

Within an hour detectives were staring down at a raven-haired, most beautiful young woman, clad only in a silk dress. Her undergarments, stockings, and shoes were missing. She was soon identified by her father, who had reported his twenty-five-year-old daughter missing four days earlier. She was Starr Faithfull, whose poetic name would soon be known to millions across the country.

At first the dead woman's end was thought to be either an accident or a su-

icide, but a closer look at the case pointed clearly to murder, a killing that Starr Faithfull may have brought on herself. She was, police learned, not a beautiful innocent struck down by tragedy, but a wild, self-destructive, and sexually abnormal creature who sought out dark violence to appease the unnatural desires implanted in her during childhood.

Starr was the daughter of Frank W. Wyman, who was divorced from her mother in 1921. Her mother then married Stanley E. Faithfull, a retired manufacturing chemist. Starr and her younger sister, Tucker, adopted the Faithfull name. The family moved into a comfortable second-floor walk-up apartment at 12 St. Luke's Place in Greenwich Village, an attractive brownstone only three doors from one occupied by dapper James J. Walker, later to be the flamboyant mayor of New York.

Though Faithfull's income was limited to his retirement pension and the few dollars he earned from inventing gadgets, the family lived well, mysteriously well according to newsmen later looking into the family's financial matters. They paid $85 a month rent for the somewhat cramped but stylish apartment, yet the flat was filled with more than $15,000 worth of exquisite antiques, a Sheraton buffet, Empire and Chippendale chests. The source of the Faithfull income was a mystery until newsmen dug up the fact that an unnamed person had paid the family $80,000 after the Faithfulls signed a legal release which held the donor blameless for any damage done to Starr.

Stanley Faithfull, when these facts became known, hastily denied receiving such an amount, stating the money was more in the neighborhood of $20,000. A lawyer in Boston, who had executed the release for an anonymous client, retorted: "If Mr. Faithfull wants to say it was only $20,000 then we're satisfied to let it rest at that."

More digging by scandal-sniffing newsmen revealed that the damage to Starr was done by none other than Andrew J. Peters, onetime mayor of Boston, an ex-congressman who had amassed a fortune, and a distant relative of Mrs. Faithfull. Starr, as a child, had lived near Peters and had played with his children. When she was eleven, Peters inveigled Starr into his home and seduced her after smothering her with ether. This was the story Stanley Faithfull finally gave out to the press. He added that his poor stepdaughter was never the same after her union with Peters, a relationship that lasted well into the girl's teens. She became, in fact, an ether addict. In addition to heavy drinking in her mid-teens, Starr consistently took all manner of barbiturates. Her rampant sexual adventures were always accompanied with heavy drug use.

The dissolute flapper Starr Faithfull, whose mysterious death aroused the nation in 1931.

A much retouched newspaper photo showing Starr Faithfull at the beach in happier days.

Faithfull, Starr

Starr Faithfull as a teenager was more active sexually than most adult women. She had one peculiarity in that she loved to tease men and admitted to a friend that the sex act itself was not as edifying to her as the foreplay. Of course her premature introduction to sex by an older man set the strange pattern of Starr's desires. Her partners, she confessed, were driven half-mad with her tantalizing. For as many times as she finally relented to her male partner, there were just as many times when her partner was driven to forcibly take his pleasures from her.

The "Mem Book" was what Starr called her diary. This revealing document was later turned over to headline hungry reporters by, incredibly enough, her stepfather, Stanley Faithfull. In it, Starr recorded her sexual adventures but referred to her partners only by initials. One of her earliest entries involved a man she called "A.J.P.," undoubtedly the generous but perverted Andrew J. Peters, a person Starr came to loathe. One entry read: "Spent the night A.J.P. Oh, Horror, Horror, Horror!" Starr went beyond confiding to her diary, which she kept in a self-styled shorthand. After a particularly bruising evening with A.J.P., she blurted out the affair to her mother; the healthy settlement Peters bestowed upon the Faithfull family followed.

Though Starr broke off with Peters, she continued to have affairs, many of them, some so brief they could be aptly termed one-night stands. In her late teens, Starr became the embodiment of the wild free-drinking, free-loving flapper, carousing through Manhattan's speakeasies, her natural beauty turning the heads of men she brought to sexual torment. One such was Joseph Collins, who took Starr to a New York hotel. A few hours later guests heard screams coming from the room occupied by Starr and Collins, and they summoned an officer. The patrolman stormed through the door to find Starr sprawled naked on a bed and Collins, in a red rage with fists clenched, yelling at her. A half-filled bottle of bootleg gin was on the bedstand. Starr was marked with welts and bruises.

The officer demanded Collins's identity and was shown his army discharge papers. With the patrolman's beefy hand on his arm, Collins gathered up his clothes—he was clad only in an undershirt—and departed, the officer shouting a warning after him. Starr, in a semiconscious state, was taken to Bellevue where she was given overnight attention. "Brought to hospital by Flower Hospital ambulance," read the Bellevue report on Starr Faithfull. "Noisy and unsteady. Acute alcoholism. Contusions face, jaw, and upper lip. Given medication. Went to sleep. Next A.M. noisy, crying. People came. Discharged."

For all that is known, Starr never saw Joe Collins again, and it is doubtful that she ever knew his name. (He could not give hers when asked for it by the intervening officer.) Yet the experience with this man provided a clue to what really happened to Starr Faithfull.

She gave it little thought at the time: her diary entry concerning the matter read simply: "I was drinking gin as far as I know. This is the first time I have had anything to drink for six months. I don't know how many I had. I don't remember. I suppose somebody knocked me around a bit."

Starr was getting used to being "knocked around a bit," so much so that she undoubtedly encouraged her male acquaintances through her insufferable sexual teasing to strike out at her in frustration.

To thwart Starr's self-destructive moves, the Faithfulls decided to spend some of the settlement money they had been given by taking Starr to Europe. Mrs. Faithfull, Starr, and Tucker sailed for London, staying at inexpensive hotels. Her mother and young sister spent most of their nights waiting for Starr to return from her nocturnal prowling. It is a matter of record, however, that Starr confined her nighttime activities to the parties of the rich, concentrating on members of the lesser nobility. She was well dressed, and her beautiful face and figure drew comment from high society columnists. However, on Starr's second European trip, one taken alone, her heavy champagne drinking undid her, and she was quickly typed an eccentric, if not an unruly, drunk.

When Starr fell from the grace of her upper-crust friends and the party invitations ceased to come, she swallowed twenty-four grains of Allonal in an abortive attempt to commit suicide. She was found and quickly revived. Her move to end her life had been obvious—she took the pills in full view of several people—one that proved her mood was anything other than suicidal. She was looking for

Stanley Faithfull, Starr's oddball stepfather, who casually released the family scandals to the press.

attention and got it. (The true suicide, as a rule, seldom announces his or her true intent.)

By the spring of 1931 Starr Faithfull's financial status was such that she could no longer return to England. Lacking the fare, she developed the odd, bittersweet habit of visiting the docks where the great liners of the day were departing. She joined in the dockside farewell festivities, running up gangplanks to kiss total strangers good-by, slipping in and out of staterooms to wish more strangers bon voyage while hurriedly sipping champagne in frenzied departure toasts. This went on for weeks, then months. The young woman tormented herself with her strange farewells, always a painful expression flooding her face when she was asked to leave a departing ship.

It was during one of these dockside visits that Starr met Dr. George Jameson-Carr, ship's surgeon of the twenty-thousand-ton *Franconia*, a popular ship of the Cunard Line. She found the mild-mannered doctor more than attractive. She fell in love with him during the brief visits she made to his ship when it was at berth in New York Harbor. Jameson-Carr was a cultured, well-read man, and Starr would engage him in desperate conversations in which she would impart to him all the intellectual sputterings she could manage from the books she read while he was abroad, books he himself had mentioned. It was as if Starr were cramming for examinations, devouring the better novels of the day in order to impress the physician when he was in port.

Her attempts failed at every turn with Jameson-Carr. They never dated, and their brief conversations were limited to Starr's frantic visits before the *Franconia* sailed. The doctor gently rebuffed her. Still she thought in her deluded mind that he was the one great love of her life. On May 29, 1931, she went once more aboard the *Franconia* to see Jameson-Carr. As was not the case on her other visits, she was drunk to near staggering, having consumed the entire contents of a large silver flask full of martinis her father had mixed for her. (Stanley Faithfull later told reporters that he was terrified of Prohibition gin, which was known to have blinded drinkers; he thought it safer if he mixed Starr's drinks for her, explaining that most often she would return home without ever touching the flask.)

Jameson-Carr politely asked Starr to leave his sitting room at sailing time. She refused and he had to order her out in a firm voice. Starr went on deck but did not leave the ship. She slipped into the lounge and mixed with other passengers as the *Franconia* began to steam out of New York Harbor en route for Southampton. Stewards finally found the familiar Starr and, while the ship was brought to a stop, she was taken off and put aboard a tug that churned back toward New York. Starr stood on the deck of the tugboat yelling out her affection for Jameson-Carr while the doctor, looking from the liner's rail, blushed with embarrassment.

Starr apparently did not return home that day, but went to a hotel. From her cheap room, on May 30, 1931, Starr sat

78

down and wrote on hotel stationery the following letter, without salutation, to Dr. Jameson-Carr:

I am going (definitely now—I've been thinking of it for a long time) to end my worthless, disorderly bore of an existence—before I ruin everyone else's life as well. I certainly have made a sordid, futureless mess of it all. I am dead, dead sick of it. It is no one's fault but my own—I hate everything so—life is horrible. Being a sane person, you may not understand—I take dope to forget and drink to try and like people but it is of no use.

I am mad and insane over you. I hold my breath to try and stand it—take allonal in hope of waking happier, but that homesick feeling never leaves me. I have, strangely enough, more of a feeling of peace or whatever you call it now that I know it will soon be over. The half-hour before I die will, I imagine, be quite blissful.

You promised to come to see me. I realize absolutely that it will be the one and only time. There is no earthly reason why you should come. If you do it will be what I call an act of marvelous generosity and kindness. What I did yesterday was very horrible, although I don't see how you could lose your job, as it must have been clearly seen what a nuisance you thought me.

If I don't see you again—goodbye. Sorry to so lose all sense of humor, but I am suffering so that all I want is to

have it over with. It's become such a hell as I couldn't have imagined.

If you come to see me when you are in this time you will be a sport—you are assured by this letter of no more bother from me. My dear— *Starr*

Starr sent this letter on May 30, addressing it to Jameson-Carr and marking it for the *Berengaria*, which was then sailing for England. On June 2, 1931, Starr wrote Jameson-Carr a short, terse note, devoid of emotion, which was a formal apology, undoubtedly a missive he could show to his superiors if necessary.

On June 4, Starr showed forced gaiety in front of her family, although she left the Greenwich Village apartment in a depressed state. She carried just $3 in her purse, the only meager pittance her stepfather could give her. That Thursday morning was the last time the Faithfulls saw Starr alive.

Later that day Starr went to a small writing room in a Manhattan department store and penned a note which was postmarked 4:30 PM Addressed to Jameson-Carr, it was sent via the *Olympic*, sailing that day for England. It read:

Hello, Bill, Old Thing:

It's all up with me now. This is something I am going to put through. The only thing that bothers me about it— the only thing I dread—is being outwitted and prevented from doing this which is the only possible thing for me to do. If one wants to get away with murder one has to jolly well keep one's wits about one. It's the same with suicide. If I don't watch out I will wake up in a psychopathic ward, but I intend to watch out and accomplish my end this time. No ether, allonal, or window-jumping. I don't want to be maimed. I want oblivion. If there is an after life it would be a dirty trick—but I am sure fifty million priests are wrong. That is one of those things one knows.

Nothing makes any difference now. I love to eat and can have one delicious meal with no worry over gaining. I adore music and am going to hear some good music. I believe I love music more than anything. I am going to drink slowly, keeping aware every second. Also, I am going to enjoy my last cigarette. I won't worry because men flirt with me in the streets—I shall encourage them—I don't care who they are. I'm afraid I've always been a rotten "sleeper"; it's the preliminaries that count with me. It doesn't matter though.

It's a great life when one has twenty-four hours to live. I can be rude to people. I can tell them they are too fat or that I don't like their clothes, and I don't have to dread being a lonely old woman, or poverty, obscurity, or boredom. I don't have to dread living on without ever seeing you, or hearing rumors such as "the women all fall for him," and "he entertains charmingly." Why in hell shouldn't you! But it's more than I can cope with—this feeling I have for you. I have tried to pose as clever and intellectual, thereby to attract you, but it was not successful, and I couldn't go on writing those long studied letters. I don't have to worry, because there are no words in which to describe this feeling I have for you. The words love, adore, worship have become meaningless. There is nothing I can do but what I am going to do. I shall never see you again. That is extraordinary. Although I can't comprehend it any more than I can comprehend th words "always"—or "time." They produce a very merciful numbness.   *Starr*

What happened in the next four days in the life of Starr Faithfull has continued to mystify the world to this day. These four days were later filled in by police theory, newspaper imagination, and much later, the creative notions of novelists, the best of these being *Butterfield 8* by John O'Hara, who fictionalized (and somewhat distorted) the life and times of Starr Faithfull. At first it was conjectured that Starr had, indeed, committed suicide by leaping from either the *Île de France* or the *Mauretania*, two gigantic liners that sailed for Europe on June 5. It was thought that Starr had secreted herself aboard one of the ships and, before being discovered, leapt unseen into the dark waves of the Atlantic, only to be washed ashore at Long Beach three days later.

Starr had been seen on board the *Mauretania*, but she had also been seen getting off the ship before it sailed. There is no evidence that Starr had ever been aboard the *Île de France*. There is also little evidence that the tragic woman committed suicide. The evidence that did present itself pointed only to homicide.

The first to make this cry was Elvin N. Edwards, district attorney of Nassau County, which encompassed the Long Beach area. The second to nod agreement to murder was none other than the unpredictable Stanley Faithfull.

On the morning of Starr's funeral—she was to be cremated at a Long Island mortuary—her family was jarred from bereavement by a man from Edwards's office who dashed to the candle-lit bier and shouted: "Stop this ceremony! The D.A. has ordered another post-mortem examination. New evidence!"

Starr's body, carried eagerly from the mortuary on the backs of volunteer newsmen, was removed for another autopsy. The following day Edwards called a dramatic news conference to add one more headline story to the millions of words that had been gushed forth on Starr's behalf. "I know the identity of the two men who killed Starr Faithfull," came Edwards's bravado. "One of them is a prominent New York politician. They took her to Long Beach, drugged her, and held her head under the water until she was drowned. I will arrest both of them within thirty-six hours."

No arrests followed. Edwards had been wrong in his statement, wrong about the suspects he had under surveillance, but correct about Starr's being murdered.

The initial autopsy performed on Starr revealed that the body contained two grains of Veronal, which might cause unconsciousness but not death. She had, as she had promised Jameson-Carr in her last letter to him, consumed a large meal

June 8, 1931—detectives and coroner's men inspecting Starr Faithfull's body on the sands of Long Beach, New York. (*UPI*)

before death. She had drowned, the pathologist said, her body having been in the water for forty-eight hours. There was no alcohol in the body, however. And her lungs were brimming with sand, pointing to murder. Many bruises—from human hands, it was determined—coated the upper part of Starr's body. At first the medical report stated that she had been raped. The second autopsy ruled out rape but insisted that she had had sexual intercourse shortly before her death.

Stanley Faithfull's murder notions were strictly emotional. He totally rejected the idea that his lovely but neurotic Jazz Age daughter had committed suicide. He was convinced she had been murdered by an unknown person. He pointed to the autopsy as signifying such a fate. His conduct following Starr's death was considered oddball in that he was so open with the press that he appeared as a sideline spectator to the entire tragedy, rather than a normally distraught close relative. Morris Markey, then a reporter covering the story, visited the Faithfulls. He would write in *The Aspirin Age*: "There were, to be sure, manifestations of eccentricity in great abundance in this family."

The minute Stanley Faithfull opened his door to this complete stranger, he blurted to Markey: "Come in. I was just trying to determine the normal weight of the human liver. There are some things in that last autopsy report I don't like, and I'd like to satisfy myself. Do you know how to translate grams into pounds and ounces?"

Some experts reconstructed Starr's end by stating that she had picked up an un-

known man, as was her custom when depressed ("I won't worry because men flirt with me in the streets," she had written Jameson-Carr in her last letter. "I shall encourage them—I don't care who they are"). He took her to Long Beach, a place she had never before visited. She taunted him by removing all her clothes except her dress (these items were never found), and after she endlessly toyed with him ("it's the preliminaries that count with me"), her companion became infuriated to the point where he knocked her into unconsciousness (the bruises, especially about the head, explained that). He may at this time have sexually attacked her.

Recovering from his passionate fit, the companion undoubtedly panicked and, to still Starr's voice against him, dragged her to the water's edge and shoved her face into the sand, holding her that way as she sucked in the grains of sand that filled her lungs. When satisfied that she was dead, the companion gathered up all of Starr's clothing—her undergarments, shoes, stockings—and left, walking through the shallow surf to eradicate his footsteps.

There were other explanations to be sure, dozens of them, but murder fit the scene and corresponded to the autopsy best of all, a murder that remains enigmatic to this day, despite the fulminations of District Attorney Edwards and the intuitive suspicions of the Faithfull family.

The dead girl with the romantically poetic name lingers in memory, conquering in death one of her greatest fears: "I don't have to dread . . . obscurity."

Farran, Rex Francis

BOMBING MURDER, 1948   ENGLAND

Captain Roy Alexander Farran had served in the Palestine police but had been removed from duties and charged with murdering a Jewish youth named Alexander Rubowitz while fighting terrorists in Palestine. Farran was court-martialed but acquitted. He returned to England, but not before Jewish militants delivered threats to him, stating that they would make him pay for the Rubowitz killing. One terrorist note read: "We will follow you to the end of the world."

On May 3, 1948, while Farran was vacationing in Scotland, a package was received at the home of his parents in Wolverhampton. Though it was addressed to Captain Farran, his twenty-five-year-old brother Rex opened the package to discover a large edition of Shakespeare's plays. When Rex lifted the book cover a violent explosion tore through the Farran cottage, devastating its interior and mortally wounding Farran, who died of his wounds two days later.

The bomb, it was later determined, had been placed inside the hollowed-out pages of the book, and it was largely believed that the death of Rex Farran was attributable to Jewish terrorists, but the killers remain unknown.

First National Bank of Chicago

BANK ROBBERY, 1977   U.S.

Examiners at the ninth largest bank in America, second largest in Chicago, could not believe their eyes. Frantic auditors combed the bank's records over and over to see if a bookkeeper had erred or the gigantic bank computer had somehow skipped a digit. But no matter how many ways the examiners checked and rechecked the records, the same stark figures jumped back at them on their calculators: $1 million dollars, precisely, was missing.

The disappearance of the $1 million occurred over a long Columbus Day weekend, between Friday, October 7, and Tuesday, October 11, 1977. By 6 PM on October 12, auditors were forced to admit that there had been no computer or bookkeeping error. The $1 million had been stolen. They called in the FBI. Bureau agents later complained that the twenty-four-hour delay by bank examiners who could not believe the money had been taken and had furiously attempted to prove an error had been made had hampered their investigation.

It was exactly this delay, authorities later stated, that the thief had counted on, had actually made part of the plan in his daring $1 million robbery. It was, of course, an "inside" job, committed by one of the many bank employees who had access to the vault area, about sixty in all out of the bank's enormous work force of more than five thousand employees.

The money was taken from cart T-12, one of twenty-four metal carts with supposedly locked compartments that contained many millions of dollars stemming from large companies and used as cash payments to other banks. There was precisely $4 million in cart T-12 when it was rolled into the First National Vault (two levels below the main floor) on Friday. Several persons entered the vault area where this cart and others were stored and locked during October 7–11. The cart was rolled into the chief teller's office on Tuesday morning and remained there all day, unlocked. The paying teller counted the money Tuesday evening to discover the money missing.

In taking exactly $1 million, the thief, in a master stroke, gave himself more time to spirit the money away, knowing that that precise amount would cause examiners to think there had been a bank error, not a theft, and that they would spend many hours checking records before realizing a robbery had taken place. The money, in neatly wrapped packs, weighed no more than twenty pounds—$800,000 in new $100 bills, the remaining $200,000 in used $50 bills. To further confound the tracing of the money, some cash on Tuesday, as the thief certainly knew it would be, was paid out from cart T-12, thus breaking the chain of serial numbers to be traced.

But how was the money transferred from the bank? One official shrugged and said that it could have been easily put into a large executive briefcase. Another speculated that it could have been removed in a industrial vacuum cleaner bag. Another guessed that a gang of white-collar confederates working with the inside man

simply removed the cash in special pockets sewn inside jackets and pants or one thief alone could have smuggled the money out that way.

The theft was certainly an inside job, FBI agents concluded. The thief knew exactly how many packages of money would make up an even $1 million. They gave him grudging respect for cool nerves in that he left $3 million in the cart.

Chicago police, who had been called into the case very late—robbery inspectors learned about the theft in the newspapers—speculated that the thief probably worked with the syndicate, transferring the money to crime cartel members who either distributed it through Nevada casinos and other areas to "wash" the bills, or flew it to the West Indies, the nearest haven for secret bank accounts. The latter had been the case in the 1974 robbery of Chicago's Purolator Security Company, in which $1.1 million of the $4.3 million taken was deposited in West Indies banks. (The Purolator thieves were eventually caught and most of the money recovered.)

Authorities began to interview bank employees. Lie detector tests were given to about a hundred workers. The chief teller and the payout teller were cleared immediately of suspicion, as were almost all others who had authority to enter the vault area where cart T-12 was stored. Everyone had to sign in and out at a guard post, and all those entering and leaving the vault areas were recorded by cameras. Agents studied the video tapes of all those entering the vault area over the Columbus Day weekend.

The tapes revealed that one man who

had worked for the bank for fourteen years appeared in the vault area three times on Saturday, October 8, when the bank was closed but internal functions had continued. "Although he had no business in the area," reported an investigator, "none of the other employees questioned his presence because they all knew him." This employee worked in the bank's lottery room, where cash from the Illinois State Lottery was received and counted, and the total reported to the state. The employee was asked to take a lie detector test and, not so surprisingly, refused. Only one other bank employee, a pregnant woman acting on her doctor's advice, had refused to take the test. The man, then knowing he was under suspicion, went immediately to a lawyer who often represented syndicate figures, according to police, paying him $1,700 as an "initial consulting fee." This attorney reportedly took cases only where subsequent fees would be enormous.

The FBI pleaded with bank officials to keep the suspicious employee at work. "Hopefully, he will make a mistake and lead us to the money," argued one agent. The bankers, however, were badly frightened. If this man could pull off one of the slickest bank robberies in American history without anything but shabby circumstantial evidence to involve him, what could prevent him from doing it again? In mid-November 1977, the employee was suspended.

Then began one of the most dogged surveillances in law enforcement history. The man was watched, followed, and monitored every waking moment of his life. He did nothing to implicate himself in the staggering robbery, continuing to lead a quiet life in the Chicago area. When he traveled, which was rarely, he was followed and watched. And, to this writing, he still is. The $1 million is also still missing.

"I don't think this guy is ever going to make a break for it," one federal agent confided to the author recently. "But he damn well sure isn't going to enjoy one penny of that loot. He probably knows it." The thief, whoever he is, may have known it from the moment he decided to put his master robbery plan into effect. He may have merely wanted to prove that he could execute such a devastating robbery; the money may have meant nothing more to the thief than a useless prize that satisfied a vainglorious ego, a superiority complex that demanded he get away with it. So far, he has.

Foster, Evelyn
MURDER, 1931 ENGLAND

The killing of twenty-nine-year-old Evelyn Foster on January 6, 1931, had all the trappings of the classic English countryside mystery. She was a woman alone, driving through the night with a strange man beside her, a gentleman turned maniac, who forced her off the road, abused her, and left her to burn to death on the lonely windswept moors. And the killer was a will-o'-the-wisp who seemed to vanish into thin air.

Evelyn Foster was the oldest daughter

85

of Joseph Foster, who owned and operated a successful garage in Otterburn, near Newcastle, England. For years she had run a for-hire car which functioned as a taxi service between the small villages about Otterburn. Good-natured, the attractive if slightly plump Evelyn frugally saved her money and was able, over the years, to purchase her own for-hire cars, her latest in 1931 being a four-door Hudson. She worked seven days a week but managed to see a boyfriend, Ernest Primrose, a Scotsman who had once worked for her father as a busman. This relationship was abandoned by Evelyn when Primrose returned to Scotland.

Preoccupied by her work and having no worries about remaining a spinster, Evelyn did begin to see another man, George Phillipson, who was a native of Otterburn and who also did woodworking jobs on Foster's buses. This was a casual relationship which Phillipson, a quiet, reserved young man, did little to alter. Evelyn and George went to dances together, took strolls on the moors, and sometimes indulged in picnics when the weather permitted, which was rare in that windy, bone-chilling northeast corner of England just below the Scottish border.

All seemed placid and predictable in the life of Evelyn Foster until the stark night of January 6, 1931. A few minutes after seven, she stopped by her home in Otterburn which was attached to her father's garage, where the buses the Foster firm operated were stored and repaired.

Evelyn walked into the kitchen to grab a bite to eat, telling her mother: "I've brought a man down from Elishaw. He wants to go to Ponteland to catch the bus." Evelyn then explained that she had driven a fare, Mrs. Esther Murray, to Birdhopecraig, and had turned around in the road to return home when she was hailed by people in a car stopped at Elishaw Road Ends, a rural way-station. A man then walked from the car and told her he had missed the Edinburgh-Newcastle bus at Jedburgh, that the people in the car had given him a lift as far as Elishaw. He wanted her to drive him twenty-four miles to Ponteland, where he could catch the Newcastle bus. Evelyn agreed, telling him it would cost him about two pounds.

"What's he like?" asked her mother.

"Very respectable," said Evelyn, "and gentlemanly-like. He looks a bit of a knut [a dandy wearing smart or stylish clothes]." She went on to say that the man had gone to the nearby Percy Arms pub to see if he could get a free lift to Ponteland (no doubt the stranger thought the fare Evelyn had quoted was too high). Nevertheless, Evelyn drove to the Percy Arms and picked up the man, who was apparently unable to get a free lift to his destination.

They drove off on the lonely road toward Ponteland. As the Hudson bumped along, the passenger smoked many cigarettes. He and Evelyn talked about her one great love, cars, and the man, who said he lived somewhere in the Midlands and told Evelyn that he owned a car himself. After going eighteen miles, Evelyn reached the small village of Belsay, its streets deserted and not a citizen in sight.

Two cars passed her at this time, one owned by William Kirsopp-Reid, a farmer from Otterburn Mill, the other driven by a stranger.

While going down Belsay's silent streets, Evelyn told her passenger: "Well, there is no bus here, but there will be one farther on."

The man's tone suddenly changed to a sinister growl: "We will turn here and go back."

"Why go back when you have come so far?" asked Evelyn.

"That's nothing to do with you," snapped the stranger.

Evelyn turned the car around and began driving back as instructed. At this moment she "felt the man creep along the seat" toward her. With a thrust of his arm he grabbed the wheel, snarling: "I will drive back."

"Oh, no," Evelyn replied, trying to push his hand away. "I will do the driving."

The man's fist suddenly smashed into her eye, numbing her. As she would later remember: "Coming through Belsay I looked out of the car to see if anyone was about the village, but I couldn't see very well because my eye felt as if it was full of sand."

The passenger had jammed Evelyn against the door and was actually driving the Hudson. When they reached a desolate stretch of roadway surrounded by the moors then howling with wind, an ominously named place called Wolf's Nick, the man stopped the car.

The passenger seemed to relax a bit. He took out a pack of cigarettes and offered Evelyn one. She refused. "You are an independent young woman," said the man in a low voice. With that he suddenly struck Evelyn twice, knocking her into the back of the car. He then, if Evelyn's later statements, given in a whisper, were properly recorded, attacked her sexually. "He did not appear to be drunk but he smelt a bit," Evelyn recalled.

A few minutes later this most bizarre of creatures threw some liquid on Evelyn and lit it, so that while she sat huddled in the backseat of her car, her clothes blazed up, flames engulfing her. (It was never determined exactly what the man threw on Evelyn, petrol or acid. He did retrieve the can of petrol kept on an outside rack and empty it inside the car, which caused the upholstery to burn.) The pain was so excruciating that the robust Evelyn passed out. Reviving, she discovered that the entire inside of the car was ablaze. Somehow she managed to get out of the Hudson, stagger several feet in front of it, and then collapse.

As she lay on the ground in agony, Evelyn distinctly "heard a car pull up and someone whistle while the car was on fire." Later she heard an explosion, which was undoubtedly the Hudson's gas tank. She remembered lying on the cold grass of the moors for "a long, long time. I was so thirsty, I lay and sucked the grass."

The whole horrible ordeal was related by Evelyn Foster herself after she had been found by two busmen who, coincidentally, worked for her father and saw the glow of her burning car flickering across the moors. The busmen wrapped Evelyn

CARRIED FROM THE MOOR. FOUND WITH HER CLOTHING BURNED. HER LAST WORDS TO HER FATHER

A British newspaper montage depicting the burning of Evelyn Foster in 1931.

in an overcoat and rushed her back to Otterburn, where she was put to bed in her own home. Most of her body was burned to a crisp; attending physicians shook their heads helplessly and told the Foster family that there was no way to save Evelyn.

She lingered for hours, however, whispering out her story. At dawn she blinked in pain at Mrs. Foster and whispered her last words: "I have been murdered. Mother, I have been murdered."

The description Evelyn gave of her attacker was hazy. She had said that he was young and dark-complexioned. He wore fashionable clothes, stood about five feet six inches, and was of medium build. He wore a dark overcoat and a bowler hat. The police, in the form of Constable Andrew Fergusson, were on hand during Evelyn's dying testimony. Fergusson proved himself to be, much like all the police involved in this case, wholly incompetent. He asked the dying woman only a few questions before strolling about Foster's garage without the slightest notion of how to proceed in the matter; Fergusson had never handled a homicide in his entire career.

He was joined shortly by Police Sergeant Robert Shanks, who also proved himself to be just this side of moronic. Both officers had no idea what to do until Gordon Foster, Evelyn's brother, suggested they take a look at his sister's car at Wolf's Nick. They reluctantly agreed, as if they did not really want to get involved. One of Foster's busmen drove the officers to the barren area, where the car was still smoldering. Fergusson and Shanks walked about the car, taking little note of anything. They found Evelyn's scarf and left it at the scene on a bumper. They found an empty can of petrol and took note that the inside of the Hudson was burned to a cinder. Then, it being a cold night, they boarded Foster's bus and headed back to town, for tea before a fire and a warm bed.

The next day Captain Fullarton James, chief constable for Northumberland County, officially took over the case. He issued an alert for the man in the bowler hat, an alarm that caused every man wearing this most popular of hats to be apprehensive of arrest (bowler hats, in fact, quickly went out of style in the district). But it was almost twelve hours after the burning of Evelyn Foster; the killer had more than ample time to escape to Newcastle or other towns and then make his way either north to Edinburgh or south to London.

Instead of calling in detectives from Scotland Yard, Chief Constable James thought to handle the case exclusively, despite his complete lack of investigative knowledge. He busied himself on visiting the car, posting guards around the moors area where the burning occurred, and shaking his head at the prospect of ever catching the culprit. He did measure the distance from the road to the spot on the moors where the car stood, approximately 198 feet, and, without any explanation, stated that the car had not skidded off the road but had been driven there. He ordered the car taken into the Foster shop for examination. No fingerprints were taken from the car. The turf from the area where the car had stood on the moors, however, was cut out in a large square and also taken away to be examined. Constable James was chiefly interested in a footprint that had been found, but by then he should have known that any footprint found after dawn, January 7, 1931, would have been useless. By then an army of police, newsmen, and curious spectators had thoroughly trampled the area. (Footprints found at the scene of any crime are generally useless in tracing down criminals anyway.)

Meanwhile, a pathologist examined Evelyn's corpse and stated that he did not think she had been raped. A coroner's jury returned a verdict of murder "by a person or persons unknown." Yet the police refused to accept such a verdict. They had, they said, investigated high and low for the car from which the killer alighted at Elishaw and could not find it or its occupants (Evelyn said the driver was a woman and that two other men had been in it). They reported that the stranger riding with Evelyn on the night of the murder did not go to the Percy Arms to wait for her; the employees at the Percy Arms never saw him. When the police hunt for the man in the bowler hat failed to turn up the suspect, high-ranking officers in Northumberland issued statements that the man simply did not exist. They then maligned the dead woman by stating that she had driven her own car off the road, set fire to it for the insurance proceeds, but had accidentally set fire to herself.

There was no mysterious stranger in a bowler hat who had murdered her.

Of course such statements were patently ridiculous. Evelyn Foster, according to all her friends and neighbors, was a hardworking and thoroughly scrupulous young woman. Further, she had no need for insurance money in that she had in the bank several thousand pounds (today's equivalent of $25,000). The rural cops had simply botched their job, knew it, and, to cover up their gross ineptitude, had conveniently indicted the dead victim out of hand, the one person who could not refute their pompous claims. Since they could not find the killer, it was simply easier to state that he did not exist, that he had never existed.

Though the maniacal killer of Evelyn Foster was never officially captured and punished, it is quite possible that the fiend did receive his just due. Less than two years after Evelyn's murder, another burning-car killing took place in rural Yorkshire. Thirty-one-year-old Ernest Brown, a widower who worked as a groom for Frederick Morton's cattle farm, had been carrying on an affair with Morton's wife. To rid himself of Morton and with wild thoughts of inheriting Morton's farm *and* wife, Brown shot his employer to death with a shotgun on September 5, 1933. He placed his body in a car inside a garage and set fire to the auto. Firemen were summoned and, as they fought the blaze, the groom smirked and said: "By God, if the boss is in there, he'll never be seen again."

The firemen were too quick for Brown;

they managed to put out the fire and preserve the remains of Frederick Morton. Enough of the body was intact so that examiners could determine that he had been shot to death before the flames reached his body.

Brown was convicted of the murder and was hanged on February 6, 1934, at Armley Jail in Leeds. The prison chaplain, while the executioner was placing a rope around Brown's neck, approached the killer and asked him to confess *all* his sins before he dropped through the trap. Brown's only remark consisted of three words: "Ought to burn," or "Otterburn." He spoke with a North Country accent that made his words difficult to understand. If Brown had truly said "ought to burn," he may have meant that his employer deserved to die or that he himself deserved to roast in the flames of hell. If he said the latter, "Otterburn," he may have been confessing to Evelyn Foster's killing.

Many factors involving Brown pointed to him as Evelyn's slayer. He had used the same modus operandi in killing Morton as had Evelyn's killer. He spoke in the same North Country accent Evelyn had described the stranger as having. He generally answered the description Evelyn had given of her assailant—he was dark-complexioned and stood about five feet six inches. (It is not known if he owned a bowler hat.) Brown was certainly, in Evelyn's words, "a bit of a knut," a snappy dresser. He certainly could have been, according to character, temperament, and murderous nature, the very stranger who killed Evelyn Foster, but no one ever knew for certain. Brown's last words make the Foster killing all the more enigmatic and vexing, which, of course, may have been Brown's malicious intent all along.

G

Getty, J. Paul, III
KIDNAPPING, 1973 ITALY

The grandson of the richest man in the world, J. Paul Getty, got drunk in Rome on the night of June 10, 1973. Before going home, J. Paul Getty III bought a comic book. As he began to walk homeward, four men grabbed him and hustled him into a car, driving him to a secret house in Calabria.

For several months the kidnappers attempted to ransom the Getty heir, but the grandfather, it was reported, ignored their demands, thinking that his grandson, an easy-living sixteen-year-old who was known as the Golden Hippie, was engineering his own kidnapping to enrich himself.

J. Paul Getty III (*right*) shown with his mother just after his kidnappers released him. (*UPI*)

Getty was convinced that the kidnapping was genuine in November when the grandson's ear, which had been chopped from the boy's head, along with a photo of the heir showing the mutilation, was mailed to a Rome newspaper. The kidnappers meant business, they said. The ear was only the first section of the boy's body that would appear; next would come fingers and toes unless the ransom was paid. Paid it was, more than three billion lire, about $2.9 million in cash, which was sent by truck to Calabria. Getty was released.

This was the largest ransom ever paid to kidnappers in modern times. Authorities later reported that they thought the crime had been perpetrated by members of the Mafia, but they did not prove it. The culprits are still at large.

Giancana, Sam
SYNDICATE KILLING, 1975 U.S.

A onetime member of Chicago's feared 42 Gang, Sam Giancana, or "Momo," as he was known to intimates, climbed steadily and cautiously up the syndicate ladder in Chicago, taking over the reins of leadership from Tony Accardo in a coup d'etat. Giancana simply went to Accardo's home, fired five bullets through the door, the story has it, and then called the boss to tell him he was retired, an edict that Accardo judiciously accepted.

As Chicago's mob boss, Giancana harkened back to the old Capone days in that he liked to swagger in the limelight. He was the typical mobster in the money, sporting a large diamond pinkie ring, wearing sharkskin suits that glistened when he walked, and taking bows in public, especially when wining and dining away from Chicago.

Though married, Giancana flaunted his relationship with singer Phyllis McGuire of the McGuire Sisters singing act. His public posturing caused his fellow syndicate members to become uneasy. Moreover, Giancana had sued the FBI for harassing him—the Bureau had assigned around-the-clock agents to trail him everywhere. Though the mobster won the suit, the ruling was overturned in a higher court.

Such goings-on were intolerable for Accardo and others in the hierarchy of the Chicago mob. It was decreed that Giancana would be killed. At about ten thirty on the evening of June 19, 1975, Giancana was visited at his large Oak Park bungalow by an unknown man (Giancana's bodyguard, who stayed in the gangster's house, had gone to bed, he later told police, and never knew who called upon his boss). Momo entertained his visitor in the basement, which had been made over into a recreation and kitchen area.

That Giancana knew the caller well enough to relax his guard was evidenced later in that he turned his back on him to fry some sausages, a late-night snack for his guest. As Giancana cooked the sausages, the killer crept up behind the syndicate boss and fired a single bullet from a .22-caliber automatic pistol with a silencer. Giancana collapsed to the floor and the killer crouched next to him, firing six more bullets into Momo's head to make sure. He then fled out the back door of the basement, got into a car he had parked in the alleyway, and drove off. (The weapon was later found in a nearby forest preserve.) Giancana's murder has never been solved.

Godfrey, Sir Edmund Berry
MURDER, 1678 ENGLAND

On the night of October 17, 1678, the body of Sir Edmund Godfrey, one of England's most respected magistrates, was found in a ditch near Primrose Hill, London. The body was carried to a nearby pub, where many townspeople examined it, startled to discover that the victim still wore three gold rings and in his pockets and purse nestled four pounds of silver and several gold pieces. Godfrey, it was safe to assume, had not been killed by thieves.

Physicians arrived to perform an autopsy. The magistrate's chest had been run through with a sword, but doctors found it odd that there was no blood on his body or clothes. Closer inspection proved that his chest was a welter of bruises and the upper portion of his body was discolored, as if he had sustained a merciless beating. There was a rope burn around the magistrate's neck, which was broken.

"Perhaps it was suicide," volunteered an official of King Charles II.

"Explain then," snorted a physician, "how it is that a man may beat and strangle himself, break his own neck, and *then* fall upon a sword. No, this act was murder."

The murder of Godfrey utterly baffled those investigating the case. Who would want the death of such a noble magistrate, a man known for his keen sense of justice and fair-mindedness? Sir Edmund had been not only the most respected magistrate in London, but one of the bravest champions of law and order who ever served King Charles. When all persons of high office and noble bloodline fled London in 1665 to escape the plague, Sir Edmund had refused to quit the city, reminding his fellow magistrates that they were duty-bound to stay behind and uphold the law. Some weeks later a widely feared felon dared officials to arrest him after he ran into a hospital jammed with lethal plague victims. Sir Edmund marched into the hospital, stepping over corpses, brushing past the fatally stricken with their open sores and running faces, to collar the felon and drag him outside. Such courage was rewarded by Charles II, who bestowed knighthood upon the magistrate.

In early 1678 Magistrate Godfrey received the formal complaint of one Titus Oates, who had named many high-level persons as being involved in a popish plot to overthrow the government and restore Catholicism as the state religion. Oates also insisted in his complaint that the plotters intended to murder King Charles II. (The rabid anti-Catholic did not know that the King had himself become a Catholic in secret, such was the persecution of that religion at the time.)

Oates was a strange creature. He had pretended to join the Jesuit order so that he could spy on Catholics and then report their plots, all of which he invented. Oates had joined other religions and been kicked out of most of them. He had also served as a chaplain in the Royal Navy, but had been expelled for his sexual attacks upon young sailors. Acting on behalf of secret sponsors such as the Earl of Shaftesbury and others who wished to compromise the king, Oates signed a sworn affidavit that the popish plot was not only real but that people like Sir George Wakeman, the queen's personal physician, were involved. Wakeman planned to murder the king, Oates lied.

Godfrey examined Oates's complaint, took the man's deposition, and did nothing, refusing to swear out warrants for the arrests of those cited by Oates. Privately he told a friend that "Oates is sworn and is perjured." He knew that the popish plot was an invention of the king's enemies and said so. He also felt that his own position was extremely vulnerable. He told another friend that he feared that he would be killed some night. On Saturday evening, October 12, 1678, Sir Edmund left his home on Hartshorn Lane and vanished. His body was found six days later.

Oates was the first to exploit the magistrate's murder for his own mad ends, publicly screaming that Godfrey had been a martyr in the anti-Catholic cause, in-

Sir Edmund Godfrey, whose murder in 1678 utterly baffled all of England.

sisting that Sir Edmund had been murdered by Catholics who knew he was about to uphold Oates's deposition. He whipped public fear to frenzy. Tradesmen and shop people went armed in the street, looking everywhere for bloodthirsty Catholics. Normally docile housewives slipped knives and loaded pistols beneath their beds before retiring in the event they had to repel invading Catholics in the middle of the night.

A Catholic silversmith named Miles Praunce drank too much one night in a London pub and loudly stated that three priests recently condemned were innocent and were being sacrificed to appease the bloodlust of the rabble. He was arrested and thrown into a dungeon at Newgate Prison. Here Praunce was tortured for several days. He was told that he would be summarily executed as a member of the popish plot. There was one way, however, he might save his life. A note from Lord Shaftesbury intimated that if Praunce was to name the Catholic killers of Sir Edmund, he might be pardoned.

Half out of his wits, Praunce agreed to name whomever he was told to name. He was brought before the Privy Council and shouted out the names of Henry Berry, Lawrence Hill, and Robert Green, all Catholics long on the death list of Titus Oates. Though innocent, these men were quickly tried and executed, along with the three priests and five Catholic members of the House of Lords, all powerful opponents of the scheming Lord Shaftesbury, who, through his lying agent Oates, managed to eliminate his personal foes by convincing many that there truly was a popish plot.

King Charles, whose Catholicism was a secret from Shaftesbury, took care of the malicious Oates. After Oates had had the effrontery to accuse the queen of plotting her husband's murder, Charles had the man brought to court on charges of libel. He was convicted and sent to prison for life. Each day Oates was taken from his cell and tied to an ox cart which traveled through different parts of London. The vindictive libeler was whipped through the streets. He died in 1705.

The question remained, as it does today, who was the actual killer of Sir Edmund? One strong suspect was pinpointed by mystery writer John Dickson Carr, who believed that the Earl of Pembroke was the real slayer of Godfrey. A dissolute young character who had proved himself to be a hopeless alcoholic with an incredible streak of savage sadism, Pembroke had stomped a man to death only months before Godfrey's murder and had been convicted of manslaughter by none other than Godfrey himself. According to Carr, Pembroke's victim bore the same strange marks upon his chest as were later found on Sir Edmund. It would have taken little to convince Pembroke to kill his prosecutor. Yet Carr's case, though impressively documented, remains circumstantial. Sir Edmund's killer is officially nameless to this day.

Gordon, Vivian
MURDER, 1931 U.S.

Showgirl, madam, blackmailer, Vivian Gordon had lived on the seamy side of life for more than twenty years. Her friends and associates were low-life Broadway types, politicians, crooked cops, and a bevy of underworld figures. Vivian both flaunted and extorted money from her sex clients, as if she were inviting her own murder—which occurred, not too surprisingly, in late February 1931.

Vivian Gordon was the daughter of John Franklin, onetime warden of Joliet State Penitentiary in Illinois. She had run away as a teenager to become a showgirl, working in burlesque choruses in New York. She met and married a salesman, John Bischoff, having a child with him, Benita; but she soon neglected her marriage, abandoned show business altogether, and became a high-class prostitute. Vivian's popularity brought enough money for her to establish her own business as a madam. Although she continued to service important clients, the five-foot-two-inch blue-eyed vixen preferred to work her own girls, taking 50 percent of their profits. She also took down in meticulous detail all the information she and her girls overheard when their loose-tongued political clients were in their revels.

This inside information served Gordon well through the late 1920s; she was able to blackmail important clients for small fortunes. Her silence on matters of the illegal in high office brought her tens of thousands of dollars. But when Judge Samuel Seabury began his investigation of the corrupt Walker regime in New York, Vivian became a talkative informant for investigators. She had, by early 1931, become vital to Seabury's probes, for she had information that could put scores of Tammany figures and cops in prison—knowing, for instance, the direct links between New York government and such free wheeling bootleggers as Dutch Schultz, Legs Diamond, Waxey Gordon, Lucky Luciano, and others. Gordon's willingness to cooperate with investigators also stemmed from the fact that she was facing a long prison term for repeated arrests for prostitution. She intended to save her own skin and turn state's evidence.

A few days before she was due to appear before Seabury's sleuths, Vivian Gordon disappeared. She was discovered, quite dead, on February 26, 1931, in Van Cortlandt Park in the Bronx. The attractive redheaded madam, then in her forties, was found dressed in a black velvet dress trimmed with yellow lace, a designer original from Paris. She wore expensive silk underwear and sheer black stockings, no shoes. Imported kid gloves still encased her small and delicate hands.

To police rushing to the scene she first looked as if she were merely asleep. Closer examination revealed that a grisly necklace had been added to Vivian Gordon's expensive and tasteful attire. Someone had strangled her to death with a thin but sturdy piece of clothesline cord, wrapping it so tightly about her throat that the cord was embedded in the flesh.

New York madam and notorious blackmailer Vivian Gordon, mysteriously murdered in 1931.

Much was missing from the corpse. Gone were a $600 wristwatch, an $1800 fur coat, and a $1200 diamond and emerald ring which Gordon had been wearing the evening she was killed. It was robbery, detectives said, that had brought the high-living Vivian to her violent end.

But given the fact that Vivian was killed only a few days before she was to testify, the motive for her murder was undoubtedly to silence her. Police Commissioner Edward P. Mulrooney stated indignantly that "until this case is cleared up there is a stain on the shield of every policeman in New York."

Scores of detectives fanned out through New York's five boroughs, interrogating the more than five hundred men listed in Gordon's little black book, extortion victims all. But in every instance, police ran into a dead end. Compounding the massive unfavorable publicity generated by the murder was the suicide of her daughter, Benita, who, on March 3, 1931, was no longer able to endure the exposure of her mother's scarlet past. The distraught teenager put her head into an oven and turned on the gas.

Police digging deep into Vivian's sordid background found mostly policemen, vice cops who had been on her payroll for years and others who were waiting to get on. Detectives did turn up a John Radeloff, Vivian's lawyer, onetime lover, and financial consultant. Radeloff, a married man, had been threatened by Vivian; if he did not return to her she would expose their sexual relationship to Radeloff's wife. The lawyer reportedly told the fiery madam that he knew "someone who can take care of you." He was referring to Chowderhead Cohen, who had once been Vivian's bouncer but who worked for Radeloff.

Radeloff and Cohen, however, proved to have unbreakable alibis and were ruled out as Gordon's killers. Another onetime bouncer for Vivian, Harry Stein, then came under scrutiny. Stein, who was represented by Radeloff, had strangled a woman to death years earlier (in much the same way Vivian had been strangled) and had served time in Sing Sing for the killing. Stein, it was also learned, appeared in the offices of a fur jobber only hours after Gordon's body had been found and attempted to sell her missing fur coat and jewelry.

Then two of Stein's friends, underworld characters Sam Greenberg and Harry Schlitten, were rounded up. They had been with Stein on the night of Gordon's death, were seen dining in a popular restaurant where some of their sinister conversation was overheard. Stein had stated to Schlitten that "if I don't put a certain party away, a friend of mine is going to end up in jail." If he was referring to Vivian he could also have been referring to any one of her hundreds of blackmail victims.

Police grilled Schlitten unmercifully until he agreed to supply them with information in return for immunity in the Gordon case. He then went on to state that on the night of the murder he and Greenberg had rented a limousine and he drove the vehicle to a lonely spot in the Bronx and waited. Shortly, Stein showed up in a cab with Vivian and they got into the limousine. Schlitten said he was then ordered to drive through Van Cortlandt Park, and he did. Stein and Greenberg then killed the blackmailing madam, he said, with Stein looping a piece of clothesline around the madam's neck and both men throwing her to the floor of the back seat, holding her down with their feet as Stein strangled her. "She only cackled once [before she died]," remarked Schlitten.

Greenberg and Stein were placed on trial. They were defended by the spectacular criminal attorney Samuel Leibowitz, who quickly showed Schlitten to be an inveterate liar and a thoroughly corrupt thug who—in Schlitten's own words, forced from him on the witness stand by Leibowitz—"went out to murder for money."

Leibowitz also proved that both Greenberg and Stein could not have been present at the time of the madam's murder; both had irrefutable alibis. Stein had been seen by scores of people at the time fixed for the murder at a bar mitzvah. With Schlitten thoroughly discredited, Greenberg and Stein were acquitted of the killing. (Stein was executed in 1955 for murdering another person.)

The killing of the extravagant Vivian Gordon remains open in the files of the New York Police Department.

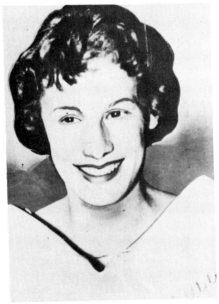

Patricia (*top*) and Barbara Grimes, abducted and murdered in Chicago in 1956, were the first victims in a rash of unsolved murders involving teenagers. (*Wide World*)

Grimes Sisters, The
MURDERS, 1956 U.S.

Two Chicago sisters, Barbara Grimes, a fifteen-year-old sophomore at Kelly High School, and Patricia, thirteen, a seventh-grade student at St. Maurice School vanished on December 28, 1956, after going to see an Elvis Presley movie, *Love Me Tender*. Their mother called police by midnight on that date to inform them that her daughters had not returned home (to 3634 South Damen Avenue). A city-wide alert went out. A little more than a year earlier the Schuessler brothers and a friend [see entry] had been brutally murdered, and Chicago police feared that the same child murderer might once again be on the loose.

The sisters were addicted to Presley movies. They had seen *Love Me Tender* eleven times; their visit to the Archer Avenue theater where they were last seen was their twelfth viewing of the film. At first it was thought that the girls had merely run away, somehow emulating Presley's life-style. The singer was contacted, and he issued the following statement to the missing Grimes sisters: "If you are good Presley fans, you will go home and ease your mother's worries."

They did not go home. Police intensified their search, picking up dozens of young men for questioning. It was reported by other teenagers at the movie theater that the sisters had been seen either talking to or getting into a car driven by a young man who looked and acted like their idol, Elvis.

Ann Landers even received a letter reportedly written by a young girl who had been at the movie that night. It read, in part:

> Betty asked me to go with her and her parents to visit her aunt. Later we decided to go to the movie. While looking for a seat Betty noticed Barbara and Pat Grimes sitting with some other kids.
>
> Outside the show we all got to talking and we exchanged phone numbers. When we got to the street where we turned off, we said good-by and we ran across the street. Then Betty forgot something she had to tell Barbara and we ran back to the corner.
>
> A man about 22 or 25 was talking to them. He pushed Barbara into the backseat of a car and Pat in the front seat. We got part of the license number as the car drove by us. The first four numbers were 2184. Betty thinks there were three or four numbers after that. We didn't think so much about it but it struck us as kind of funny. When we heard that they were missing we didn't know what to do.

This unsigned letter was never verified as having been written by a true eye witness. In fact, it was later suggested that the letter was written by the very man who abducted the girls, his motives as baffling as the fate of the Grimes sisters. Many strange events and people accompanied the investigation.

Police Sergeant Ernest Spiotto, who stayed on the case for years, questioned a young man arrested for cutting off a lock of hair of the girl sitting in front of him in a movie theater. This was only about a week after the Grimes girls had disap-

peared. The young man claimed to be a psychic and told Spiotto that he had had a dream about the Grimes sisters. Reported Spiotto: "He told us that he had this dream about a field with trees and a tiny creek. He said there were two naked bodies there—bodies looking like mannequins lying in the field."

That's exactly what Leonard Prescott thought he saw on January 22, 1957, when driving his car near the DuPage County line, two mannequins lying in a ditch. It was the sisters, as inseparable in death as they had been in life, both bodies frozen and naked, found fifteen miles from the Grimes home. The youth who had had the psychic dream about the Grimes girls was pulled in by Spiotto for more questioning, but he had a perfect alibi and was released.

The pathologist examining the bodies announced that the sisters had died from exposure to the severe winter cold; they had simply frozen to death. He did not explain how they came to be naked and tossed like rag dolls in the ditch. The sisters had apparently been beaten and sexually molested. A coroner's jury and the police insisted the girls had been murdered. According to one report, the killer had chopped away a piece of Barbara's thigh and had repeatedly stabbed Patricia in the chest and had cut away her lips.

Though scores of detectives answered thousands of tips on the case and interviewed hundreds of suspects and so-called witnesses, not one concrete clue developed in the Grimes sisters slaying. Police are still waiting for that clue or a confession.

101

H

Hall-Mills Case, The

MURDERS, 1922 U.S.

In its time no other trial in American history received more attention than the Hall-Mills case. It had everything—illicit sex, violent murder, revenge, extraordinary passion, and above all, mystery. In the end the case did not have an actual killer who could be named and punished, although the reading public had its pick from a number of prospects. The Hall-Mills case was the greatest real life whodunit of the Jazz Age.

There was no roar at the beginning. Two lovers, Raymond Schneider, twenty-two, and Pearl Bahmer, fifteen, strolled for three miles beyond their New Brunswick, New Jersey, homes, going down De Russey's Lane, famous as a lover's area, early Saturday morning, September 16, 1922. They walked into Phillips Lane, named after the nearby Phillips farm, and toward some crab apple trees, intending, they later said, to "pick mushrooms," a euphemism for spooning hastily contrived by Raymond. Pearl suddenly stood ramrod-stiff, spotting a couple lying in a half-embrace beneath one of the crab apple trees.

At first Bahmer and Schneider thought the couple were making love, but when they edged closer they realized that there was an unnatural stillness about the pair. Raymond spoke to them and got no answer. He moved even closer to see that both man and woman were dead, shot in the head. He grabbed Pearl's hand and yanked her down the lane. They ran to a nearby farmhouse to report the discovery. New Brunswick police were called and two patrolmen answered. They were led back to the crab apple tree by Schneider and began to take gruesome inventory.

The man was flat on his back, a round-crown Panama hat covering his face. It was no chore identifying him. His killer, apparently a waggish sort, had propped one of the victim's own calling cards against his foot. He was the Reverend Edward Wheeler Hall, the good-natured, balding, and somewhat chubby Episcopal minister of the Church of St. John the Evangelist of New Brunswick.

Dead next to the forty-one-year-old Hall was petite Mrs. Eleanor Mills, thirty-four. Her head was cradled by Hall's arm as they lay side by side in death. Mrs. Mills

102

had been the lead soprano in Hall's church choir. The Reverend Hall had been shot only once, a .32-caliber bullet (the casing was found near the body) crashing through his brain. The killer had obviously savored the slaying of Mrs. Mills, shooting her three times in the forehead. Her throat was not only slashed from ear to ear but (an autopsy revealed almost four years later) her slayer had cut off her tongue and hacked away her vocal cords, in sinister mockery, no doubt, of the lady's once lovely voice.

The bodies, even to the untrained eye, had been placed beneath the crab apple tree, and very carefully, as if the killer wished to maintain the propriety the couple had outwardly represented in life, even though they were adulterous lovers. It was later speculated that Hall and Mills had been discovered naked in the act of sexual intercourse, had been shot and slashed, and then had been dressed neatly, she in a blue lawn dress with red polka dots, blue velvet turban, black hose, and brown oxfords; he in a gray worsted suit, white shirt with high stiff collar, white tie, black socks, and black shoes. The killer had even taken the trouble to button Hall's coat, although, when the victim was turned over, the back was torn. When the Panama hat was removed it was noted that the minister's glasses had been carefully placed on the bridge of his nose. Mrs. Mills's face had been covered by a long scarf. It was if a stage manager had meticulously set up the scene. All of it embodied a sneering mockery—dragging the unfaithful dead lovers to New Bruns-

The Rev. Edward Wheeler Hall, murdered with his mistress in 1922.

Mrs. Eleanor Mills, the petite choir singer, who joined her lover in violent death.

De Russey's Lane, outside of New Brunswick, New Jersey, a trail leading to one of America's most sensational unsolved murders.

The crab apple tree (to the left) where the bodies of the pastor and his favorite choir singer were found.

wick's most famous lover's lane, placing the bodies in death embraces. Moreover, scattered over the corpses were many love letters Mrs. Mills had written to the rector, torrid missives for that sedate year of 1922 that would serve to shock and titillate the nation.

The Reverend Hall had addressed his lover as "My Gypsy Queen" and she had, in her childlike scrawl, called him "Babykins." (The letters found from Mills to Hall were written in pencil on school notebook paper; Hall's letters to his paramour were later unearthed by James Mills, the cuckolded husband, who sold the steaming *billets-doux* to the newspapers for $500.)

In one letter Mrs. Mills had gushed:

Dearie, what a gay, happy girl I am today . . . I love your dear note of last night and went to sleep happy after reading it. Of all the people that I know, no one understands me but you. But of course I have never shown my real self to others.

I am looking over toward the trees by the elms and dreaming . . . I am holding my sweet babykins' face in my hand and looking deep in his heart . . . Oh, honey, I am fiery today. Burning, flaming love. It seems ages since I saw my babykins' body and kissed every bit of you.

In another, the choir singer mixed gratitude with lust:

Sweetheart, my true heart, I could crush you—oh, I am so happy tonight! I'm not pretty. I know there are girls with more shapely bodies, but I'm not caring what they have. I have the greatest part of all blessings, a noble man's deep, true eternal love, and my heart is his; poor as my body is, scrawny as my skin may be; but I am his forever. How impatient I am and will be! I want to look up into your dear face for hours as you touch my body close.

The Reverend Hall was no less tempestuous when he openly committed to paper his passions for Mrs. Mills. In one missive he waxed:

Darling Wonder Heart—I just want to crush you for two hours. I want to see you Friday night alone by our road [perhaps a reference to De Russey's Lane]; where we can let out, unrestrained, that universe of joy and happiness that will be ours.

While police at the scene stood about, news of the bodies lying beneath the crab apple tree brought scores of curious residents to the scene, including several newsmen. A reporter dashed back to his office and called Mrs. Francis Noel Stevens Hall, the pastor's heavyset, matronly wife who was seven years his senior. Mrs. Hall was the richest woman in New Brunswick; she and her husband lived at 23 Nichol Avenue, in a gigantic mansion having gardens and lawns that sprawled over an entire block. Mrs. Hall, upon receiving the news of her husband's death, abruptly hung up on the reporter.

A half hour later her wealthy cousin,

Henry de la Bruyere Carpender, a member of the New York Stock Exchange, went to the newspaper office and was then taken to the murder site on the Phillips farm. Carpender stared at the bodies, then knelt next to the dead rector, taking the lifeless hand and saying: "Well, old fellow, you never did this yourself."

Carpender then turned away, without commenting on the dead Mrs. Mills lying next to his brother-in-law, and spoke privately with William E. Florence, New Jersey state senator and lawyer to the Hall family, whom Carpender had brought with him. They left without telling police anything.

It was at this juncture that the authorities began an internecine war that was further to confuse the already baffling murders. Although the bodies had been found approximately 350 feet inside Somerset County, Azariah Beekman, prosecutor for that county, insisted that the couple had been killed in Middlesex County, which contained New Brunswick, and had been deposited inside his county. The case, boomed Beekman, logically belonged with Middlesex authorities. Joseph E. Stricker, prosecutor for Middlesex County, said no, it was a Somerset County case plain and simple; the bodies had been found in Somerset County and jurisdiction for the case properly belonged in Somerset.

This squabbling would continue for years. But that morning police, after dozens of gaping citizens had had their fill of staring at the bodies, finally removed the corpses to the Somerset County morgue for examination. Somerset detective George Totten, before leaving the scene, picked up several .32 cartridge shells. These later matched the caliber of bullets that had been fired into the couple.

Little else could be found at the scene since police were soon overrun by stampeding spectators, hundreds of them rushing into the area in search of souvenirs. Vendors magically appeared to hawk hot dogs and popcorn. It was impossible to detect any concrete clues as to the killer's identity in this carnival atmosphere. The crab apple tree itself was the object of dozens of souvenir hunters who produced knives and began whittling away at it. Before the day was done nothing of this little tree, including its very roots, would be left.

Police, however, did interview James Mills and Frances Hall, on the day the bodies of their respective spouses were found. Mills, who was eleven years older than his wife and worked as the sexton and janitor at the Reverend Hall's church, was a mild-mannered fellow who apparently knew that his wife was seeing Hall, but insisted that he had believed all along it was a platonic relationship. He admitted that his wife for months had been slipping out of their small house at 49 Carmen Street, a short distance from the church, at all hours of the night. (A New York newspaper would later describe the Mills house as "a small, dingy, four-room apartment in a ramshackle building.") The Reverend Hall frequently visited the Mills home, often staying for dinner.

Mills told police that his wife had left home at seven thirty Thursday evening.

It was the last time he saw her alive. He asked her at the time where she was going, and Eleanor Mills replied tartly: "Why don't you follow me and find out." He did not follow her, he said, but did wait up for her until midnight. He went to bed, then woke up fitfully at 2 AM. Not finding his wife in bed with him, Mills woke up his two small children and went in search of Eleanor. He visited the church, which was dark, and then returned home. On Friday morning, at nine o'clock, Mills went again to the church, where he saw Mrs. Hall. He told her that his wife had been gone all night. Mrs. Hall told Mills that her husband, too, had not returned home since early Thursday evening. (Mills, it was later said, was having a chocolate phosphate in a New Brunswick drugstore at the time of the murders, the couple having been dead for about thirty-six hours by the time the strolling lovers discovered their bodies.)

Mrs. Hall, police discovered, was equally ignorant, or appeared to be, about the torrid relationship that existed between her dallying husband and the choir singer. Her past relationship with Eleanor Mills appeared to bear this out. The wealthy woman had become a second mother, it seemed, to Mrs. Mills, taking her on outings and into her home for social affairs. She had also paid for an expensive operation Eleanor had undergone some months earlier.

The relationship between Hall and his wife appeared to be a tranquil one. The pastor had married the rather dumpy and phlegmatic Frances Stevens in 1911, two years after he had been installed as rector of St. John the Evangelist Church. Frances was the leading parishioner and the marriage, all said, was a happy one. The fact that Hall, twenty-nine at marriage, wedded a woman then thirty-six did cause the gossips among New Brunswick's thirty-thousand souls to whisper that he was after the woman's considerable fortune.

By 1922, when the Reverend Hall took up with Mrs. Mills, his wife had grown heavy; her hair was flecked with gray and she wore a pince-nez to read. At forty-eight, she looked twenty years older and was never seen without a dowager's dress. By comparison, Eleanor Mills was a great beauty, at least in the roving eye of the Reverend Hall.

Mrs. Hall told investigators that her husband had left home on Thursday night, at seven-thirty, giving the exact time Mills had given. The pastor had told his wife that he had "some business to attend to," and that was the last she saw of him. She remembered having, as had Mr. Mills, a "sleepless night" when discovering her husband had not returned. In the morning she called New Brunswick police to ask if any "casualties" had been reported. She was told that there were none. She later saw Mr. Mills at church and was surprised, she said, when he told her that his wife had vanished at the same time her husband had left his house.

Household servants in the Hall mansion testified that Mrs. Hall and her brother Willie, who lived with the Halls, were on the premises at the time of the murder. But a watchman in the exclusive neighborhood told police that he had seen a woman in a gray coat go into the Hall mansion at the side door at about two thirty on Friday morning. He was not sure if it had been Mrs. Hall. Detectives raced back to Mrs. Hall and she reluctantly confirmed the fact that she was the woman seen by the watchman. She added that, unable to sleep, she had roused her brother Willie, and the two of them had gone to the church in search of her husband. Finding the church dark, she concluded that "someone might have taken ill and Dr. Hall had gone to their assistance." With that she and Willie went to the Mills home. Why she arbitrarily picked that home to visit when she claimed to be ignorant of her husband's affair she could not say. Seeing no lights in the Mills home, Mrs. Hall and Willie Stevens returned to the mansion on Nichol Avenue.

Willie Stevens, Mrs. Hall's oafish-looking brother, denied that he had gone anywhere on Friday morning, but he later admitted that he had accompanied his sister in search of her husband. Willie was to become the subject of great speculation in this mysterious murder case, a prime suspect in the minds of most because of his strange habits and behavior. He was much like the eccentric uncle portrayed in *Arsenic and Old Lace*, a wealthy oddball who wore suits too large for his hulking frame, making him appear twice as large as he really was. His thick, uncombed hair shot skyward like a fright wig, and bushy eyebrows curled about glasses with thick lenses. His walrus mustache, never trimmed, hid large, sensuous lips.

Stevens had been left $150,000 in a trust fund but was given only a $40-a-week allowance to ensure his not spending his money foolishly. The Stevens brother did a lot of foolish things, or, in the eyes of his very proper peers, performed acts that were wholly unpredictable and unnerving. He was a volunteer in the New Brunswick Fire Department and spent a good deal of time at the station, where he would cook steaks for the regular firefighters, choice cuts of meat he purchased from his allowance. He proudly wore his fireman's hat on his strolls through the town's Hungarian quarter—a place where bizarre apparrel was commonplace and his unusual appearance did not cause him to be taunted by children.

Stevens was allowed to carry the fire department flag (which he had purchased for $70) in all parades and was often permitted to ride on the fire truck during routine alarms. So much was Willie enamored with firefighting that he once started a fire in his own backyard, then raced inside his home to don his fireman's hat, then dashed back into the yard to douse the fire. He had never held a full-time job, yet he became a self-taught authority in the fields of entomology, botany, and metallurgy, studying for endless hours in his book-lined rooms inside the Hall mansion on Nichol Avenue.

Another Stevens brother, Henry, also enormously wealthy, who lived in Lavalette, New Jersey, fifty-five miles from the murder site, also came under suspicion because he was a hunter and a crack shot, although it would have taken no marksman to shoot Mrs. Mills and the Reverend Hall from close range. His brusque manner with police and reporters made him seem as if he might be hiding something. But, like all the Stevens clan, along with James Mills, Henry was found to have an alibi that could not be broken. He was, during the time of the murders, at a waterfront party with dozens of others.

Having no real suspects, police unexpectedly turned to the couple who found the bodies. Raymond Schneider and Pearl Bahmer, who admitted that they had been on the Phillips farm on Thursday night, had what prosecutors termed "tainted backgrounds." Schneider and Bahmer were arrested and interrogated. Schneider had left a wife he had married only two months earlier and was nothing more than a shiftless idler who picked up pocket money in pool halls. Bahmer had been arrested several times as a vagrant and was pronounced an incorrigible.

Schneider said a youth named Clifford Hayes had murdered Hall and Mills, finding them beneath the crab apple tree and shooting them mistakenly, thinking they were Pearl Bahmer and her father! Why Hayes would want to kill Pearl, whom he had dated only a few times, and a man he had never met, Schneider could not explain. Hayes proved to be absolutely innocent, and Schneider later stated that he had invented the story, again not giving a reason. He was later tried and convicted of perjury and sent to the state reformatory for two years.

It appeared to police and the press, desperately keeping the story on the front page, that the case was hopelessly bogged down in dead ends. Then a woman, undoubtedly the strangest of the strange characters involved in the Hall-Mills case, stepped forward. She gave her name as Mrs. Jane Gibson (she was also know as Mrs. Jane Easton, after one of her three husbands). She was a hog farmer who became the state's chief witness against the Stevens family.

Called the Pig Woman by the press because of her occupation, the leathery-faced, hoarse-voiced Mrs. Gibson said that she had been on the Phillips farm on the night of September 14 and had witnessed the killing of the pastor and his mistress, stumbling upon the scene while riding her mule Jenny in pursuit of poachers who had been stealing corn from a field she kept.

The Pig Woman, however, gave hazy testimony, describing a fight between some men and women in the far-off gloom of the crab apple orchard, and then hearing some shots. She then fled. Her testimony at the time was as incomplete as sixty-six other witnesses'. The grand jury, on November 27, 1922, following eighteen hours of deliberation, returned a "no bill" verdict, which meant no one was indicted for the murder of Hall and Mrs. Mills.

The case evaporated. James Mills went back to ringing church bells, Mrs. Hall went on a year-long vacation in Italy, and the Pig Woman returned to her hogs. Almost four years went by without comment on the case by police and press. Then, at the stroke of midnight, on July 28, 1926, several squads of state police surrounded the illustrious mansion of Mrs. Hall in New Brunswick. Detectives arrested the

Mrs. Jane Gibson, called the Pig Woman, shown with her mule Jenny; she was the chief witness for the prosecution.

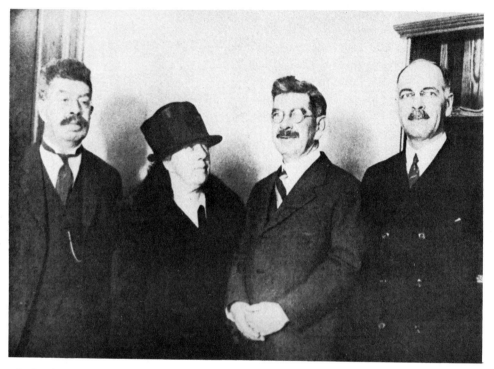

Defendants Willie Stevens, Mrs. Hall, Henry Stevens, and Henry de la Bruyere Carpender, charged in 1926 with killing the Reverend Hall and Mrs. Mills.

startled woman in her nightgown and hustled her off to jail, after serving her with a warrant that charged she had "willfully, feloniously, and with malice aforethought killed and murdered" the Reverend Hall, her husband, and the hapless choir singer, Mrs. Mills.

This incredible police move had been brought about by a New York newspaper after a divorce suit had been filed. Louise Geist, a maid in the Hall household, had married a piano salesman, Arthur M. Riehl. The marriage had ended in 1926 when Riehl filed for divorce. In his peti-

tion, to blacken his wife's name in shifting favor to him in the divorce, Riehl had incidentally charged that Geist had had many sexual encounters with the murdered Reverend Hall and had received about $6,000 to keep silent about this and for corroborating Mrs. Hall's account of her wherebouts on the night of the murder.

The divorce suit was brought to the attention of Philip Payne, managing editor of Hearst's New York *Mirror*. Payne, who had sensationalized the 1922 murders, always believed the Stevens clan had done the killings. Using the Riehl divorce papers, he pressured New Jersey authorities, chiefly Governor A. Harry Moore, into reopening the case and charging Mrs. Hall, her brothers Henry and Willie, along with the cousin, Henry Carpender, with murder. Payne also claimed that a fingerprint expert in his employ had found Henry Stevens' thumbprint on Dr. Hall's calling card, the very card found at the murder site. (The expert's findings were later dismissed as inconclusive.)

Mrs. Hall was promptly released after posting a $15,000 bond, but she and her brothers were put on trial for murder. (Carpender was not indicted). The trial began on November 3, 1926, in the jam-packed courtroom in tiny Somerville, New Jersey. The courtroom was designed to hold 250 people but more than five-hundred squeezed into the place. So many lawyers packed the table areas that there was little room for movement.

Charlotte Mills, the flapper daughter of the slain Mrs. Mills, had turned news-woman and busied herself by grinding out endless copy on Mrs. Hall's drab attire for a New York paper. Somerville was inundated with reporters, more than five-hundred of them descending like locusts upon the tiny community. The *Mirror*, leader in the effort to convict the Hall family, rented an entire small hotel for its visiting staff members. Sixty leased wires were set up in the basement of the courthouse, and over these twelve million words were sent forth describing every detail of the twenty-four-day trial.

James Mills was a witness for the prosecution, but he offered little other than

James Mills, the cuckolded husband who sold his wife's love letters to the press for $500.

Charlotte Mills, the victim's flapper daughter turned reporter, shown here rattling off a gossip column about those who stood accused of murdering her mother.

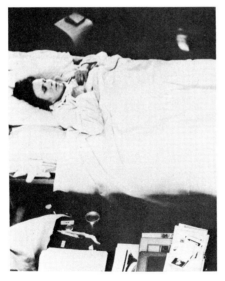

The Pig Woman, dying of cancer, dramatically testified from a makeshift hospital bed in court during the sensational 1926 trial.

his belated knowledge that his wife and the Reverend Hall had been carrying on an affair. Again, the star witness for the prosecution was the flamboyant Jane Gibson. The Pig Woman by this time was ill, having undergone an operation for cancer, and had to be rolled into the courtroom on a portable bed. She moaned her dramatic testimony while tossing and turning in the bed, craning to stare at Mrs. Hall, who sat with quiet dignity with her brothers at the defense table.

Special Prosecutor Alexander Simpson, a New Jersey state senator, took the fifty-six-year-old Gibson through her almost four-year-old testimony once again. But this time, the Pig Woman's memory of that long-ago night on De Russey's Lane allowed for more detail than she originally provided. Embellishment many called it, as she played her role for all it was worth. While on her patrol to guard her corn from thieves, she said, she tied up her mule Jenny and by a moon, "shining bright and pretty," she said she saw Willie and Henry Stevens and Mrs. Hall alight from a car and walk into the crab apple orchard. "I was peeking and peeking and peeking," croaked the bed-ridden Pig Woman.

Simpson asked: "Then what did you hear or see?"

Gibson: "I heard mumbling voices to the left of me. Men's and women's voices. I stood still. They were coming closer all the time."

Simpson: "Were you able to make out any words?"

Gibson: "Well, the men were talking and a woman said very quickly, 'Explain these letters!' And the men were saying 'God damn it' and everthing else . . . all that kind of stuff. Somebody was hitting, hitting. I could hear somebody's wind going out. And somebody said, 'Ugh!' Then somebody said, 'God damn it, let go!' "

Simpson: "A man hollered, 'God damn it, let go?' "

Gibson: "Yes, then somebody threw a flashlight toward where they were hollering. I see something glitter and I see another man like they were wrestling."

The man wrestling with the Reverend Hall, insisted the Pig Woman, was Henry Stevens. She then said she heard a shot and ran for her mule. A nurse, who was attending Jane Gibson, applied cold cream to her lips so she could continue talking. Gibson stated that she heard one of the two women in the orchard say, " 'Oh, Henry,' easy, very easy, and the other began to scream, scream, scream so loud, 'Oh, my, oh, my, oh, my,' so terrible loud."

Simpson: "Then what?"

Gibson: "I run for the mule and I just about got my foot in the stirrup when bang, bang, bang—three quick shots. Then I stumbled over a stump getting on the mule and I run for home." She had lost a moccasin, however, and returned minutes later to retrieve it. It was then that she said she saw "a big, white-haired woman doing something with her hand, crying, something . . . bending down, facing something. Kneeling down, fixing something."

Simpson: "The same woman you say was Mrs. Hall?"

Gibson: "Yes."

The defense later pointed out that Mrs. Hall was not a "big white-haired woman," but was short and had gray hair. Sitting behind the defense table, paid to do so, was Jane Gibson's ancient mother, who chanted through the Pig Woman's testimony: "She's a liar, she's a liar, she's a liar!"

Moreover, the defense asked the Pig Woman how many times she been married. She could not remember, nor could she recall the names of her husbands, nor where she had married them and when or if she had been divorced. Here the woman could remember exact details of a four-year-old murder, exclaimed the defense, but she could not recall her marriages. The point was well taken with the jury, and Gibson's testimony was all but obliterated.

The Pig Woman's big moment was over. Burly policemen lifter her from her bed and onto a stretcher. As they began to carry her from the courtroom, Jane Gibson raised herself on a elbow and, turning to face Mrs. Hall and the Stevens brothers, she yelled from her moving litter: "I told the truth, so help me God! And *you* know it—and *you* know it—and *you* know it!"

"She's a liar, she's a liar, she's a liar!" droned her mother.

Gibson was carried to a waiting ambulance which sped off in the direction of a Newark hospital. En route, the Pig Woman spotted an ice cream stand and asked the driver to stop. An attendant bought her a pint of ice cream and she wolfed this down, happily chatting with the ambulance crew, saying, "I feel better than I have any time during the last four years, now that I've got that [her testimony] out of my system."

Mrs. Hall took the stand in her own defense and proved to be a remarkably cool and reserved witness. She remained calm through all the prosecution's badgering and insinuations, a demeanor that earned her the sobriquet of the Iron Widow. Her unflappable composure impressed the jury, especially when the prosecutor asked if her dead spouse had always been "a loving, affectionate husband." At this moment she wept openly and answered one word: "Always."

Simpson, who stood only five feet tall, then rushed to the stand and shouted: "Now, Mrs. Hall, did you kill your husband?"

"I did not," replied the widow in an even voice.

"Did you play any part in that dreadful tragedy?"

"I did not."

On December 3, 1926, the jury retired for four and a half hours, then returned a verdict of "not guilty" for all three defendants. The "Million Dollar Trial"—the amount reportedly spent by the Stevens family on their defense— was over. (The total amount spent was a little more than $400,000.) The defendants filed a $3-million lawsuit against the New York *Mirror*; the newspaper's lawyers later settled with the Stevens family out of court for an undisclosed sum. Editor Payne, who had brought about the 1926 courtroom carnival, vanished the following year on a Maine to Rome flight in a monoplane called the Old Glory, disappearing somewhere over the Atlantic with pilot Lloyd W. Bertaud. (Payne and his tabloid antics were later profiled by Edward G. Robinson in the motion picture *Five Star Final*.)

Though her testimony was allegedly a deathbed oration, the Pig Woman did not perish immediately after her courtroom appearance. She lingered in the limelight until February 7, 1930, dying of cancer in Jersey City. The Stevens family resumed their lives without further crisis: Mrs. Hall continued to attend her dead husband's church, living for two more decades without remarrying, continuing to be one of New Brunswick's Civic leaders, but from afar. She spent most of her days behind the walls of her mansion with her brother Willie, who gave up being a volunteer fireman altogether.

But the question remains: Who murdered the fun-loving Reverend Hall and the choir singer he took as his mistress?

Haskell, Edwin
MURDER, 1908 ENGLAND

One of the most baffling slayings in Edwardian England was that of Edwin Richard "Teddy" Haskell, a crippled twelve-year-old who lived alone with his mother, Flora, in Salisbury, Wiltshire. Edwin's mother, a laundress of meager means, displayed great affection for the child who walked on a crutch; she hoped some day to buy him a cork leg.

Mrs. Haskell's nephew, Percey Noble, knocked on the back door of his aunt's house at about 10:30 PM, on October 31, 1908. The door was flung wide and Noble was met by a hysterical Mrs. Haskell who screamed: "Run for a doctor! A man has killed my poor little Teddy!" Neighbors responded to Mrs. Haskell's screams of terror.

A constable came on the run and discovered Teddy in his upstairs bed, his throat cut from ear to ear. Mrs. Haskell stated later that after putting her boy to bed she sat in the kitchen. She heard a noise and went to the front door and, just at that moment, a man raced down the stairs, pushed her aside, and dashed into the street, pausing only to hurl a bloody knife, the murder weapon, in her direction.

The story seemed incredible, and police, having no other suspect, arrested and charged Mrs. Haskell with the slaying. In court she was branded a "mercy killer," in that she believed her child would grow up to be a helpless cripple, and unable to bear his sorrowful lot, she murdered him. The woman's compassion for her son and the fact that she had never expressed doubts or worries for his future mitigated against euthanasia. Mrs. Haskell was fortunate in being defended by Rayner Goddard, one of the keenest legal minds in England at the time (Goddard later became Lord Chief Justice of England). She was acquitted after two brief trials.

The man Mrs. Haskell said she saw run from her house was never found; she gave an incomplete description of him, and she was also the only person to see him. Why he would kill a helpless child asleep in bed remains a nagging mystery, but it must be remembered that there are many unsolved murder cases, where total strangers have committed homicide without apparent motives [see Evelyn Foster].

Hiker Slayings
MURDERS, 1980 U.S.

Thirty miles northwest of San Francisco in the placid woodlands of Point Reyes National Seashore, one of America's most beautiful spots, an unknown madman began murdering defenseless hikers in 1980. The first known victims of this stalking terror were two women from the Sierra Club. A third woman barely missed the fate of her hiking companions. Diana O'Connell, twenty-two, and Shauna May, twenty-three, had got separated from their companion on a narrow trail. Their bodies were found nude, face down, and crisscrossing each other the day after Thanksgiving 1980 in a thickly wooded area. Both victims had been shot through the head.

As officers fanned out over the heavily wooded area they found, to their shock, another couple, two teenagers who had been missing for seven weeks, both dead, but fully clothed, at the base of a giant fir tree. They too had been shot in the head. More than fifteen months earlier three other women had been killed in a similar manner. Officials reluctantly concluded that they were dealing with a mass killer responsible for at least seven deaths. There

Hiker Slayings

Police composite sketch of the suspect in the California hiker slayings of 1980.

was one witness who caught a glimpse of a man fleeing the scene of the earlier murders and thus a police sketch was produced. The witness described the man as a "clean-cut white man in his late twenties or early thirties, of medium build with medium-length hair." He wore hiking clothes and a knapsack.

The ritualistic pattern of the slayings caused analysts to conclude that the victims had been forced into submissive positions before being shot with a high-powered weapon. The killer was apparently appeasing a thick streak of sadism, employing, according to Marin County Sheriff Al Howenstein, "mental torture in which the victim pleads not to be murdered." The sheriff, working from a psychologist's profile, added that part of the ritual in the killings was the necessity of the killer to force hikers off the trail and to select victims who appeared to be vulnerable. "The man very carefully and deliberately plans these acts in his effort to achieve some degree of psychological relief. The problem is that the murders will not satisfy those needs, and they will get worse."

R. William Mathis, a criminal psychologist, later commented: "He [the killer] gets his maximum excitement by mentally terrifying his victims."

To Reno Taini, a wilderness instructor who found the teenagers slain in the fall of 1980, the killings constituted a sacrilege. "To have it happen in such a sanctuary," he lamented, "it's like shooting somebody in church."

To the time of this writing the hiker murderer is still at large.

I

Irish Crown Jewels
ROBBERY, 1907 IRELAND

In 1830 British King William IV presented to the Order of St. Patrick a collection of jewelry—a diamond star, a diamond badge, and five collars studded with rare gems—which were to be worn on all state occasions by the Lord Lieutenant of Ireland who was also the Order's Grand Master. These jewels, which would have been worth well over $1 million today, were known as the Irish Crown Jewels and were kept in a large safe inside Bedford Castle tower.

Some time in early July 1907 the Irish Crown Jewels were reported missing by their keeper, Sir Arthur Vicars, and his assistant and nephew, Pierce Mahoney. Vicars himself was unsure of just when burglars could have stolen the rare jewels. He could not pinpoint the exact time, let alone the day, when the jewels were taken, since, when he had inspected them some time in early June 1907, instead of returning them to the safe, which had a rusted lock, he had merely placed them in a large tin box, storing them in the castle's library.

Vicars, who happened to be distantly related to Sir Arthur Conan Doyle, wrote to the creator of Sherlock Holmes asking for advice on how to proceed in his investigation to recover the lost jewels. Doyle, who was quite an amateur sleuth, began his own probe. He learned that Vicars was involved in a homosexual group that included Francis Shackleton, the famed explorer and adventurer.

Shackleton and Mahoney, Doyle apparently learned, were notorious liars and cheats, as well as lovers. As did Vicars, they had keys to the strongbox that had contained the jewels.

While Doyle was snooping about, Vicars held a much-publicized séance in his home. He and other society friends were told through a medium, allegedly speaking to a "control" force from "the other side" that the jewels could be found in a nearby Dublin graveyard. Vicars and his assistants then raced to the closest graveyard and began to dig about haphazardly, spending several days on their useless quest. Vicars was widely lampooned by journalists of the day for embarking on the senseless search. Before they could dig further, Vicars and his assistants were fired by King Edward VII.

Conan Doyle, however, continued to

Sir Arthur Conan Doyle, creator of Sherlock Holmes, was asked to solve the riddle of the crown jewels theft; he failed.

dig, discovering that Vicars and Shackleton, who lived extravagantly and clearly could have used the money the stolen gems would have brought, were associated with Edward VII's brother-in-law, the Duke of Argyll, in what may have been a homosexual relationship. To avoid scandal, Doyle and others concluded, the king had dismissed Vicars, rather than prosecute him as the logical culprit in the jewelry theft. The exposure of a homosexual ring so close to the throne, it was reasoned, might have brought ruination down upon British royalty. Police were ordered off the case, and the theft was conveniently forgotten.

All of those responsible for the Irish Crown Jewels, however, later met violent ends. Mahoney was killed in an apparent hunting accident in 1914 when he tripped the trigger of a shotgun while climbing a fence. Some later claimed that the accident was staged. Shackleton died drunk and dissolute in 1925, his once considerable fortune shrunk to nothing after years of paying off blackmailers who threatened to expose his high-placed homosexual liaisons. Vicars was assassinated by members of the IRA. He was summoned from his elegant house at Listowel on April 14, 1921, then shot dead as he stepped into the street. His house was burned to the ground. Police later found Vicars's body propped against a tree with a placard hanging about his neck which read: "A warning to Spies."

It was never learned why Vicars was considered a spy, although he had expressed little sympathy for the Irish revolutionaries of the period. It was speculated that he had been killed for his part in stealing the Irish Crown Jewels and that he may have died at British hands. His killers, like the lost gems, were never found.

J

Jack the Ripper
MURDERS, 1888 ENGLAND

The most enduring uncaptured fiend of the nineteenth century was that butchering and taunting slayer known as Jack the Ripper, a title the boasting killer bestowed upon himself. No other single murderer up to that time left his bloody mark upon society with such impact as did this demonlike creature. He was crafty, intelligent, and always lethal. From the filthiest hovel in London's East End to Queen Victoria's throneroom, Jack spread his calculated terror with the casual air of a chestnut vendor. He was England's greatest nightmare, a slaughterhouse killer who proved that evil could exist for its own sake.

The killings attributed to the Ripper were five in number, but he may have committed as many as nine, from April 1888 to February 1891. Most experts, however, agree that the real Jack the Ripper committed only five murders, the most gruesome of the lot, in less than a three-month period. These five murders, beginning with the slaying of Mary Ann "Polly" Nichols on August 31, 1888, and ending with the slicing up of Mary Jane Kelly on

120

November 9, 1888, all bear the hallmarks of the same madman, the same kind of throat slashing, disemboweling, and general mutilation, particularly of the female organs.

Then again, this period of slaughterhouse killings may have been chosen by authorities and crime experts simply because the most likely suspects could have operated only during that three-month period, if, indeed, the suspects were likely candidates for the role of the mass murderer. Never having caught the killer, the British at least narrowed the field of the Ripper's activities, conveniently claiming that his insane bloodbaths stopped at a fixed point because he simply died or was shut up in a lunatic asylum, a tidy solution to a dreadful dilemma. For most Ripper students it is inconceivable that the killer went undetected for years, perhaps decades, surviving his own fits of carnage, his name never joining the long list of suspects. Such a comfortable fate is undoubtedly too terrible to contemplate for those insisting upon an explainable and justifiable end to this horror story.

Years before the Ripper may have died, scarecrow children in London's impoverished East End, near the narrow lanes and byways where Jack stalked his victims, chanted the following ditty:

Jack the Ripper's dead
And lying on his bed.
He cut his throat
With sunlight soap.
Jack the Ripper's dead.

One could easily conjure the vision of the real killer passing a group of children spewing forth these lines, smiling benignly, patting them on their heads and continuing over the cobblestones to his job, his home, his family, the sinister secret of his continuing unmolested existence giving him solace and gratifying his lust for permanent black fame. As the Ripper's letters to authorities prove—at least two of them are genuine out of the thousands sent by cranks, pranksters, and the ghoulish-minded—he was a grandstander, a killer who coveted the limelight and challenged the police to find him.

The London police in 1888 were never equipped to track down such a clever, shifty madman. They could barely hold in check the destitute thousands that inhabited the East End where the meanest streets in the world were to be found. Police had to contend with hordes of prostitutes, thugs, drunkards, uneducated immigrants, muggers, thieves of all stripes in the East End, which had a burgeoning population in the Ripper's day of more than 900,000 souls, about 80,000 people in the Whitechapel district where he concentrated his lethal deeds.

This squalid terrible area teemed with more than 1200 prostitutes of the lowest class, most of these raggedy streetwalkers unfit for service in the district's sixty-two brothels. Most of the 233 lodging houses at that time consisted of one-room affairs where prostitutes paid on a night-to-night basis, bringing their customers to tiny, filthy rooms provided with small charcoal-buring stoves for heat and single candles for light. Often as not, these women serviced their crude customers on the street, selecting a secluded spot for a quick assignation.

The streetwalkers were generally middle-aged women with no income other than what they could pick up in the street. uneducated, diseased, alcoholic, these prostitutes formed the pool of flesh into which the Ripper dipped his long knives. The first of these who may have been a victim of the Ripper was Emma Elizabeth Smith, forty-five, as she was returning to her hovellike room at 18 George Street, Spitalfields, in the early hours of April 3, 1888.

She had been seen talking to a distinguished-looking gentleman wearing dark clothes and a white scarf. Hours later she was found staggering into her lodgings by a constable. She had been horribly beaten about the face, her ear had been slashed and an object, she said, had been inserted into her vagina and broken off, causing her horrible internal injuries. She claimed that she had been attacked on Osborn Street by four men, one of whom she thought was a teenager, but she could not be sure. Emma Smith died of peritonitis some hours later.

Martha Tabram (or Turner) was next. A middle-aged whore, she was found on the first landing of George Yard Landing,

An 1888 newspaper illustration of how the body of Mary Ann Nichols was found in Buck's Row, Whitechapel; she is considered the Ripper's first victim.

later Gunthorpe Street, in Whitechapel, at 3 AM on August 7, 1888. She had been stabbed thirty-nine times, most of the wounds centered about the area of the female organs. In both the Smith and Tabram killings the attacks took place in very public areas, and it puzzled police that no one had seen anyone fleeing from the scenes. Moreover, not a single cry for help from either victim was heard.

The third such killing of a prostitute, who many experts later insisted was the Ripper's first actual victim, was the ghastly murder of Mary Ann "Polly" Nichols, forty-two, a drunken, barroom-brawling whore whose body was found by two tradesmen and a constable on Buck's Row about 4 AM on August 31, 1888.

Nichols had died of a slashed throat, two sweeping incisions an inch apart that ran the width of her neck, deep penetrations to the vertebrae that left her almost decapitated. Her abdomen had been repeatedly slashed and cut, as had been her vagina. Physicians examining the body believed the killer had used a knife with a six- to eight-inch blade, and had used it with some degree of medical experience in post-mortem examinations. William Nichols, the victim's husband, who had not seen his wayward wife for more than three years, was summoned to the morgue to make a positive identification. He took one look at the mutilated body and moaned: "I forgive you for everything now that I see you like this."

As in the cases of Smith and Tabram, there was no apparent motive for the crime; Polly Nichols had nothing to steal and very little to give in the way of sexual

Jack the Ripper was depicted in many ways by the terrified British press; here he slinks down a London street dressed uncharacteristically in shabby clothes.

gratification. Detectives concluded that the only reasonable motive was that the killer had an intense, abiding hatred of prostitutes. A search was then conducted for any lowlife man who had publicly mistreated whores in the area. One name, "Leather Apron," kept popping up. The reference was to a man named John Pizer, a bootmaker who detested whores and generally knocked them about when in his cups. He was tracked down to his lodgings where a half-dozen sharp, short knives were found among his belongings. Pizer explained that he used these knives in his trade. His alibi was strong. He had been at home during the murders of the three prostitutes, and his entire family swore to this claim. Pizer was released as innocent.

Detectives, in their search for Leather Apron picked up a man resembling Pizer who had been drinking in a Gravesend pub and acting queerly. His clothes were bloodstained and he had cut marks on his hands. The man, William Piggott, said he had tried to help a woman having a fit in Whitechapel but she had bitten his hand, the wound having caused the bloodstains. Piggott was held for questioning but acted like a lunatic in his cell and, within three hours, was shipped off to an asylum.

By this time the populace in the East End began to panic. A stalking maniacal killer was loose in the streets and the police seemed helpless against his attacks. They had no clues, no suspects, no notions of what to do or where to look for the fiend. Eight days went by before the killer struck again, September 8, 1888. His

Police sketch of Annie Chapman, mutilated by the Ripper.

next victim was forty-seven-year-old Annie Chapman. In the early dark hours of that Saturday morning, Chapman, drunk and demanding a room in Dorset Street, was turned away because she lacked the money for a bed. She staggered down Hanbury Street and was seen by a woman to stop and talk to a stranger at approximately 5:30 AM, a half hour before her hacked-up body was found. The stranger was described as dark, about forty, perhaps a foreigner, who wore dark clothes that gave him the appearance of a gentleman. On his head was a deerstalker hat with duckbills fore and aft, the kind of hat later associated with Sherlock Holmes. The witness, a park keeper's wife, said she did not get a good look at the man's face but heard him ask Chapman in a low voice: "Will you?" To this, "Dark Annie" replied: "Yes." The two of them went off.

Dark Annie Chapman was found behind 29 Hanburg Street in a small yard, her head almost completely cut away from her body, held in place by a handkerchief. (This was a scarf Chapman was wearing when murdered.) She had been savagely mutilated as the police report stated: "[She was] lying on her back, dead, left arm resting on left breast, legs drawn up, . . . small intestines and flap of the abdomen lying on the right side above right shoulder attached by a cord with the rest of the intestines inside the body, two flaps of skin from the lower part of the abdomen lying in a large quantity of blood above the left shoulder; throat cut deeply from left and back in jagged manner right around the throat."

The killer had removed the kidney and ovaries from the body. Chapman's two front upper teeth were missing; in the case of Nichols, five front teeth were missing. This time, there were clues, however, even though the diabolical murderer had probably planted them to mislead police. Following the Nichols murder, the cry for Leather Apron had gone out and this was reported in the papers. Pizer, the bootmaker, was not picked up until September 10 (two days after the Hanbury slaying) and was still being sought at the time Chapman's body was found. Knowing police were still searching for Leather Apron, the killer of Annie Chapman conveniently left a piece of a leather apron under a nearby tap. He had also undoubtedly kept the many newsclippings reporting the slaying of Martha Tabram, who had been seen hours before her death with a soldier, and how a knife and a soldier's bayonet might have been used on her. The newspapers had reported how the company of soldiers in the Tower had been paraded before supposed witnesses and how no trooper was identified. To resurrect suspicions of a military man being the murderer, Chapman's slayer left another false lead—the torn corner of a blood-soaked envelope imprinted with the crest of the Sussex Regiment. Both of these so-called clues, the apron and the piece of envelope, were dismissed by police as false.

Further confusing police investigators were the thousands of letters, notes, and postcards sent to authorities. Most of these missives put forth harebrained schemes on how to catch the killer or provided generally useless information. The first of the real "Jack the Ripper" letters, or, at least, the first letter to use the name, was postmarked September 28, 1888 (and dated three days earlier), mailed from London East Central. It was sent to the Central News Agency and read:

Dear Boss,

I keep on hearing the police have caught me but they won't fix me just yet. I have laughed when they look so clever and talk about being on the right track. That joke about Leather Apron [undoubtedly a reference to his leaving the false clue] gave me real fits. I am down on whores and I shan't quit ripping them till I do get buckled. Grand work the last job was. I gave the lady no time to squeal. [Most likely a reference to Chapman, who apparently let out no cry when he attacked her; she was slain only a few feet from the open windows of a boardinghouse where seventeen persons were sleeping.] How can they catch me now. I love my work and want to start again. You will soon hear of me with my funny little games. I saved some of the proper red stuff [blood from Chapman, who was gored like an ox] in a ginger beer bottle over the last job to write with but it went thick like glue and I can't use it. Red ink is fit enough I hope *ha ha*. The next job I do I shall clip the lady's ears off and send to the police officers just for jolly wouldn't you. Keep this letter back till I do a bit more work, then give it out straight. My knife is nice and sharp and I want to get to work right away if I get a chance. Good luck.

Yours truly, JACK THE RIPPER

126

Don't mind me giving the trade name. Wasn't good enough to post this before I got all the red ink off my hands curse it.

The last reference is to published reports in which pathologists examining the Ripper's victims had stated that his incisions, removal of organs, his manner of wielding the knife, displayed surgical skill, which led police to suspect they were dealing with a deranged doctor or, at least, with a demented medical student. The Central News Agency received a second missive, a postcard postmarked September 30, 1888. Predicting Jack's next victims, it read:

I was not codding dear old Boss when I gave you the tip. You'll hear about Saucy Jack's work tomorrow. Double event this time. Number one squealed a bit. Couldn't finish straight off. Had not time to get ears for police. Thanks for keeping last letter back till I got to work again.

JACK THE RIPPER

The "double event" referred to by the sender involved the bestial murders of two more East End prostitutes, which occurred in the early hours of the very day the Ripper sent off his last postcard, on September 30, 1888. At approximately 1 AM, a deliveryman, Louis Deimschutz, drove a horse and cart into the backyard of the International Working Men's Educational Club on Berner Street and came upon the body of Elizabeth "Long Liz" Stride (real name Elizabeth Gustaafsdotter, also known as Annie Fitzgerald), a forty-five-year-old Swedish immigrant. The prostitute's throat had been slashed by one long incision. More than two quarts of blood had flowed from the victim's wound, yet when Deimschutz and members he summoned from the club lifted the body, it was warm to the touch. Apparently the cart driver had turned into the courtyard just as the Ripper was about to begin his mutilation. (The card had read: "Couldn't finish straight off.") He undoubtedly fled down the cobblestone lane as he heard the cartman approaching.

While the Ripper was running from this scene, Catherine Eddowes, a forty-three-year-old prostitute, was released from Bishopsgate Police Station, where she had been jailed for drunkenness. It was a little after 1 AM. Eddowes stepped into the gloom of the street, turned to the constable at the door and said, "Night, old cock," and sauntered in the direction of Houndsditch and Mitre Square.

Within the next forty-five minutes Catherine Eddowes met Jack the Ripper and stepped into a dark corner of Mitre Square with him for what she presumed to be a quick trick. At 1:45 a passing constable saw a heap of clothing bunched into a corner against a brick wall. He threw his light in the direction and winced to see the woman, her skirts and petticoats pulled up to her waist, her throat gashed. This time the Ripper had done his work with thoroughness and had done it speedily. He had slashed the victim's face repeatedly, perhaps to prevent identification, nicking the eyelids. There were gashes about one of Eddowes's ears. ("Had not time to get ears for police.") The vic-

A press portrait of Liz Stride, one of two Ripper victims on the same night.

127

tim's privates had been cut to pieces, the abdomen cut wide open and the left kidney and entrails removed. Some intestines had been thrown over the shoulder of the deceased. It had been as bloody a disemboweling as that performed on Annie Chapman.

No more letters were sent by the Ripper until October 16, 1888, when George Lusk, head of the Whitechapel Vigilance Committee received a small parcel and a note. The note read:

From Hell

Mr. Lusk

Sir I send you half the Kidne I took from one woman prasarved it for you tother piece I fried and ate it was very nise I may send you the bloody knif that took it out if you only wate a whil longer signed   Catch me when you can Mishter Lusk

The small parcel contained a human kidney. This was matched to Catherine Eddowes's corpse, proving that this note was the most genuine Ripper communication sent to date.

It was little consolation to the police. The fiend that terrorized the East End seemed to taunt them. Although patrols had been doubled and tripled and hundreds of suspects had been pulled in for questioning, the killer consistently eluded detection. "The man vanishes into thin air," complained one official.

By then the frenzy of London's citizens reached epic proportions. Pickets marched up and down in front of police headquarters and petitions signed by thousands of alarmed residents flooded Buckingham Palace, begging Queen Victoria to do something about Jack the Ripper. The Queen spent many restless hours pondering the moves of the mysterious killer.

In a note to the Home Secretary, Victoria asked: "Have the cattle boats and the passenger boats been examined? Has an investigation been made as to the number of single men occupying rooms to themselves? The murderer's clothes must be saturated with blood and kept somewhere." After Mary Jane Kelly was slaughtered by the Ripper on November 11, 1888, Queen Victoria sent an urgent note to her prime minister, Lord Salisbury, stating: "All these courts must be lit and our detectives improved. They are not what they should be."

Lord Salisbury actually called a cabinet meeting to discuss how to handle the elusive Jack, but little in the way of helpful directives came out of these lofty deliberations. The police were stymied; Police Commissioner Sir Charles Warren appeared to be dumbfounded by the mass slayings. His every move in the case emphasized the archaic stereotype of the stodgy, unimaginative British bureaucrat. He had no idea, really, of how to conduct an investigation into such affairs; the Ripper was more than his match and, by openly killing long after Warren's police dragnets had been thrown out, the murderer seemed to be smugly sneering at the efforts of the law to catch him.

Warren contemplated such measures as equipping his constables with shoes made of India rubber so that their approach on night patrols could not be heard by Jack upon the cobblestone streets. He gave long and tedious hours of thought to this proposal and then abandoned it as too expensive a proposition. Next Warren thought to use bloodhounds to track down Jack. Warren hired two supposedly excellent bloodhounds, called Barnaby and Burgho, and spent many hours training them to follow the scent of the killer. He even pretended to be the killer himself and had the hounds chase him for a mile or so through the narrow streets of London. (He lost them.) The dogs themselves got lost and had to be tracked down by police. They proved utterly useless in the hunt for the Ripper.

Moreover, Warren was guilty of obliterating possible clues to the killer's motives, if not his identity. In Goulston Street, after the "Double event" killings, a patrolman found a scrap of apron that had been torn away from Catherine Eddowes's body, used to wipe clean the killer's bloody knife. Throwing his lamp on a nearby wall, the constable saw the following words scrawled:

> The Juwes are not the
> men that will be blamed
> for nothing.

The words had been written only hours after Eddowes had been killed and they were attributed to the Ripper, as if he had intended to put the killings onto the vast number of Jews living in the East End. Sir Charles Warren was called to the spot and, after reading the message, ordered that it be wiped out. It was later claimed that the police commissioner had this done to prevent any racial or religious unrest, as anti-Semitism was then rabid in London. However, in not waiting for the message to be photographed so that the writing could later be analyzed, Warren foolishly wiped away what might have been an important clue. (The odd spelling of the word "Juwes," instead of "Jews," some later said, was an archaic usage stemming from ancient Masonic writings. Also, the ritualistic disemboweling of several victims where the entrails were thrown over the right shoulder reportedly had something to do with Masonic rites. This gave rise to the theory that the murders were part of a Masonic conspiracy to rid British society of prostitutes.

Despite the precautions taken by police and the warnings spread through the East End, prostitutes continued to solicit customers as usual. One of these nonchalant hustlers was Mary Jane Kelly, an attractive twenty-four-year-old streetwalker. Unlike the middle-aged, broken-down whores who had served as the Ripper's earlier victims, Mary Jane (also called Mary Ann) was fairly intelligent. She maintained regular lodgings, a first-floor room at 26 Dorset Street off Miller's Court. Behind on her rent, Mary Jane began soliciting briskly, bringing men back to her small room. On November 11, 1888, about 4 AM, Elizabeth Praten, who occupied the room above Kelly, heard a low cry of "Oh, murder!" coming from nearby but she did not respond; such cries in that crime-ridden area were commonplace.

Mary Jane Kelly, the youngest and prettiest of the Ripper victims, who suffered incredible mutilation at the fiend's hands.

At 10:45 AM that morning Thomas Bowyer, a rent collector, knocked on Kelly's door. He got no response, so he looked through the broken pane of the first-floor window to see if Mary Jane was present. He shrank back in horror. He saw two mounds of flesh piled on a table next to the bed and the carved-up body of Mary Jane Kelly, a huge pool of blood beneath the bed that held her; she looked as if a wild beast had been gnawing at her bones. Bowyer ran off to tell his employer, who, in turn, came to gape at the mutilated corpse before calling police.

Officers cordoned off Miller's Court, posted a guard before the locked door to Kelly's room, and sent for Police Commissioner Warren, asking that he employ the bloodhounds to track down the fiend. No one entered the Kelly room as officers waited almost three hours for Warren, who, along with the bloodhounds, could not be found. It was Lord Mayor's Day and huge crowds had already assembled for festivities.

Word soon filtered out of Miller's Court about the Ripper's latest victim and, within hours, newsboys were hawking extra editions, shouting: "MURDER, HORRIBLE MURDER!" The Ripper had apparently chosen this day to feed his gigantic ego once more, upstaging the Lord Mayor of London.

When Warren failed to appear, Superintendent Arnold ordered the door to Kelly's room battered down. Police rushed inside, many of these burly officers taking one look at the awful bloodletting and turning away to retch. It was the most revolting of the Ripper killings. Jack had, for the first time, murdered inside a building, and he had taken his time in cutting up the victim, indulging himself in a wild, insane orgy of mutilation.

The *Illustrated Police News* quoted directly from the official report:

> The throat had been cut right across with a knife, nearly severing the head from the body. The abdomen had been partially ripped open, and both the breasts had been cut from the body, the left arm, like the head, hung to body by the skin only. The nose had been cut off, the forehead skinned, and the thighs, down to the feet, stripped of the flesh. The abdomen had been slashed with a knife across downwards, and the liver and entrails wrenched away. The entrails and other portions of the frame were missing, but the liver etc., were found placed between the feet of this poor victim. The flesh from the thighs and legs, together with the breasts and nose, had been placed by the murderer on the table, and one of the hands of the dead woman had been pushed into her stomach.

Nothing ever had been seen like this in the murder annals of English history. The repulsive ferocity of the killing was not human in the eyes of those who witnessed the body. It was the worst sort of butchery, and police photographers were summoned to record the gory sight. The Ripper had spent at least two hours at his slaughter, police concluded, providing himself light from a small stove in which

News sketch of Jack leaving Mary Jane Kelly's tiny first-floor flat on November 9, 1888.

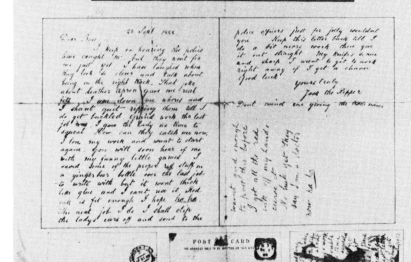

Police reproduced the first postcard and letter received from Jack the Ripper, hoping someone would recognize the writing.

he burned rags and some clothes (not his own but female garments and a hat. It was never determined just whose these clothes were; Kelly's own clothes were folded neatly on a nearby chair.)

Police Commissioner Warren was informed of the grisly slaying and shortly thereafter, tacitly admitting his own ineptitude in dealing with the archfiend, he resigned his post. With Kelly, for most serious Ripper historians, Jack's killings came to an end.

But there were two, possibly three more murders that fit his modus operandi. In June 1889 the headless body of Elizabeth Jackson, a Chelsea prostitute identified by scars, was found floating in the Thames. On July 18, 1889, Alice McKenzie, a Whitechapel prostitute, was found with her throat slashed and her privates hacked out. The last such killing was that of prostitute Frances Coles, whose body was found on February 13, 1891, in Swallow Gardens in Whitechapel. Her throat had been cut and she had been mutilated about the abdomen.

Coles lingered unconscious for a few hours before dying. Apparently a constable, Ernest Thompson, who was out for the first time on night duty, interrupted the killer as he turned into Swallow Gardens. According to Frederick Porter Wensley, onetime head of the Criminal Investigation Department of Scotland Yard, "a man came running out of Swallow Gardens towards him. As soon as he perceived the officer he turned tail, made off at speed in the opposited direction, and was in a few seconds lost to view." A minute later Thompson stumbled over the near dead Frances Cole. This was, perhaps, the closest, any police officer may have come to the enigmatic Jack the Ripper.

Yet there were others who later came forward claiming to have seen the Ripper talking with one or more of his victims. He was alternately described as a small, stout man of five feet five inches or a tall (five-foot-ten-inch), slender dark man in his early thirties who gave the appearance of being a gentleman, dressed in clothes belonging to the upper class, from casual to elegant attire. He was often described as "foreign-looking" because of a sallow complexion and black hair, although witnesses uncannily never saw much of his face as he stood, purposely so, in the shadows when others were about. Much play in the press was given to the "foreign-looking" aspect of descriptions. It was obviously understood that such a fiend could not really have been a British subject graced with genteel British education, manners, and morality. He *had* to be a foreigner.

George Hutchinson, who had known Mary Jane Kelly, said he saw the unfortunate woman at 2 AM, only an hour before she was murdered on November 11, 1888, going toward her lodgings with a well-dressed gentleman who stood about five feet six inches. This man, who Hutchinson thought was Jewish, tapped Kelly on the shoulder as she passed him on Thrawl Street and both began to laugh. He appeared to be thirty or thirty-five-years old with a pale complexion and a trimmed mustached with the ends curled. A well-tailored, long dark coat fit loosely

133

Reproduction of the "From Hell" letter, sent to George Lusk, along with a piece of his latest victim's anatomy.

about him. Beneath this were a dark-colored jacket and a light-colored waist-coat, which held a thick gold chain. His trousers were dark and he wore black button boots with gaiters that had white buttons. His shirt was white and his black tie was fastened with an expensive horseshoe pin. This was the image of Jack the Ripper that was to last through the ages, the handsome but unhinged gentleman luring his victims to horrible death.

"All right," Hutchinson heard Kelly say to the man after a brief conversation.

"You will be all right for what I have told you," he heard the man reply.

"All right, my dear," Kelly told the man as he put his arm around her shoulder and began to lead her away. "Come along, you will be comfortable."

Hutchinson followed the couple to Kelly's place and waited, curious to see what kind of aristocratic customer Kelly had picked up. He tired of waiting and left at about 2:30 AM. At that moment, Jack the Ripper was undoubtedly preparing to cut his victim's throat.

A Mrs. Paumier, who sold roasted chestnuts only a block from Miller's Court, was approached by a well-dressed man with a black silk hat, black coat, and thin black mustache. He was carrying a shiny black bag. This was only hours after police had arrived at Miller's Court.

"Have you heard that there has been another murder?" asked the man casually.

Mrs. Paumier replied: "I have."

The man grinned and said: "I know more of it than you do." He then walked away.

Mrs. Paumier later stated that this very man had stopped three of her friends on the night Kelly was murdered. One of these women, who pulled away from him, asked: "What's in that bag you're carrying?"

The man turned on his heel and began walking away, but not before saying in a surly voice: "Something the ladies don't like." (Shiny black bags, such as doctors then used to carry their instruments, went quickly out of style; many men were arrested simply for carrying them.)

On other occasions, a man carrying a parcel that could have held surgical knives as easily as the shiny black bag was seen talking to the Ripper victims. He was certainly a methodical killer, employing his medical knowledge to kill and disembowel his victims. He was also careful to make sure that he himself was not coated with his victim's gore, which most probably would have led to his identification. Here, again, the Ripper enacted a well-thought-out procedure in killing his victims. A study of the post-mortem reports reveals that the Ripper's angle of throat-cutting did not place him in front of his victims but behind them.

Aside from the Kelly girl, who was the only victim murdered indoors, all the other victims were accosted in the street and taken to a secluded area, ostensibly to have sex in the open. The women, rather than lying on the ground, stood up, as was then the custom, lifting their cumbersome skirts and petticoats, not from the front as originally suspected, but from the rear, and probably at the request of the killer,

who told them he preferred anal intercourse, which was not unpopular at the time (in fact, preferred by most whores in order to prevent pregnancy; Mary Jane Kelly, incidentally, was three months pregnant when murdered).

With her back to the killer, and lifting her skirts and petticoats to bulk up to the waist, the victim was then absolutely helpless and wholly ignorant of his intentions. He then easily reached forward with one hand—it was said, from the types of incisions he made, that Jack was ambidextrous—to cover the victim's mouth, muffling her cries and, at the same time, suffocating her. With the other hand he brought forth the eight- to nine-inch blade, a surgical tool of some sort, and quickly slashed the victim's throat, killing her instantly. He then placed the body on the ground and went to work with his methodical mutilations. In this way, the killer would not be coated with his victim's blood from the throat slashing. This would spurt down her front, splashing perhaps only his hands, since he was to her rear, a position he had cleverly worked out in advance.

After satiating himself with his gory games, Jack walked casually off through the streets of Whitechapel, relatively clean of blood. When police became more attentive and increased patrols threatened, the Ripper could easily have entered any one of the hundreds of all-night boardinghouses and rented a room for the night, washing away what bloodstains he might have gotten and then departing early the next morning.

Jack the Ripper

The Ripper's modus operandi was one thing, his identity another. The police officially sealed the Ripper files after the killing of Mary Jame Kelly, ordering that they were not be be opened for a hundred years, in the year 1988. The files however may be a disappointment to those present at their opening, for they reportedly contain only a few old, yellowed press clippings and copies of autopsy reports, along with unverified eye-witness reports. The original Ripper letters have long since vanished from the file, along with the police photos taken of the victims, stolen mostly by souvenir hunters within London's police ranks.

Jack the Ripper's identity, according to some of the scores of reporters, crime buffs, and historians who wrote of the case, may have been known to the police all along but, in keeping with the ever-popular idea of unholy conspiracy, the insane killer was either shut up in an asylum shortly after the murders and there died, or committed suicide. It was also said without much authority that neither fate befell him; that Jack was a berserk member of the royal household and his activities were therefore necessarily shielded by police.

There were many nominees for the role of the Ripper. Here are the foremost candidates:

1. Michael Ostrog—a mad Russian doctor who was judged to be a homicidal maniac and who was sent to a lunatic asylum in 1888. Ostrog's whereabouts at the time of the Ripper murders were wholly unknown. As a suspect Ostrog was ambiguous at best.

2. Dr. Stanley (first name unknown)—a Harley Street surgeon whose son had reportedly died of syphilis contracted from Mary Jane Kelly. Stanley went in search of Kelly in Whitechapel, killing his way toward her, as it were, until finally finding her and mutilating her more than any of his other victims. This improbable suspect, according to Leonard Mattes, who published his *The Mystery of Jack the Ripper* in 1929, died in Buenos Aires, confessing his murders to a one time pupil on his deathbed. There is little beyond conjecture to support this story, let alone to verify the existence of Dr. Stanley, who does not appear as a practicing physician in any of the well-kept medical records of the General Medical Council of Great Britain for the years 1888–89.

3. Thomas Cutbush—who was taken into the Lambeth infirmary as a lunatic on March 5, 1891, a month after the possible last Ripper victim, Coles. (He promptly escaped from this institution four hours later.) Cutbush, a resident of Kensington, had stabbed several girls in the buttocks, a peculiar sexual aberration which he had been practicing for years. This did not, however, qualify him as *the* homicidal maniac.

4. G. Wentworth Bell Smith—soilicitor of a trust society in Toronto, Canada, who boarded at 27 Sun Street in Finsbury Square. Smith, who was to become the prototype of the fearful "lodger" in innumerable stories and films (e.g., Marie Belloc-Lowndes' *The Lodger*), was essentially a social misfit who hated prostitutes and complained long and loud about their

walking the streets and visiting churches. He told his landlord, E. Callaghan, that "They should all be drowned." All of this suspect's actions were peculair; he left his room late at night wearing a heavy over-coat and rubber-soled shoes, returning in the early hours. When asked the reason for his nocturnal prowls, Smith would merely mutter that he could not sleep or that he wanted an early edition news-paper. He paced constantly in his room at night when not going out, undoubt-edly a confirmed insomniac. Callaghan later reported that his lodger kept three loaded revolvers in his bureau and would stand nervously against the bureau, his hands ready to open the drawers and clutch the weapons any time someone en-tered his room. This paranoid fellow, however, was gone from the Callaghan house by 1889, yet he could have com-mitted the murders, given his 1888 residency, of the five women univer-sally accepted as definite Ripper victims (Nichols, Chapman, Stride, Eddowes, and Kelly). Smith was never located.

5. Kosminski (first name unknown)—described as "a vice-ridden Polish Jew" who lived in Whitechapel during the time of the murders and was known for his hatred of women in general and prosti-tutes in particular. After exhibiting hom-icidal tendencies, Kosminski was sent to an asylum in March 1889. There was no medical background in this man's history, however, to confirm the fact that he pos-sessed surgical skill.

6. Montague John Druitt—the most popular suspect among police officials who

Suspect: Montague J. Druitt, who committed suicide shortly after the "official" Ripper killings stopped.

worked on the Ripper case. Druitt came from a prosperous middle-class family, although he himself was left little in his father's will. An Oxford graduate, Druitt may have studied medicine for about a year, which would allow for his surgical knowledge in cutting up the victims, if indeed he was the Ripper. He later became a barrister, although his practice failed and he took up the duties of a schoolteacher in Blackheath, where, in 1888, he was dismissed because he "had gotten into trouble," which meant that he had taken homosexual liberties with some young boys, according to one report.

Druitt's mind at this time was unstable; his mother was already in an institution. He began prowling about Whitechapel, but his exact whereabouts at the time of the murders is uncertain. One report had it that he was in a mental institutuion at the time of some of the Ripper murders. Another had it that he was free at this period.

But not a bit of evidence has ever been found to prove Druitt to be the fiend of Whitechapel. He had no real criminal background and was generally a despondent young man, fearful that he was going insane. A note later found among Druitt's effects by his brother stated: "Since Friday I felt I was going to be like mother and the best thing for me was to die." Some days after writing this note, on December 3, 1888, Druitt vanished. His floating body was found in the Thames a month later. He had loaded his coat pockets with huge stones and leaped to a watery suicide. The only reason why Druitt would be considered a likely Ripper suspect on the part of the police was the convenient fact that he committed suicide less than a month after the murder of Mary Jane Kelly, the last Ripper victim, if Kelly was the last. Druitt's candidacy, when all is considered, is that of a police scapegoat.

7. George Chapman—a Polish immigrant, real name Severin Antoniovich Klosowski, who was a medical student and later a junior surgeon in Poland. He moved to London in 1888, working in Whitechapel as a hairdresser under the name of Ludwig Klosowski. Chapman was always one of the strongest suspects in the Ripper murders in that he had access to the victims and found an easy escape into his own Whitechapel home. Yet Chapman's movements at this time were not known to police and he was not investigated until fourteen years later when he was charged with poisoning three women, including his wife, for financial gain. He was convicted and hanged on April 7, 1903, without ever admitting that he was the Ripper.

What most discounted Chapman as being the notorious Jack was the fact that his method of killing, administering poison to his victims, was wholly unlike the savage butchery practiced by the Ripper. Crime authorities reasoned that no killer would so drastically alter his modus operandi. However, H. L. Adam, writing in *The Trial of George Chapman*, was firmly convinced that Chapman was the Ripper. His physical appearance coincided with the scant descriptions of the Ripper. He used American slang in his speech and often told people that he was an American. This dovetailed, said Adam, with the American argot in the letters and notes the Ripper sent to authorities wherein he used such words as "Boss."

The Ripper murders ended about the time, according to Adam, that Chapman left for America in May 1890, going to Jersey City, New Jersey, where several Ripper-like murders occurred while Chapman was a resident there. Early in 1892 the Ripper murders ceased in Jersey City. In May of that year Chapman left the U.S. and returned to London. Chapman's attitude was also similar to that of the Ripper's; he callously joked about murder. There was much that pointed to Chapman as being bloody Jack, yet concrete proof was missing.

8. A Jewish *shochet*—the slaughterer who performs the ritualistic killing of animals according to Talmudic law. There were many such workers and abattoirs in Whitechapel, which held a large Jewish population. The slaughterer of the time possessed the knives and skill to perform the Ripper killings, but motive in this instance is completely lacking, along with any identification. This is a peripheral theory without much substance, strictly advanced to comply with Jack's technique.

9. Frederick Bailey Deeming—who murdered his wife and four children for gain, then skipped to Australia in 1891, where he murdered another wife and was about to kill yet a third woman, his intended, when he was apprehended.

Suspect: George Chapman, who poisoned prostitutes twelve years after the Ripper slayings; he was a favorite police candidate for Jack's role.

139

Suspect: Dr. Thomas Neill Cream, whose last words were "I am Jack the—"

Deeming was an eccentric killer with an inflated ego who bragged that he was Jack the Ripper, but there is little evidence to support his claim. He was nowhere in the vicinity of Whitechapel when the killings took place. Deeming was executed on May 23, 1892.

10. Dr. Alexander Pedachenko—a Russian immigrant who was reportedly sent to England by anti-British Russian police circles to embarrass British police procedures. This highly imaginative theory held that Pedachenko killed the prostitutes so that he could record the inept police moves in tracking him down. Another Pedachenko theory is that he had murdered several women in the Russian town of Tver and, because of his high-born position, the Ochrana, the Czarist secret police, merely shipped the madman to England to get rid of him. It was also reported that this story was confirmed by no less a figure than Rasputin, in an unpublished manuscript entitled *Great Russian Criminals,* found in the Mad Monk's apartment after he had been assassinated. The manuscript never surfaced but was allegedly seen by journalist William LeQueux. The Pedachenko story is about the most impossible of the theories as to the Ripper's identity.

11. Dr. Thomas Neill Cream—a poisoner of East End prostitutes, Cream was sent to the scaffold on November 15, 1892. Just before he fell through the trap, Cream's last words were: "I am Jack the—" The rope cut off the last word, presumably "Ripper." What discredited Cream's egotistical claim was the hard fact that

during the Whitechapel slashings, he was inmate No. 4274 in Joliet State Prison, Illinois. Cream had been convicted of murdering several women in Chicago and was sent to prison on November 1, 1881. Prison records confirm the fact that he was not released until July 31, 1891, long after the Ripper killings had been committed. (The author personally checked these and other records, which irrefutably place Cream in Illinois up to the summer of 1891 and which completely dispel the theory that Cream had bribed his way out of prison and returned to London to enact Jack's crimes.) Moreover, Cream was a sneaky, almost timid murderer who slyly poisoned his prostitute victims in London, dashing off when even the slightest remark on the part of an intended victim might appear suspicious of his motives. He had neither the psychological stamina nor the physical ability to perform the Ripper's slaughterhouse deeds. In short, Dr. Thomas Neill Cream lacked the audacious nerve displayed by Jack.

12. Prince Albert Victor, Duke of Clarence—the eldest son of the future King Edward VII, who had apparently contracted syphilis in an East End men's club which brought about his premature death in 1892, after being confined in an asylum. Dr. Thomas Stowell, in 1970, working from the private papers of Dr. William Gull, personal physician to the royal family, claimed that Eddy, as the prince was nicknamed, was the insane fiend Jack, performing his grisly killings in retaliation for contracting syphilis from a Whitechapel whore. Stowell's own research papers

Suspect: Prince Albert Victor, the Duke of Clarence, grandson of Queen Victoria and a recent though unlikely nominee for the role of Jack the Ripper.

were destroyed by his family after his death and the Gull papers were never seen by anyone else.

The hypothesis that a member of the royal family was the true culprit, and that he was know to be the Ripper by his family, including Queen Victoria, was carried to absurdity in Frank Spiering's *Prince Jack*, published in 1978, and written as a novel. It was Spiering's contention that the police and governmental authorities covered up the prince's identity as the Ripper in order to gain more power from the throne. Queen Victoria paid political blackmail for the official protection of her grandson in relinquishing her absolute powers.

Actual facts, documentation, witnesses, and direct statement written or spoken by those authorities are not in evidence in Spiering's work, which is no more than a preposterous piece of fiction. Making Prince Eddy into the Whitechapel monster appeals only to those who insist that a sacrosanct conspiracy lies behind every controversial event in history. In the reality of crime detection, this theory is, at best, amusing.

13. James Kenneth Stephen— Eddy's youthful tutor at Cambridge, with whom the prince had had a reported homosexual relationship. A known hater of women, Stephen, who was Virginia Woolf's cousin, allegedly went on the Whitechapel murder spree because the Duke of Clarence rejected him! It was Stephen, some Ripper scholars said, who was the real killer and author of at least two of Jack's letters, including the one where the

Suspect: James Kenneth Stephen, woman hater and loving friend of Prince Eddy.

human kidney was mailed. They maintained, further, that it was his own bloody thumbprint he had affixed to the Ripper postcard.

A cynic who thought little of life, it was said that Stephen purposely misspelled words and left out punctuation in the Ripper's letters to convince police that the sender was uneducated. (In another version, Stephen sent the letters to cover up Prince Eddy's actions.) Analysis of Stephen's handwriting and the Ripper's reveals a few similiarities but not enough to prove conclusively that they are one and the same.

14. Sir William Gull—physician to the royal family. This eminent doctor, who apparently did treat Prince Albert Victor for syphilis, was himself thought to be the Ripper, a man approaching senility who had frequent losses of memory and during those blackouts became the Whitechapel killer. Spiritualist R. J. Lees, who had held séances for Queen Victoria and was considered to be the greatest medium of the era, predicted the first three Ripper murders, describing them in detail. He so shocked himself that he fled to Europe during the times he said the Ripper would strike. Lees, when returning to London, bumped into a distinquished-looking gentleman when getting off a bus. He followed this man, whom he "intuitively felt" to be the Ripper, to a fashionable West End house at 74 Brook Street, which proved to be Gull's. The story goes on that Lees entered the house and confronted the doctor, who admitted that he had been suffering memory losses since

Suspect: Sir William Gull, Queen Victoria's physician; some said he was Jack because of his mental blackouts.

suffering a stroke in 1887. In the following year Gull reportedly roamed the East End at all hours—he did visit a surgery there—and returned home with blood on his shirt. This tale is, of course, completely unsubstantiated by facts.

15. Jill the Ripper—Some adventurous armchair sleuths have suggested that Jack the Ripper was not Jack at all, but Jill, a powerfully built midwife. This included, some years after the Ripper killings, Arthur Conan Doyle, who deeply believed that Jack the Ripper was a berserk midwife who had been sent to prison for performing abortions, turned in by a prostitute. The midwife, upon her release, vented her spleen upon prostitutes in Whitechapel, murdering and dissecting them with her limited surgical skill, taking particular vengeance upon the hacked-out female organs that represented her abortionist trade.

Doyle, in a strange way, owed the Ripper a sideways nod in that his first Sherlock Holmes story, *A Study in Scarlet*, appeared in 1888, when Jack was scaring London out of its wits. Doyle presented a sleuth, unlike the inept detectives in the Ripper killings, who could track down any menace, capture the most evil geniuses of crime. Holmes's popularity was rooted in the public's frustration at not seeing bloody Jack captured. At least Holmes in fiction triumphed where Scotland Yard in reality failed.

And Doyle was not above employing the Ripper's techniques. In his story *The Cardboard Box*, the grisly contents of same consist of two ears, a male and a female.

The Ripper, Doyle's readers easily recalled, had promised in one of his more boisterous letters to send police the ears of the next prostitute he slew.

In all the hundreds of published and unpublished sources examined by the author regarding the perpetually fascinating Jack the Ripper case, the motive for the murders remains consistently that Jack was an intense hater of women, which has caused most writer-researchers to look to the obvious, a homosexual killer such a Prince Eddy or Stephen, albeit homosexuals by and large *are not* woman haters.

The author's contribution to the myriad speculations about the Ripper is a simple one, but one that I have yet to see stated anywhere else. It deals with the backgrounds of the all the women murdered by the Ripper, definite and possible victims alike. *All nine* women, from Emma Smith to Frances Coles, had been, at one time or another, married, and most had had children. Mary Jane Kelly was to have a child, being three months pregnant. All of these women had left their husbands and families to take up prostitution, and not as a way of survival, since most had been modestly supported by their working-class spouses. They were attracted to prostitution because they believed it offered a more carefree, easy life.

It was not a homosexual venting his hatred for women (and why would a homosexual feeling thus select only the low-class prostitutes?) who slashed his way through Whitechapel, but a married—or once married—heterosexual, not neces-

The immortal Sherlock Holmes, shown with Dr. Watson in an illustration from *The Strand Magazine*, was created in the same year that the Ripper reportedly disappeared; the fictional supersleuth triumphed where London police searching for Jack failed. (*Illustration; Sidney Paget, 1888*)

sarily a man who had ever contracted the then untreatable syphilis, but one, perhaps with children, who had been deserted the same way the husbands and families of all the victims had been deserted. In the Victorian era, the morality of the family, no matter the class, was passionately clung to. To abandon the abiding concept of marriage and the family was to commit the unforgivable sin, the unpardonable betrayal.

Jack the Ripper was no aberrant homosexual, but a husband cuckolded a hundred times over, it appears to the author, much like the betrayed Philip Carey, a medical student, by the way, in Maugham's *Of Human Bondage*. But how, the reader may ask, would the killer, this abandoned husband, know that all of those women selected for his vengeful wrath had once been married women? The prostitutes practicing in the East End regularly went to nearby clinics for checkups, and it was here that the records contained their past marital status—records that any doctor, medical student, or assistant could examine, files from which the Ripper could easily select his victims. But then the police never looked for a married medical man whose wife had turned prostitute. The answers in that direction were too prosaic; they were looking for something more bizarre, someone as exotic as the utterly macabre actions of Jack the Ripper misleadingly suggested.

They found no one and produced legend after legend, myth after myth, creating the most vexing enigma in English murder history. But they did not really look in Whitechapel for that smooth-talking gentleman, assuming he only made raids into that terrible district, then fled to the comforts of middle- or upper-class areas. They did not look deep into the backyards of the murders. Their perspective did not look for a cuckolded, deserted, angry husband.

Jack the Stripper
MURDERS, 1964–65   ENGLAND

Emulating Jack the Ripper, a psychopathic killer began killing prostitutes in London in early 1964, his first victim being Hannah Tailford, whose body was found

A police sketch of "Jack the Stripper," who terrorized London in 1964–65.

floating in the Thames on February 2. She had been suffocated. In the next year and a half, five more prostitutes were similarly murdered, either strangled or suffocated, their bodies tossed into the Thames or dropped along lonely stretches of road. The last victim was Margaret McGowan, who had testified in the Profumo scandal. Police quickly proved that McGowan had been killed without any connection to the Profumo affair.

An army of detectives combing London for clues were unable to pinpoint the killer's identity. The maniac was obviously very careful to cover his trail. All of his victims had been found naked; he had murdered the women and then stripped them, thus earning the sobriquet "Jack the Stripper."

After closely inspecting the bodies, police discovered that four of the six corpses were flecked with spray paint. Since the victims vanished between 11 PM and 1 AM, it was concluded that the killer worked a nightshift and that he picked up the women and took them to a place where paint spray equipment was stored. Thousands of garages and small plants where such equipment might be kept were inspected and thousands of night workers, particularly drivers, were investigated, yet police were unable to turn up a single clue.

The killings suddenly ceased in late 1965. Shortly thereafter, a security guard who had a night driving job committed suicide, leaving a note to his family that read: "I am unable to stand the strain any longer." Investigators checking the man's personal effects and background, however, found nothing to incriminate the man in the killings. But since the murders stopped at the time of his suicide, police conveniently theorized, as had detectives in the Ripper murders almost eighty years earlier, the dead man had been the slayer of the London prostitutes. The file on these murders is nevertheless still officially open.

Jackson, Kate
MURDER, 1929 ENGLAND

On the night of February 4, 1929, a neighbor heard wild screaming coming from the grounds of a cottage owned by Kate and Thomas Jackson, located in the town of Kenilworth. The neighbor ran to the Jackson home to find Mrs. Jackson in the arms of her husband, who was carrying the battered woman into the cottage through the back door. She was unconscious and bleeding from savage head wounds. She died while in a coma two days later.

Thomas Jackson told police that he had been sleeping when his wife's screams aroused him. He had raced to the back yard of the cottage and found Kate unconscious eight feet from the back door. Detectives, however, found a tire wrench under a cushion in the Jackson home. Though this was not proved to be the murder weapon, Jackson was charged and stood trial for murder.

During the husband's trial Kate Jackson's nefarious background was brought to light. She had been a notorious free-lance prostitute who had selected wealthy men to compromise, blackmailing them for large amounts of money. One victim embezzled more than £20,000 from his firm to pay her, for which he was sent to prison for five years.

It was soon evident that Mrs. Jackson had a number of lethal enemies who could have murdered her. The defense introduced a letter Kate had received shortly before her death which read:

Dear Madame,

We are still watching and waiting. The pleasure is ours. When you don't expect us we will drop on you, and when we have finished with you your own mother won't know you. You foul thing. Call yourself a woman, do you? You are a disgrace to the name. How many more men have you blackmailed until they have to pinch money to shut you up?

Prosecutors argued that Thomas Jackson had written this letter himself to throw suspicion on a secret enemy as having been the killer. They failed, however, to prove that Jackson had penned or written the letter.

Given the double life Kate Jackson had been leading and the apparent innocence of her cuckolded husband, Thomas Jackson was adjudged not guilty and released. Mrs. Jackson's killer was never found.

K

Kenosha Killings

MURDERS, 1967–81 U.S.

Seven murders within fourteen years, 1967 to 1981, occurred in the vicinity of a small unpaved alley running the length of three blocks in Kenosha, Wisconsin. All of the victims lived between 64th and 67th streets, the first being high school student Mary Ellen Kaldenberg, a seventeen-year-old who left her home at 2007 64th Street on February 9, 1967, to buy a soda in a drugstore. The girl never returned. Her body was found in the back of an abandoned 1948 Packard hearse at the city auto pound, a mile from her home, on February 13.

In the late 1970s, six more murders were committed in or near the alley. These included Jerald A. Burnette, a fifty-two-year-old factory worker beaten to death with a tire iron on January 30, 1978 (Steven Gross was later sent to prison for this robbery-slaying); Herman Bosman, an eighty-year-old man whose beaten body was found in his burning home—the killer had set the fire to cover the murder—at 6612 20th Street on May 27, 1979; Alice Alzner, an eighteen-year-old Lake Forest, Illinois, college student who had been raped and strangled with her own brassiere on June 23, 1979, and then buried in a shallow grave in a rose garden adjoining the alley (Thomas J. Holt, who lived in the house on the lot where the girl was buried was later sentenced to death in Illinois for the killing); Mrs. Alice Easton, sixty-three, Raphael Petrucci, sixty-three, and John F. Amann, fifty-one, all stabbed to death in Mrs. Easton's home, which backed onto the alley on January 26, 1981 (Mrs. Easton's grandson, Robert McRoberts, nineteen, was charged with the murders and is still awaiting trial at this writing).

Thus there is no final disposition regarding the last three murder victims, and the Kaldenberg and Bosman killings have yet to be solved.

Kenosha Coroner Thomas J. Dorff, following the last three murders, began to feel that the alley itself represented some sort of evil. "Those three murders are not going to be the end," he predicted. "There is something strange out by that alley, sort of a 'Bermuda Triangle of Murder,' I'd say. What seems to be going on is unexplainable."

Kensit, John
MURDER, 1902 ENGLAND

Kensit, who was the founder of the Protestant Truth Society and the leader in ferreting out popish traditions in the Church of England, addressed a Roman Catholic crowd in Liverpool on September 25, 1902, his biting anti-Catholic remarks infuriating those in attendance. He had to be smuggled out a back door of the hall, but his bus was blocked as it tried to depart.

With two supporters brandishing umbrellas, Kensit attempted to fight his way through the violent throng surrounding his bus. He was highly visible in that he was wearing a shiny top hat. Someone in the crowd hurled an iron file at the religious leader, striking him above the eye. He was taken to the hospital for treatment of what doctors initially thought to be a superficial wound.

Kensit's condition, however, grew rapidly worse, and he died of meningitis and septic pneumonia on October 8, 1902. The furor over Kensit's death was tremendous; he was hailed as "the first Protestant martyr of the twentieth century," and thousands demanded that his killer be brought to justice.

Though it was impossible to select the true killer from the hundreds in the crowd attacking Kensit, police charged eighteen-year-old John McKeever with hurling the iron file. McKeever was an ardent foe of the Protestant religion and was undoubtedly chosen for this reason to stand trial for the crime.

Although McKeever had been in the crowd, there was no way in which the prosecution could establish the fact that he was the person who had killed Kensit. Moreover, competent witnesses quoted the victim clearly stated, after being struck: "*She* has blinded me!"

McKeever was quickly found not guilty and, upon hearing the verdict, the accused whipped a harmonica from his pocket and began to play jubilantly in court. Partisans ran forward and lifted the youth onto their shoulders, carrying him, amidst triumphant cheers, from the courtroom.

Kensit's killer was never found.

King, Dot
MURDER, 1923 U.S.

Born Dorothy Keenan, Dot King came from an impoverished New York slum family, a short but attractive natural blonde with blue eyes who left home in 1915 at age nineteen to become a model in a Fifth Avenue dress shop. Dot became popular along Broadway during World War I, a showgirl, most believed, who had once been in the *Follies*, albeit there is no record of Dot's ever appearing in any of Florenz Ziegfeld's extravaganzas.

The playgirl, who was escorted everywhere by millionaires and theater magnates, became the Jazz Age prototype of the bobbed-hair flapper who danced, drank, and partied through nighttime New York during the early 1920s. She became a hostess for a speakeasy when Prohibition became law, and her early notoriety in that murky, booze-sodden world almost rivaled Texas Guinan's. Her name began to appear in gossip columns, where she was referred to as the "Broadway Butterfly." With this transitory fame came money, mostly from stage-door johnnies and, later, from wealthy sugar daddies. One of these fun-loving sponsors—King allegedly knew him only as "Mr. Marshall"—paid for her apartment at 144 West 57th Street, which was a short walk from Carnegie Hall. Moreover, her rich Maecenas showered her with cash and jewelry estimated to be worth $30,000 (gems that would be worth ten times that amount today). Her baubles included two diamond bracelets, a ruby necklace, a diamond and emerald studded wristwatch, and assorted pearl necklaces.

Marshall, it was later reported, would appear at King's door only late at night, twice a week, having his bodyguard, a hulking giant named Walter, first knock and then step into the showgirl's apartment to make sure that she was alone. When all was right, Marshall would enter to spend the night. When not entertaining Mr. Marshall, Dot spent most of her waking hours, the hours of the night, carousing through Manhattan's lively speakeasies. In one dive she met and became enamored of a Latin gigolo named Alberto Santos Guimares, a man who had no income other than what he received from admiring females.

Guimares moved in with King, but was careful to absent himself whenever the bountiful Marshall appeared. His clothes

The Broadway Butterfly, Dot King, whose mysterious murder in 1923 still baffles New York police.

were furnished by Dot, who also turned over large amounts of Marshall's money to him. Being a generous sort, she regularly sent her mother cash and bought one of her older brothers a taxicab.

Unknown to King, Guimares, an active fellow, was seeing a rich socialite, Mrs. Aurelia Dreyfus, who was also helping to support him. The bought lover turned vicious in 1922, beating Dot mercilessly. She was often seen with bruises on her arms and face and, on one occasion, with two black eyes. Though her friends and brothers, who knew of Guimares's wild temper, told her to get rid of her gigolo, Dot desperately clung to the Latin lover. "Someday Alberto will marry me," she told a confidante. Some said she was simply a masochist wanting to be punished for living the life of a kept woman.

Dot King's marital aspirations evaporated on March 15, 1923. On the morning of that day, her maid, Billie Bradford, found the fun-loving Dot lying dead on her bed. The maid spotted a pair of men's yellow silk pajamas nearby and quickly stuffed these under the cushion of the couch in the living room before running for the police.

Detectives arriving at the scene first thought that King had committed suicide, but Chief Medical Examiner Dr. Charles D. Norris decreed that the woman had been murdered. Her arm had been brutally twisted behind her back. Norris noticed that Dot's nose, eyes, and cheeks had been scratched and that burns about the mouth indicated that a rough murderer had chloroformed her, causing the scratches when applying a wad of chloroform-soaked cotton to her face; the wad of cotton was found under some bedcovers and an empty chloroform bottle was discovered beneath the bed.

The apartment was a wreck. Someone had ransacked it, and King's jewels were missing. It was a robbery-murder, detectives said. But then investigators unearthed some torrid letters written to Dot by her sugar daddy, Marshall. One read:

Darling Dottie:
    Only two days before I will be with you. I want to see you, o so much! And to kiss your pretty pink toes!

The letters were traced to J. Kearsley Mitchell, alias Marshall, son-in-law of Edward T. "Uncle Ned" Stotesbury, fabulous multimillionaire and the top name on Philadelphia's Four Hundred list. Mitchell admitted that he had supported Dot, that he had tucked $1,000 bills under her pillow when ending his nocturnal visits to her. The yellow silk pajamas were also his, confessed the mortified millionaire, but under no circumstances had he slain Dot King, who was now called by the press the "Broken Butterfly."

Mitchell said he had spent the whole day, March 14, with Dot in her apartment, taking her to dinner that night and returning to the apartment about midnight. He left at 2:30 AM, he swore, although the elevator boy did not see him. "Well," said Mitchell, "I had to consider the boy's feelings." He claimed to have walked down the private stairs to the street.

152

Even though Mitchell was the prime suspect in the murder, police inexplicably released him, an action which caused many to state that his social prestige, power, and money had eased him from an indelicate situation. (Mitchell's involvement with Dot King, however, ruined him socially in Philadelphia.)

What may have altered the course of police detection in this sensational case which held the newspaper headlines for weeks was the discovery of Alberto Guimares. King's friends and brothers informed detectives that the Latin lover had been abusing her; this dangerous, calculating entrepreneur was a much more likely suspect. Guimares was tracked down and hauled in for questioning. With cool aplomb, the lover casually informed detectives that, at the time of King's death, he was making the rounds of several speakeasies with none other than Mrs. Aurelia Dreyfus, the wealthy socialite he had been seeing and who was also, like Mitchell, a Philadelphia aristocrat.

Mrs. Dreyfus backed up Guimares's statements, insisting that the gigolo had been with her all through the night of March 14–15, 1923. Police had no choice but to release the grinning Guimares. They went back to the robbery theory and announced that two men, unknown to this day, had broken into Dot's apartment, held her arm behind her back until she told them where her jewels were hidden, then chloroformed her to death to prevent her from identifying them before they fled down the stairs with the gems.

The case was left open with this rather feeble explanation, and soon the Dot King name shrank to nothing in the newspaper columns. In the following year, 1924, Mrs. Aurelia Dreyfus mysteriously fell to her death from the balcony of her luxurious Washington, D.C., hotel suite. Found some weeks later in her papers was a sworn affidavit by Mrs. Dreyfus that she had perjured herself when providing Guimares with an alibi in the Dot King case. The document, lamentably, gave no specific details, and investigators, who could not prove that Guimares had pushed Mrs. Dreyfus from the balcony, again released the gigolo after a routine grilling.

Mrs. Anna Keenan, Dot's mother, nevertheless insisted that Guimares had murdered her daughter and plagued the press for years to pursue the matter. Guimares drifted about the country until 1953, when he died without ever hinting that he had had a hand in killing Dot King or Mrs. Dreyfus. To this day no one is quite sure who killed the Broadway Butterfly and took the jewels she had so passionately earned.

L

Lawn, Alice Maud
MURDER, 1921 ENGLAND

Shopkeeper Alice Maud Lawn was found dead, her head crushed with the blunt edge of an ax, on the side stairs of her small shop in Cambridge, England, on July 27, 1921. The crime appeared to police to be the work of a burglar surprised by the fifty-year-old Miss Lawn as he was rifling the till; a small amount of money had been taken from the register.

Arrested for the murder was a garrulous laborer named Thomas Clanwaring, mostly, it seemed, because he was one of Cambridge's leading eccentrics. Clanwaring had the habit of telling imaginative but untrue tales about himself that painted him in heroic terms. He claimed that he had been drinking at the Rose and Crown pub at the time of the Lawn killing, but he was nevertheless put on trial.

Prosecutors were unable to prove that Clanwaring could have left the pub, gotten to Miss Lawn's shop, killed the woman, and returned to the pub in a short amount of time. The defendant was acquitted and released. Miss Lawn's killer was never found.

Levine, Peter
KIDNAPPING MURDER, 1938 U.S.

Taken from his New Rochelle, New York, home on February 23, 1938, twelve-year-old Peter Levine was held by one or more kidnappers who apparently had not formalized their plans so that adequate ransom arrangements could be made. No payment for the boy's return was demanded. The boy's dismembered body was unearthed on May 29, 1938, and his kidnapper-killers remained at large. Though the FBI lists this unsolved crime as a kidnapping, it may have been an abduction for purposes of a sex killing (the boy's body was too badly decomposed for examiners to determine if he had been sexually molested or not).

Liberty Bell Replica
ROBBERY, 1893 U.S.

Children all over the U.S. contributed more than 250,000 pennies toward the construction of a six-foot-tall, six-and-a-half-ton replica of the Liberty Bell which was

154

displayed at the Chicago World's Fair of 1893. The bell, which was part of the exhibit of the Daughters of the American Revolution and was subsequently to become a traveling exhibit, vanished after the first day of the fair.

Security guards were nonplussed as to how the enormous bell had been smuggled out of the fairgrounds during the night. No one ever saw the bell again.

Lincoln National Bank & Trust Company
BANK ROBBERY, 1930 U.S.

The officials of the Lincoln National Bank & Trust Company never knew what or who hit them on the morning of September 17, 1930. At exactly 10:02 that Wednesday morning, three men dressed in business suits and carrying briefcases entered the giant bank in Lincoln, Nebraska, which was then thronged with customers. Another man casually took up a guard position outside the front door of the bank, cradling a submachine gun in his arms and pointing it at no one in particular.

Though the street was thick with people, no one paid special attention to the machine gunner. He and his three companions had been seen to drive up to the bank in a late-model Buick, the kind of unmarked car detectives used. It was felt that the men going into the bank were officials of the bank or bank examiners and that the man in front of the door was

simply a plainclothes bank guard. Further, the Buick parked in front of the bank was affixed with a siren, making it appear to be an official car.

Once inside the bank, the three men ordered the fifty-some customers and bank employees on hand to lie down on the floor. A customer and a teller who were slow in obeying were hit on the head by one of the gunmen. Two of the men went straight to the vault which had been opened at exactly ten o'clock, two minutes before the robbers had entered the bank. They filled up their large briefcases with cash and an enormous quantity of negotiable bonds and other securities.

After spending less than five minutes inside the bank, the men departed, walking slowly from the bank, the machine gunner stationed outside joining them. Once inside the Buick, the men sped off with the siren wailing, which cleared the streets, allowing the robbers to escape safely without police interference.

The haul was enormous, the largest bank robbery in the U.S. up to that time in the twentieth century—$2,702,796 in cash and securities. Most of the loot was in negotiable bonds. The identity of the thieves remained a mystery to police. After some weeks, however, three men were named as the robbers—Tommy O'Connor, Howard "Pop" Lee, and Jack Britt, all residents of Lincoln. Britt was released, but O'Connor and Lee were convicted on flimsy evidence and sent to prison for twenty-five years each. Both men were released after serving ten years; they had been proved innocent, and authorities finally and reluctantly agreed that they had been nowhere near the bank when the robbery took place. Neither O'Connor nor Lee received any compensation for his wrongful imprisonment.

There were many other suspects, but investigators could not prove their guilt. Bank robbers Eddie Bentz and Harvey Bailey were named, but no charges on this robbery were brought against them. Members of the Capone mob were also named, undoubtedly on the assumption that the bank robbers had employed the same modus operandi as the killers of the Moran gang at the St. Valentine's Day Massacre a year earlier in Chicago; the slayers in Chicago had dressed as policemen and escaped in an unmarked detective car with a police siren.

Gus Winkler, a crafty sometime member of the Barker gang, was later picked up in Chicago. He was about to be charged with the robbery when he suddenly made a deal with authorities. Winkler stated that he would arrange for the return of approximately $600,000 of the negotiable bonds. He was granted immunity from prosecution, particularly after he established an iron-clad alibi, and turned over $575,000 in bonds taken from the Lincoln Bank. He also gave authorities a signed affidavit that almost $2 million in negotiable bonds were burned, but there was no evidence to support Winkler's statement. Winkler was later executed gangland style with more than a hundred machine gun bullets pumped into his body.

More than $100,000 in cash and $2 million in bonds were lost to the Lincoln National Bank & Trust Company; it was a blow from which the institution never recovered. It closed its doors forever the following year. The men who actually committed the robbery have never been identified.

Lloyd, Dora Alice
MURDER, 1938 ENGLAND

The murder of London prostitute Dora Lloyd on February 21, 1932, caused a sensation in the press in that it was a public killing. Though the woman's slayer was described in exact detail, he was never apprehended. The killer, tall, slim, clean-shaven, about thirty-five years old, and wearing horn-rimmed glasses, picked up Lloyd on Air Street, a notorious area for streetwalkers. Several women had been approached by the man before he went off with Dora. He had stated that, though he was unemployed, he had fifteen shillings to spend for a woman.

The couple took a taxi to Lloyd's apartment at Lanark Villas, arriving a little after 1 AM. A half hour later neighbors heard Dora scream and cry for help for several minutes, then came what sounded like "gurgling noises." Dora, at the time, was being strangled by her guest, police later concluded. No one came to Dora Lloyd's rescue.

Her killer left the apartment house unmolested and was never found. The coroner's verdict in the Lloyd case: "Willful murder by some person unknown."

Los Angeles Slasher, The

MURDERS, 1974–75 U.S.

Los Angeles's Skid Row, close to the downtown library, was terrorized by an unknown maniac who caused the deaths of at least eight men, all derelicts, from December 1, 1974, to January 31, 1975, an orgy of murder that has yet to be explained. In each instance, the killer sought down-and-out alcoholics and precisely slit their throats from ear to ear in what psychiatrists later described as a "murderous frenzy" that indicated a sexual obsession.

The first victim found was Charles Jackson, forty-six, slashed on the lawn of the Los Angeles Public Library some time in the early morning hours of December 1, 1974. Next was Moses August Yakanak, forty-seven, who was found slashed to death in an alley on December 8. On December 11, Arthur Dahlstedt, fifty-four, was found murdered in the doorway of a vacant Skid Row building.

David Perez, forty-two, was found slashed to death in some bushes on Flower Street on December 22, 1974. Following this killing, a cancer-ridden derelict named Casimir Strawinski prophetically told a friend: "I won't be around too long." On January 8, 1975, the fifty-eight-year-old hobo was found in his third-floor room in the Pickwick apartment hotel, murdered by the slasher. (Strawinski's prediction was undoubtedly a reference to his fatal disease, not an expression that the slasher would seek him out.)

Forty-year-old Robert "Tex" Shannahan was slashed to death on January 15, 1975. His body was found in an apart-

These two sketches by a Los Angeles Police Department artist were assembled from various descriptions of the notorious slasher who terrorized Skid Row in the winter of 1974–75.

ment close to where Strawinski died. Ten days later, on January 25, the butchered body of Samuel Suarez was found in his fifth-floor room in the Barclay Hotel.

The final victim, Clyde C. Hay, thirty-four, was found slashed in the manner of the others in his cheap Hollywood apartment. In this killing, as in the others, only skimpy information concerning the killer was provided—a wiry man with long, stringy hair. Detectives called the madman a "human jackal." Police Lieutenant Dan Cooke told the press: "We're dealing with a real monster."

To this date, however, detectives have been unable to track down the Los Angeles slasher, even though the killer left a "signature" which only he and the police knew about, according to Lieutenant Cooke, a gruesome clue reminiscent of that left by the Los Angeles slayer of the Black Dahlia [see entry].

Luard, Mrs. Caroline Mary
MURDER, 1908 ENGLAND

Fifty-eight-year-old Caroline Mary Luard, a warm-hearted person without known enemies, accompanied her husband, Charles, on a walk outside of Ightham Knoll, their home near Sevenoaks in Kent. It was 2:30 PM, August 24, 1908. Charles Edward Luard, a retired major general, sixty-nine, intended to collect some golf clubs at the nearby Godden Green golf course. Mrs. Luard parted from him at Crown Point village, saying that she would

stroll to an unoccupied summerhouse called La Casa, which offered a resplendent view of Fish Pond Woods.

General Luard returned home to Ightham at about 4:30 PM. A Mrs. Stuart, who had been invited to tea by the Luards, arrived. She had tea with the general, who told the woman he was surprised that his wife had not yet returned from her walk; it was unlike her to ignore company. A short time later General Luard went in search of his wife and found her in the empty summerhouse, shot to death. Two bullets had been fired point blank into her head. Four expensive rings were missing from the victim's fingers, along with her purse, which contained a small amount of money.

The time of Mrs. Luard's murder was fixed at 3:15 PM by the local coroner. Daniel Kettle, a farm worker, and Annie Wickham, a housewife, both of whom lived nearby, later testified that they had heard two shots coming from the summerhouse at precisely 3:15. (They did not investigate.) The Reverend R. B. Cotton, who had seen the general on the golf course, later stated that he saw a "sandy-haired tramp" coming from the direction of the summerhouse.

General Luard was the primary suspect in the case as far as local residents were concerned, despite the fact that police proved he was definitely at the golf course at the time when his wife was murdered. Luard received scores of insulting and accusatory letters. Further, he was put through two agonizing coroner's inquiries which exhausted the old man. It was established that he and his wife were on the best of terms and were wholly compatible. Luard was released without charges, but the loss of his wife unhinged him.

Putting his home up for sale, the general went to live with a friend, a Colonel Ward. He repeatedly told Ward that he found the pressure of being suspected as his wife's killer unbearable. He sent a note to a friend which read:

"I have gone to her that I loved. Goodbye. Something has snapped." With that, Major General Charles Luard walked to the train junction at West Farleigh, lit his pipe, and waited for the express. When the train arrived, Luard threw himself in front of the racing engine. The suicide caused a sensation in England, and police redoubled their efforts to apprehend Mrs. Luard's killer. They failed, concluding that she had been murdered by an itinerant worker bent on robbing her.

Some time later John Alexander Dickman, convicted of murder in 1910, was named as Mrs. Luard's killer; but this was long after Dickman had been hanged in a controversial execution, and nothing could be proved to link Dickman to the Ightham killing.

A man later confessed to the murder in London, but he was dismissed as being insane. Even later police found a man's jacket and boots on the shoreline of Re-gents Park Lake and beside these items a letter signed "Jack Storm," written to his father, in which Storm confessed to killing Mrs. Luard and stated his intention to drown himself. No body was ever found, even though the lake was repeatedly dragged. The suicide note and clothes may have been part of a twisted prank.

The Luard murder remains a classic mystery to this day.

Lufthansa Airlines
ROBBERY, 1978 U.S.

On December 11, 1978, six masked gunmen entered the Lufthansa Airlines cargo hangar at New York's Kennedy International Airport, overpowered one employee and handcuffed eight others, breaking into the airline's high-value safe cage from which, within a few minutes, they removed more than $5 million in American currency, and almost $1 million more in gold, jewels, and foreign currencies.

The robbers, still sought today, had acted in a precision-timed raid, according to police. The manner and modus operandi of the raid had striking similarities to a Wells Fargo robbery [see entry] in Staten Island committed less than two weeks later.

M

McElroy, Kenneth Rex
MURDER, 1981 U.S.

He was thought of as the town bully, a roughneck who settled his arguments with fists, feet, and firearms. Thick-necked, overweight Kenneth Rex McElroy, forty-seven, had held the small village of Skidmore, a community of 440 souls in northwest Missouri, in terror since he had dropped out of school. On July 10, 1981, McElroy and his wife, Trena, drove to town from their farm. They parked their pickup truck outside the D&G Recreation building, a local bar and pool hall on Skidmore's Main Street. They sat quietly in the bar drinking beer, and suddenly the place filled up with sixty to eighty residents who had just come from a town meeting at the American Legion Hall.

The local citizens had been talking about the worst nuisance ever to plague their town, McElroy, whom they called Kenrex. "A large crowd gathered and the bar owner began to give them free beer," Trena McElroy later stated. "It was unusual for morning time. They just stared at it." Minutes later McElroy and his wife got up from their bar stools, walked outside to their pickup, and climbed in.

160

The crowd of men followed the couple, milling about the truck so that McElroy could not drive it away.

According to Mrs. McElroy, it was at this time that "a man walked across the street, pulled a rifle out of his pickup, and started firing. Four times he fired and I kept begging him to stop." McElroy, hit squarely by the bullets which smashed the glass of the driver's door, slumped forward. Most of the crowd dove for cover as the rifleman commenced firing. "Others just stood and looked," lamented Trena, "but no one tried to stop it. No one screamed, just me. And the man that did it didn't run away. He stayed right there."

McElroy was dead, and few in the rural farming community lost any sleep over the killing. Kenrex had been a terror to most people since childhood. Spoiled as a youngster, McElroy quit school in the sixth grade, accusing teachers of ignoring him. He later bragged long and loud that he never learned to read and yet he grew rich. How he grew rich required little speculation on the part of the residents. He was suspected of hog rustling in four states, chiefly in Missouri. Red Smith, bartender at the D&G, where McElroy hung out, remembered that "sometimes he made your eyes pop out, especially when he took thousands of dollars out of his pocket and laid it on the bar."

Kenrex was a surprise to a lot of people. The 230-pound farmer, who sold antiques on the side, never went to town without carrying a rifle or shotgun. He shot at things and people whenever the whim urged him to do so. McElroy was accused of riddling the side of a corrugated metal garage on Main Street, spraying shotgun pellets into the local grocery store ceiling, and shooting Romaine Henry in the leg after overtaking the farmer on the road and accusing him of "talking bad" about him. McElroy also shot Ernest Bowencamps in the face with a shotgun blast when the seventy-two-year-old grocer disagreed with him in early July 1981.

Though convicted of this assault, McElroy was let loose on a substantial bond. The fact that the bully was at large infuriated the townspeople. Four days after he had shot the elderly grocer, McElroy sauntered into town carrying a carbine with a bayonet attached, as if to dare anyone to interfere with his amusements.

The much married Kenrex (he had twelve children through different marriages) had often boasted how he could do anything he pleased and get away with it. "He always said he never would get convicted," commented one Skidmore resident.

When McElroy was released on bond after shooting grocer Bowencamps, the entire town held a meeting to decide what should be done. Apparently it was determined that Kenneth Rex McElroy

Town bully Kenneth Rex McElroy, who was executed vigilante-style in Skidmore, Missouri, in 1981. (*Wide World*)

Mrs. Trina McElroy claimed to have seen her husband's killer coldly shoot him in front of more than sixty people; the entire town of Skidmore refused to identify the executioner of the town bully.

should die. Following his execution, a Nodaway County grand jury refused to indict anyone for the slaying. The local prosecutor refused to file charges. Stated County Prosecutor David Baird: "I file charges when I can prove a case beyond reasonable doubt. [The grand jurors] simply were not convinced there was probable cause. If they're not convinced of probable cause, then we don't have reasonable doubt."

Mrs. McElroy's identification of the slayer was not corroborated by a single soul in Skidmore. All present at the murder site said they could not name the killer. "It was a vigilante killing," according to Richard McFadden, the McElroy family attorney. "It was murder frontier style."

But few people agreed with McFadden. Citizens and police were relieved that the local terror had been eliminated. "Good riddance," exulted a state patrolman. "What happened was an example of peer democracy in action. The legal system didn't work. So they made a new system for that day. It was war. McElroy was the enemy. So the people drafted an army. The enemy was conquered. Everyone was discharged. And everyone went back home to get ready for the Pumpkin Festival in October."

The killer of Kenneth McElroy is still at large, unnamed by a very closed-mouth community, at this writing.

Mad Butcher of Cleveland, The

MURDERS, 1935–38 U.S.

Little remembered, the mass slayings attributed to the Mad Butcher of Cleveland rival in many ways the dismemberment murders committed by Jack the Ripper [see entry]. The first two victims of this apparently deranged killer were found by boys playing in Cleveland's industrial valley, Kingsbury Run, on September 23, 1935. In a weed-covered ravine the boys stumbled over two naked bodies which had been decapitated.

Police arrived and laid out the bodies. The genitals of the victims had been sliced away, and these were later found in a rusty bucket a short distance from where the bodies had been discovered. The heads of the murdered men were later found embedded in the side of a muddy embankment and these were matched to the bodies. Fingerprints were taken of the corpses, but only that of the younger one yielded an identification. The man was Edward Andrassy, a small-time thug, womanizer, and bisexual who had had sexual associations with several young boys even though he was married and had a child.

Andrassy and his nameless companion had been butchered by a professional, pathologists easily determined. The severing of their heads had been performed in clean surgical strokes. Since the neck muscles of the victims had retracted, it was concluded that the murdered men had either been alive when the decapitation took place or had died only mo-

ments earlier. The bodies had been drained of blood and then taken to the ravine by the killer.

No other clues were forthcoming and police, conditioned to violent crimes among Cleveland's burgeoning immigrant population, credited the murders to some clannish vendetta and marked the gruesome murders unsolved. Thickening this file four months later was the report of another victim who police thought had been slain by the same killer. On January 26, 1936, a butcher was told that there was a basket full of "some meat" in an alley next to his shop. The butcher found the dismembered limbs and the lower torso of a female cadaver wrapped in newspapers and stuffed into a bushel basket. Police investigating days later uncovered the missing sections of the body inside a deserted house nearby; the head was never found.

Fingerprints taken from the victim revealed the body to be that of Florence Polillo, a thirty-six-year-old whore. She had been dismembered with the same precision marking the first two bodies found. Though all of the woman's friends and associates were interviewed and every possible lead followed up, these were slim, and police were unable to determine who might have murdered Florence Polillo.

The same vexing situation presented itself when another headless corpse was discovered by boys on June 6, 1936, as they played in Kingsbury Run. The body of a young man was found sticking out of an embankment. His head, half-buried in the clay, rolled out after detectives dug

163

One of the Mad Butcher's early victims, Mrs. Florence Polillo, a Cleveland prostitute, murdered and dissected in 1936. (*Wide World*)

up the area. The decapitation had been performed in one decisive stroke. Though the man's fingerprints failed to identify him, the body had six different tattoos, some with initials.

All the owners of Cleveland's tattoo parlors were grilled, but none could identify the markings. In frustration, police put the body on display in the morgue and more than two thousand persons filed by in an attempt to identify the victim. None did. A moulage was made and this death mask was also put on display during the Cleveland Exposition of 1936–37, yet none of the thousands of people who stared at it in grim fascination could identify the face.

Bodies kept turning up. On July 5, 1936, a workman found a decapitated male so badly decomposed that identification was impossible. This corpse, the only one discovered on Cleveland's west side, was located at Big Creek near Clinton Road. On September 10, a tramp trying to hop a freight in Kingsbury Run, stumbled over a body face down in a pool of water. The body had been castrated; the arms, head, and genitals were never found. Identification was impossible, which is what the killer clearly had in mind when performing his grisly chores.

Three more headless corpses were found scattered all over Cleveland during 1937. In the following year three more victims, again decapitated, with arms and legs cleanly cut away at the joints as a butcher might dissect a steer, were found, the last two bodies discovered in a Cleveland dump.

Even though scores of detectives were permanently assigned to investigate the senseless killings, not one solid suspect was put under arrest. For some unexplained reason, the Cleveland killings came to an end in 1938, either because the murderer left town, police theorized, or because he may have died. The former idea was the most realistic, especially when a headless body was found in late 1938 outside of Newcastle, Pennsylvania. Three more murder victims, found in a boxcar with their heads removed in Pittsburgh in 1939, enforced the notion that the decapitating killer had moved on to other areas. As late as 1942 the same strange slayer was apparently at work in Pittsburgh, where two more mutilated bodies were found.

The Mad Butcher of Cleveland, who had claimed twelve lives in that city and most probably six in Pennsylvania, was never identified.

Police removing the chopped-up remains of a headless corpse from the shoreline of Lake Erie in Cleveland in 1937, the eighth victim attributed to the Mad Butcher.

Mekler, Michael
MURDER, 1981 U.S.

On the evening of September 26, 1981, Michael Mekler, a twenty-six-year-old insurance claims adjuster in Chicago, went out on a date with his fiancée, Janet Lawler. Mekler, a hardworking and conscientious employee, carried a beeper for messages and, while driving with Lawler, received a message from his office requesting that he go to the 5800 block of W. Eastwood to estimate damage done to a Cadillac that had reportedly been involved in a traffic accident.

Mekler immediately responded, driving his Mercedes-Benz to the area. Getting out of his car at 5807 W. Eastwood, Mekler began to look about for the Cadillac, but no such car was in sight. The claims adjuster took a few steps and suddenly two shots rang out. Mekler fell, hit twice in the head, as his terrified fiancée screamed for help. The claims adjuster was dead on arrival by the time he was rushed to the Northwest Hospital.

The case has continued to baffle police. Detectives are convinced that a secret enemy had phoned in the report to Mekler's office, the Nisha Auto Body Shop, and the shop foreman had unwittingly relayed the message in a clever setup in which Mekler "was beeped to his death." Though a thorough investigation is ongoing at this writing, no suspects have been arrested.

Money, Sophia
MURDER, 1905 ENGLAND

A twenty-one-year-old bookkeeper for a dairy in Lavender Hill, Clapham Junction, Sophia Money told Miss Hone, a fellow employee, that she was going for a walk on the evening of September 24, 1905. At about seven o'clock that night, she called another friend in a candy shop, stating that she might be going to Victoria Station in London. Inside the Merstham tunnel on the Brighton Line, a workman routinely checking the tracks at 11 PM came across the mangled dead body of a young woman—her head had been crushed and a leg had been severed—lying on the tracks. It was Sophia Money.

The question for police was whether Money's death was due to suicide, an accident, or perhaps murder. They questioned a train guard of one of the trains that had passed through the tunnel at the time. The guard reported that a woman answering Sophia's description had been with a man, "acting furtively," on board the train at East Croydon. Then a signalman reported that he had seen a man and woman struggling, the man attempting to force the woman down into a seat, as the train passed him.

It was concluded by investigators that Money had kept a secret date with a man who had convinced her to go to Victoria, that he had attempted to rape her in their compartment, and that she had been hurt during the struggle, perhaps knocked unconscious. To cover his assault, the killer had hurled the woman from the train (British trains then having separate exit doors from all compartments).

Though a coroner's jury, on October 6, 1905, could not determine the cause of Money's death, all signs pointed to murder. The woman had been found with a white veil in her mouth, as if it had been used as a gag. Further, police were able to pinpoint two trains as being the only ones on which Sophia could have been traveling: the London Bridge to Brighton train, which passed through the Merstham Tunnel at 9:13 PM, or the train from Charing Cross to Reading, which went through the tunnel at 9:33 PM. Both of these trains emerged from the tunnel with all their doors closed. It was safe to assume that someone closed the door of Sophia's compartment after she was thrown to her death (if she was not already dead; her body was so disfigured that there was no way of knowing if she had been murdered before being thrown from the train).

The classic Merstham Tunnel Mystery, as it later became known, was embellished in 1912 by the insane actions of Sophia's unbalanced and incestuous brother, Robert Henry Money. A dairy farmer, Money had a long career of illicit activities. Though he was thought to be an upstanding citizen, Money secretly seduced two of his sisters, having children with both of them. He took them all to Eastbourne on a vacation and there went berserk, shooting both sisters and killing the children—one wounded sister escaped—before setting fire to a cottage to cloak his mass murder and shooting himself.

The brother may have been the killer of Sophia Money, murdering the one sister who refused to have an incestuous affair with him, and tossing her body from the moving train that shot through Merstham Tunnel. It was the kind of callous, bestial act that suited the brother's personality and character.

Montesi, Wilma
MURDER, 1953 ITALY

The body of voluptuous Wilma Montesi was found on the morning of April 11, 1953, at Tor Vajanica, a beach about twenty miles outside of Rome by a carpenter going to work. He alerted police who inspected the young woman on the beach. She was half in the water, waves lapping her face, wearing only a pink slip. It was later determined that her dress, shoes, stockings, and garter belt, items she was known to be wearing when last seen, had vanished.

Detectives at first announced that Wilma had committed suicide but could not explain the absent clothes. They had simply been "swept out to sea," a police official stated. It was an open-and-shut case. The Montesi family, however, its members being substantial citizens—Wilma's father owned a highly successful sawmill—cried out that in no way could the attractive Wilma have killed herself. She was a happy woman unencumbered with emotional problems. The Montesis pointed out that she was not pregnant, nor was she mentally unbalanced. In fact, she was engaged to be married to a local constable.

Police suddenly reversed their statement and announced that Montesi had died accidentally—had somehow fallen into the water while wading and had drowned. This, too, held little logic in that the woman, a good swimmer, would have had to have drowned in less than three feet of water.

The accident theory nevertheless appeased the scandal-fearing Montesi fam-

Montesi, Wilma

Attractive Wilma Montesi's strange death led to a national scandal in Italy.

ily, and the young woman was laid to rest wearing the wedding gown she never wore in life, her tombstone declaring that she had died by mishap. Wilma Montesi would have been forgotten in her grave had it not been for a wealthy young man named Silvano Muto who published a gossip magazine. Five months after Montesi's burial, Muto published an article in which it was stated she had participated in a sex and drug party given by wealthy Rome playboys. She had been drugged to death, claimed the article, but the host of the party, who arranged for the body to be dumped on the beach, was not named.

Muto was hauled into court on an old Mussolini-era charge of "spreading false and alarming news capable of disturbing public order." This occurred after crowds of volatile Italians had demonstrated before public buildings, demanding that the Montesi case be reopened. Muto faced a tribunal in early 1954, and to the shock of the court, disclosed the identity of the man who had hosted the "sex and drug orgy"— one Marchese Ugo Montagna, a rich member of the gentry.

As a result of Muto's statements, the paramilitary police organization, the Carabinieri, reopened the Montesi case, claiming that Wilma had been willfully murdered. Seventeen people were indicted and put on trial, with witnesses openly naming Italian Chief of Police Tommaso Pavone as one of Montagna's high-level governmental contacts. Pavone resigned. Other resignations followed.

Prosecutors attempted to prove that

Wilma had been running around with the Montagna crowd and had attended a party where she had been drugged and, while in the middle of a sex orgy, dropped dead. Her body was then unceremoniously dumped on the beach. None of the scores of witnesses at the trial, however, could pinpoint the person responsible for drugging Wilma or name those who dragged her body to the beach. In the end no one was convicted of murdering the girl, although her enigmatic death caused wild demonstrations and arguments to break out on the streets of Rome for years after the trial. The hardest hit by the scandal was the forty-three-year-old Montagna, whose estranged mistress, Anna Maria Caglio, testified that he had given her a half-million lira.

Montagna, listening attentively in court, leaped to his feet after this statement, yelling: "That's a lie! You're only saying this so they'll increase my taxes!" The playboy's taxes were increased but Wilma Montesi's killer was never pinpointed.

Mossler, Jacques
MURDER, 1964 U.S.

Millionaire banker and financier Jacques Mossler was found brutally beaten and stabbed to death in his Key Biscayne, Florida apartment on June 30, 1964. His wife Candace, then forty-five, and her nephew, twenty-four-year-old Melvin Lane Powers, were accused of killing the millionaire in a scheme to obtain Mossler's

Candy Mossler at her sensational 1966 murder trial, with lawyer Percy Foreman.

169

wealth. Both were tried, with Percy Foreman handling the defense.

Although there seemed to be a strong case against Candy Mossler and Powers, Foreman won their release after a masterful defense. Mossler's killer was never brought to justice.

Moxley, Martha
MURDER, 1975 U.S.

Fifteen-year-old Martha Moxley of Greenwich, Connecticut, left her home with friends on Halloween night, 1975. Her body was found by a friend walking across the Moxley property on Walsh Lane, only two hundred yards from her front door, hidden somewhat in a clump of pine trees. The girl was dead, bludgeoned by an unknown killer using a golf club.

Police later found the golf club nearby, its handle broken off, but were unable to identify its owner. Martha was a well-liked girl in her community and without apparent enemies. Detectives interrogated more than five hundred persons in the case, but the murder was never solved.

Mullendore, E. C., III
MURDER, 1970 U.S.

Gene Mullendore was the kind of western hero found in the books of Edna Ferber and Zane Grey. He had slaved to put together one of the richest ranches in the Southwest, more than 130,000 choice acres of cattle land which stretched from Oklahoma into Kansas. Upon this land thousands of white-faced Hereford cattle grazed, and from beneath the soil, through ninety wells, millions of gallons of oil were pumped into the Mullendore coffers. The Cross Bell Ranch was the largest in Oklahoma, an empire inherited by Gene's college-trained grandson, E.C. Mullendore III.

The grandson was an enterprising youth who thought to make Cross Bell an agricultural model and, from 1959 on, spent a fortune on improving the cattle herds, acquiring more and more land, and filling in huge tracts of swamps in an attempt to convert these marshes into grazing lands. Old Gene Mullendore had originally worked the land with convict labor, paying near slave wages. E.C. changed all that, hiring hordes of high-priced workers, many of whom had shady backgrounds, and some of whom later became suspects when the Mullendore heir was mysteriously murdered on September 26, 1970.

Though he was worth about $40 million on paper, by early 1970 the younger Mullendore was hopelessly in debt, with more than $9 million in mortgages accruing against the Cross Bell Ranch. In the late 1960s Mullendore had taken out countless loans and had even kited checks to pay for his extravagant way of life. A wheeler-dealer, the grandson loved the good life, flying about the country whenever he had the notion, going to Los Angeles to frequent low-life clubs where he was once beaten up by bouncers after jumping up on a table to get a better look at the show.

E.C.'s attractive wife, the former Linda Vance, ordered her clothes and household goods from such exclusive stores as Neiman-Marcus; these were flown from Dallas to the Oklahoma ranch, as were all the luxuries the high-living couple ordered.

Even though he was facing bankruptcy, the impetuous Mullendore had arranged to buy $341,000 in Thoroughbred horses for his million-dollar stable. In July 1970, Mullendore spent $90,000 redecorating his $200,000 house, which was already in receivership. Though faced by enormous debts and hounded by creditors, chiefly banks that had made him loans in the millions, Mullendore was not worried. He was arranging for a multimillion-dollar loan to cover all his debts and give him the capital to put the Cross Bell Ranch on a paying basis. Or so he thought.

To cover the huge loan, Mullendore had taken out two insurance policies, one for $10 million against his own life, another in the amount of $5 million for his wife. His was the largest insurance policy ever written for one man up to that time. E.C. had offered the policy as security against the "super loan" he was expecting. Beyond the insurance policy was Cross Bell itself, valued at approximately $38 million, a highly inflated estimate. How the policies came to be written was a strange story in itself. E.C.'s brother-in-law, John W. Mecom, Jr., Texas oil tycoon and owner of the New Orleans Saints, had suggested the life insurance policies as a method whereby Mullendore could drag himself out of his miring debts.

The agency writing the Mullendore policies was headed by Atlanta-based Leroy Kerwin and Leon Cohen. This agency, which had promised to arrange a gigantic loan for Mullendore once he took out the policies, farmed out the policies to several other insurance firms eager to underwrite a man they believed was enormously wealthy. A few small loans were arranged by Kerwin and Cohen, but nothing like the millions they had promised.

Meanwhile Mullendore began to drink heavily, so much that his wife moved out of the house and filed for separate maintenance. More and more the paper tycoon in his drunken meanderings made vague references to the "Mafia" when talking with ranch hands and his friend and bodyguard, Damon "Chub" Anderson. The bodyguard took little note of these statements but remembered them well after the night of September 26,1970.

At 11:45 PM Anderson heard shots explode in the living room of the Cross Bell Ranch headquarters, which was located outside of Hulah, Oklahoma. The bodyguard was then upstairs running a bath for Mullendore, who was downstairs eating some stew. Anderson raced downstairs at the sound of the gunfire to see his employer in a sitting position on a couch. He had been beaten, and there was a bullet hole in his forehead which trickled blood across his face.

Acccording to the bodyguard, the minute he entered the room a "sharp blow"

171

knocked him down; he realized that he had been shot in the right arm. He jumped up, taking out a .25-caliber automatic pistol, and fired at two men fleeing in the dim light. He emptied his weapon at them, smashing the glass of two sliding doors leading to a patio. Anderson then called police but could not give them accurate descriptions of the two invaders, only that they were "of medium build." No tracks were found of the killers.

E.C. Mullendore was dead, his dreams of empire punctured by a single bullet. His body was whisked to a nearby morgue and, before it could be properly examined, bloodstains and other clues were washed away. It was later said that he committed suicide, but since E.C.'s hands were washed at the morgue no traces of paraffin on them could be detected.

The only definite information on the killing ascertained by police was that Mullendore had been shot with a .38-caliber pistol. Several pistols of that type were owned by workers at Cross Bell Ranch, but apparently none of these was used in the killing.

As the investigation deepened, it was revealed that Mullendore had hired, for exorbitant fees, a number of strange characters to obtain loans for him. One of these was George Aycock, who had received $30,000 to secure an enormous loan for E.C. The Mullendores had reportedly agreed to pay Aycock a 10 percent commission on the multimillion-dollar loan, one that never materialized. In a later deposition Linda Mullendore stated that

"George Aycock told me that if he did not receive his million and a half commission off the top, he would kill me and my husband." Aycock denied this charge.

Kent Green, a burly, thick-necked entrepreneur who had served four prison terms for assorted crimes such as grand theft and interstate auto theft, had also been a "loan consultant" to E.C. It was said that Green, who had lived on the ranch with his girl friend Jennie (both of whom carried .38 pistols at the time), was busy arranging huge loans for Mullendore "from questionable sources."

Even the two insurance magnates, Kerwin and Cohen, were identified as highbinders. Cohen had been convicted of rape and fraud. Kerwin had a fraud conviction. Both of these men, who had "hyped" the enormous Mullendore insurance policies at the expense of unwitting insurance companies taking on parcels of the insurance packages, had played upon the gullibility and business ineptitude of Mullendore when convincing him that they could arrange a loan after he took out his policies; they gleaned enormous commissions from the policies before moving into other fields, leaving the insurance companies underwriting the Mullendore policies holding the bag.

In 1971 Kerwin was found shot twice through the head and buried in a shallow grave outside of Toronto, Canada. His death was rumored to be Mafia-connected.

What the Mafia hoped to collect in the Mullendore murder, if indeed the Mafia was involved at all, was unclear. The financial chaos created by the muddled Mullendore certainly would not have benefited organized crime.

In the end, Gene Mullendore was forced into bankruptcy, but not before he erected a monument to his murdered grandson. Insurance payments of $8 million were finally made—E.C. had miraculously paid about $300,000 in premiums shortly before his death—$3 million to Linda Mullendore, the remaining money paid out to the many panting creditors of Cross Bell Ranch.

No one was ever indicted for the murder of E.C. Mullendore III.

N

Nathan, Benjamin

MURDER, 1870 U.S.

Wealthy Benjamin Nathan, a man of fifty-seven, returned to New York City from his summer home in Morristown, New Jersey, with two of his four sons, Frederick and Washington, on July 28, 1870, to stay at the family mansion on West 23rd Street. Since he was not expected and decorators were at work in the house, Mrs. Anne Kelly, the housekeeper, made up a room on the second floor of the mansion where the head of the house was to sleep. The sons slept on the third floor of the sprawling Victorian building.

Early in the morning of July 29, the neighborhood was aroused by the shouts of Washington and Frederick Nathan, who were running down the street calling for help. Washington's socks and nightgown were coated with blood. He had entered his father's room to wake him that morning and found the patriarch battered to death. Washington had stood in a pool of blood and brushed up against the body, which is how he came to be coated with gore.

Police rushed to the scene and found Nathan lying on the floor. There was ample evidence that a violent struggle had occurred; the businessman had obviously fought for his life. The walls, floor, and door frame of the makeshift bedchamber were splattered with blood. Nearby lay an iron bar, also covered with blood, which had apparently been used to crush Nathan's head.

Robbery was the obvious motive. A small safe in the room was open and a small cash box on a table was empty. Yet little money had been taken, since Nathan kept only household funds on hand. When the news broke that the prominent business leader had been senselessly slain, the mayor offered a large reward for the capture of the murderer. Rewards from the city and the Nathan family later totaled $47,000, a great amount of money in those days. The killing shocked the public and caused the New York Stock Exchange, of which Nathan was a much respected member, to lower its flag to half mast. The Exchange itself offered a $10,000 reward for the culprit. Newspapers throughout the country, particularly the Jewish press, gave enormous space to the murder, and, even in European publications, the Nathan killing dominated the news for months.

Frederick and Washington Nathan were investigated but were cleared of any complicity in their father's murder. Washington Nathan was known to be a "man about town", one who spent lavishly on his pleasures, yet he was not in need of money and certainly did not murder his father to obtain an inheritance that was already his, along with a handsome income from family interests.

Several notorious New York burglars, chiefly Johnny Irving and George Ellis, who were later serving time for robberies, claimed that some fellow burglars murdered Nathan when invading his house. Irving said a burglar named Kelly had entered the Nathan mansion on the night of July 28–29, 1870, and inadvertently stumbled over Nathan in a room not normally used as a bedchamber, killing him with the iron bar, a burglar tool called a "dog," which was also used by carpenters. Ellis named a safecracker, Billy Forrester, as the killer. Evidence against both of these men was utterly lacking, and police concluded that Irving and Ellis were lying, merely supplying names in order to have their sentences reduced.

The killing, which New York's Police Chief Byrnes later called the city's "most famous mystery murder," was never solved.

Wealthy Benjamin Nathan, whose classic murder in 1870 is now called the Twenty-third Street Mystery.

Nitribitt, Rosemarie
MURDER, 1957 WEST GERMANY

Born in Hitler Germany in 1933, the daughter of a laundress, Rosemarie Nitribitt had little education as a child, and by the time Germany was invaded by the Allies in 1944, she had become a street waif. She later claimed that she was raped by one of the invaders. In 1945 she was found sharing a tent with a French soldier and, being underage, was interned in Koblenz.

Within five years the unschooled Rosemarie had blossomed into a voluptuous teenager who worked the streets. She was self-taught in the ways of glamour and style; voraciously reading French magazines, she copied the latest hairstyles and dressed in the most stylish clothes her sporadic income could afford. In 1950, seventeen-year-old Rosemarie Nitribitt moved to Frankfurt, then the postwar boom town where modern skyscrapers were being erected overnight and money for almost any enterprise, including high-class hustling, was plentiful.

Rosemarie began working Frankfurt's sleek, swanky bars, where she would sit upon high bar stools, her tight dresses displaying her long, mannequinlike legs, rounded thighs, and ample bosom. With pouting lips, faintly slanted eyes, small, white, even teeth, high cheekbones, her face would appease the most particular sensualist.

Any man who approached her wearing a business suit and flashing substantial cash was an acceptable customer. Nitribitt worked hard at her trade, walking any-

where to save bus and cabfare, hoarding her illicit income, spending her money only to beautify her attractive body. Men without cash to spend were of no interest to her. "Don't waste time with the shrimps," was her advice to fellow hustlers. "The big fish are the only ones worth a worm." And she began to land the big fish, especially brokers whom she sought out, exchanging her sexual favors for inside market tips; she invested her streetwalker's loot in stocks and prospered.

Nitribitt continued to ply her scarlet trade, but only in the best hotels and lounges. She acquired bigger and more expensive cars, until she was sitting prettily behind the wheel of a custom-made black Mercedes-Benz. Next she moved into a luxury apartment on the Stiftstrasse.

The car was used as a come-on; Rosemarie would sit with the door open in parking lots, the radio blaring, the top down, her long and inviting legs jutting, and call over any man who looked well-to-do. The curious male would approach, taking in Rosemarie's blatant beauty, and be asked to go for a "spin." Most agreed and were soon being whisked along the autobahn. She would suddenly pull into a gas station and order the tank filled. She would eye her companion coquettishly. If he withdrew a wallet ample with bills to pay for the gas, she would invite him to her apartment. If he did not offer to pay, he was taken back to the parking lot and courteously thanked for his companionship and shooed away.

Nitribitt graduated from this ploy when she began to move in the higher-echelon circles of bankers and businessmen. Visiting diplomats from America, Britain, and France were given her name in Frankfurt's most exclusive clubs. She became the most sought-after courtesan in West Germany, the country's super–call girl. The young woman by 1957 had scores of rich international playboys in her address book yet she had no man to call lover nor even a solitary girl friend. No pimp was ever associated with her; she managed her own affairs from the start. And she was lonely. Yet Rosemarie was ever optimistic and full of plans. She told her favorite bartender that she had all the money she ever wanted. Her plan was to select some handsome American, marry him, and move to the United States, where she would buy her husband anything he desired, from cars to houses.

In 1957 Rosemarie Nitribitt began to change. She whispered to casual acquaintances that someone was "out to get me," but never mentioned a name. Some of her clients, while riding to her apartment in her car, noticed that she kept stopping and turning around to see if she was being followed. One badly unnerved customer later informed police: "We were driving to Miss Nitribitt's apartment when she suddenly turned into a small side street, stopped her car, and looked back at the main road we had left. A few seconds later I saw a large beige-gray Mercedes shoot past. I couldn't see the driver's face, but Miss Nitribitt murmured in a hoarse voice: 'That vermin has been following me since we left the Frankfurter Hof.' As we drove on her hands on the wheel were shaking so badly that I was afraid she would lose control of the car."

This same beige-gray Mercedes-Benz was also seen parked several times in the early hours just outside Nitribitt's apartment by her janitor and a postman, but they did not write down the car's license plates. The janitor and Erna Kreuger, the charwoman who cleaned Rosemarie's apartment, learned that the rich hustler had purchased a pistol. (One of her clients taught her how to use it.) She began to substitute code names for her own, insisting that clients call her "countess Maritza" (after the Austrian opera) or "Rebecca." When someone calling her to arrange an assignation did not use these passwords, the nervous Rosemarie would hang up.

After having her car checked one day, Nitribitt chatted briefly with a garage attendant. "You must have a lot of wealthy friends to have a car like that," remarked the mechanic.

"Yes, they're all very nice," she said in her low voice à la Marlene Dietrich, but added ominously, "but you wait, one day they'll all do me in!" She mentioned no names. To her doctor who had told her to drink less liquor, Rosemarie snapped: "Why? I'm going to die young anyway!"

On November 1, 1957, Mrs. Kreuger, the char who later complained to the police how sloppy Rosemarie was, knocked on the door of Number 36 in the Stiftstrasse apartment building. She could hear Rosemarie's poodle wildly yelping behind the door. Mrs. Kreuger thought that Rosemarie was drunk again—she had been drinking heavily in recent weeks—and would have gone away except for the hysterical-sounding dog. She opened the door with her passkey.

177

Nitribitt, Rosemarie

Rosemarie Nitribitt was sprawled face forward on her expensive couch, her tightly fitting blue skirt hiked high in the air to reveal nylon-clad legs, one arm outstretched as if she had been reaching for the telephone only inches away. Police were called and found that Germany's most famous courtesan had apparently been strangled; there were blue-black marks about her throat. There was also a deep wound in her head as if she had been bashed by a blunt instrument. The dead woman had not been sexually molested, a later examination revealed. Also, she had not been murdered for her valuables. Jewels worth thousands of dollars were found on tables in plain sight. Several stacks of bills were also found.

When the news was announced that Rosemarie Nitribitt had been murdered, scores of wealthy businessmen and government leaders suddenly took vacatiions. It did them little good. The police had already found her so-called green dossier, a burgeoning address book containing the names and numbers of hundreds of her clients. Detectives embarked on an investigative odyssey, intending to interview each and every one of Nitribitt's clients, having concluded that one of these men had to be her killer.

Dozens of respected figures in the international set were confronted by police and nervously sputtered out their sordid relationship with Nitribitt, but all provided concrete alibis. One tycoon, rather than reveal his association with the woman, blew out his brains, even though police later proved that he was innocent of the murder.

178

The police got nowhere and desperately took out advertisements in all of Germany's daily newspapers requesting that anyone having an association with Nitribitt come forward and aid them with information. The ads also stated that police had all the names of those who had dallied with her. A flood of men deluged the Frankfurt police headquarters in a frenzy to clear their names, but none of them proved to be a likely suspect.

Police Chief Kalk did learn that Rosemarie had made more money blackmailing her customers than performing in bed. She would call a client and claim to be pregnant, demanding a large sum of money to have an abortion. Either she received the money or she would inform the client's wife of their liaison. The payments were made.

Nitribitt went to her grave leaving about $50,000 in cash, her Mercedes-Benz, and about $20,000 in furs and jewelry to some distant relatives. Not until four months later did police manage to produce a live suspect, one Heinz Pohlmann, from the hundreds who had patronized the very active Rosemarie.

Pohlmann was a traveling salesman who had met Nitribitt only a few weeks before she was murdered. He insisted that he was innocent and provided an alibi that could not be challenged by police. The salesman, while being detained, sold the story of his association with Rosemarie to several magazines for an enormous amount of money and retired when he was released. [Pohlmann was rearrested in 1960, but no real case could be mounted against him and he was again released.]

The case was not even cold when German film producers made a quickie movie, Das Mädchen Rosemarie ("That Girl Rosemarie"), starring Germany's top sex symbol Nadja Tiller. It was a box-office smash.

Whoever killed Rosemarie Nitribitt went undetected and remains so at this writing.

Noel, Mrs. William
MURDER, 1893 ENGLAND

William Noel, a wealthy butcher living with his wife in Ramsgate, England, had breakfast on Sunday, May 14, 1893, before going off to church. Since each practiced a different faith, Noel went to his church that morning alone. Later he strolled about the village visiting friends before returning home at 4:20 PM. He tried the kitchen door at the rear of his shop-home and found it locked. Peering through the door window, he saw his wife sprawled on the floor, her head against the door.

Noel ran to the home of a next-door neighbor, crying for help. Police were summoned and, as constables stood by, Noel climbed through a window, moved aside his wife's body, and opened the door. He told the constables that he did not have a key to the back door. At first, investigators believed that the woman, who had been shot once through the head, was the victim of an intruder intent on robbing the shop, but Mrs. Noel's valuables and cash in the shop were still on hand.

Having no other suspects, the police arrested Noel, despite the fact that no murder weapon was found, no motive on Noel's part could be remotely established—he and his wife were on very good terms—and that Noel established the fact that he was in church at the time of her death as fixed by the coroner. Moreover, the rural constables handled their investigation like country bumkins. A chief inspector and two constables later searched the Noel shop and home with cavalier disdain to police protocol; the inspector sat on Mrs. Noel's bed while two constables rummaged through her closets and bureau, all of them drinking beer and smoking pipes, further allowing neighbors to walk about the confines of the Noel establishment as sightseers.

Nothing to incriminate Noel was found. He was nevertheless put on trial at the insistence of local police, who promised to bring forth evidence that would convict the husband of murdering his wife. The evidence was not forthcoming. When Justice Grantham learned of the unorthodox police investigation and the utter lack of proof against the accused, he exploded: "There is not enough evidence in the case upon which I would like a dog to be whipped, much less than a man to be hanged, and the case ought not to have been sent for trial!"

Noel was dismissed. His wife's killer, who had murdered for reasons that still baffle crime historians, was never found.

O

Oakes, Sir Harry
MURDER, 1943 BAHAMAS

Harry Oakes was a self-made man and one of the richest in the world, a man who could reportedly write a check for $200 million and have plenty to spare. By 1943 Oakes was Sir Harry, having obtained through influence and money the title of baronet, and was the most important citizen of the Bahamas, owning one-third of the island of New Providence, where Nassau is located. On July 8 of that year, Sir Harry Oakes's enormous wealth and power became useless to him. On that day he was found murdered in Nassau, his skull caved in by a blunt instrument, his body horribly burned in bed, his flesh covered with pillow feathers. It was a case that would stump crime experts for decades to come.

Born in Maine, Oakes left his middle-class home while in his second year of law school, announcing that he was off to seek his fortune. "I was born to be a millionaire," he told one and all before going to the Klondike to dig for gold at the turn of the century. He found nothing but poverty and misery, yet he went on drifting about the world in search of gold, bumming his way to Africa and Australia, returning to the American West, and then moving north into Canada, where he finally struck it rich in Ontario, discovering the Lake Shore Mines, which proved to be the second largest gold find of recent times.

Overnight Harry Oakes became the potentate he had many years earlier predicted he would be. The Canadian government, however, moved quickly upon his empire to levy gigantic taxes. Oakes bristled at the thought of such taxation. A friend, Harold Christie, offered Harry a solution. Christie was a wealthy businessman from the Bahamas, a place where no personal taxes were levied. Why not move to Nassau, suggested Christie, and save your fortune? Why not indeed, said Harry Oakes, and he promptly moved to the Bahamas to take up permanent residency and become a Bahamian citizen. Oakes also began to buy up huge tracts of land on the island until he owned one-third of that sunny dot in the silver sea. He became the island's most important resident, overshadowing even the island's British governor, the Duke of

Windsor, the royal playboy who had abdicated a throne to marry the American commoner Wallis Simpson.

From 1932 to 1943 Oakes was the most powerful man in Nassau. Businessmen came to him to seek permission to build stores and offices. Farmers who worked his lands listened attentively as he dictated what crops were to be planted. Hotel and airline owners did his bidding in establishing Nassau as a pleasure resort for tourists. In the late 1930s Harry Oakes felt that with all kinds of British royalty and nobility visiting the islands he, too, should join the upper crust in an official capacity. Through influence and, some said, a great deal of money, he was made a British baronet in 1939.

Sir Harry reveled in his power, his money, his title. Yet he was considered by the social leaders in the islands to be an uncouth barbarian, the one person never invited to elite functions. Harry scooped up beans with his knife, spat out seeds from grapes at dinner, and had the manners of a warthog. Oakes had never taken the time to learn the etiquette of the rich. Moreover, his speech was peppered with profanities, his mannerisms with obscene gestures. Though he owned a resplendent estate and manor house called Westbourne, maintained servants and an expensive wardrobe, Sir Harry Oakes was definitely persona non grata among the more civilized folks.

It mattered little to the supertycoon. He had cronies like Harold Christie to keep him company. It was Christie who came to Oakes with a proposition in early 1943

Sir Harry Oakes, self-made multi-millionaire and enigmatic murder victim.

Sir Harry's elegant estate at Nassau, Westbourne, where he was found dead, his body burned in bed and coated with feathers in 1943.

Oakes, Sir Harry

Oakes's close friend, Harold Christie, who found the body; his business connections included the notorious Meyer Lansky.

involving syndicate financier Meyer Lansky, who had built a billion-dollar gambling empire in Cuba through the local dictator Fulgencio Batista. Lansky wanted to build casinos in Nassau for the increasing tourist trade; he was willing to pay a cool $1 million for the exclusive gambling rights. Sir Harry, of course, was the man to approve of such an enterprise. At first Oakes gave a tentative yes to the scheme, deferring to the island's governor. It was reported that Christie met with the Duke of Windsor, who agreed to Lansky's idea.

Entrepreneur Christie then went back to Sir Harry, but Oakes suddenly did a turnabout, refusing to have anything to do with Lansky, the proposed gambling casinos, and the national crime cartel of America, for which Lansky acted as a banker.

Some weeks later, on July 8, 1943, Sir Harry was found in his bedroom by Harold Christie. Oakes was sprawled in his large bed quite dead, his head caved in by what police later described as "a long blunt instrument." His body had been set on fire and was grotesquely charred, his pajamas burned away. The killer had then, through some mad caprice, dumped all over the body feathers from a pillow, which clung to the mottled flesh, making the tycoon all the more hideous in death, a grim mockery, as it were, of the tar-and-feather treatment administered to confidence men of old by irate citizens discovering their schemes.

Christie, who had been staying with Sir Harry at the time, went screaming through Nassau's streets to announce the murder before going to the authorities. The Duke of Windsor was contacted and he ordered police to seal Westbourne from the public. A short time later the Duke inexplicably ordered local police off the case and contacted Miami police, asking that they take over the exclusive investigation. It was considered strange procedure for a British Crown Colony to ask detectives from another country to investigate a murder on its soil, but everything about the Oakes murder was strange. It was later suggested that once the Duke realized that the killing might be linked to the American syndicate, he felt that Miami police, well versed in the operations of the ubiquitous Meyer Lansky, would bring more expertise to the investigation.

Yet no member of American organized crime was ever indicted for the crime. Instead, the playboy son-in-law of Sir Harry Oakes, Count Marie Alfred Fouquereaux de Marigny, was charged with the homicide. De Marigny, who had arrived in Nassau in 1937 from Mauritius, ostensibly to invest in land, had married Oakes's daughter, Nancy. Oakes himself hated his son-in-law, although Sir Harry's wife had encouraged de Marigny to court her daughter.

The murder was simply a family affair, insisted police. De Marigny had killed Oakes to gain his fabulous fortune. Untrue, screamed the devoted Nancy, and she quickly hired the best defense attorneys available, the team headed by Godfrey Higgs. Moreover, Nancy de Marigny hired a famous Miami private detective, Raymond C. Schindler, to investigate on

Count Alfred de Marigny, in police custody a day after Harry Oakes's body was found.

Harry Oakes's daughter, Nancy, who was utterly loyal to her husband, de Marigny.

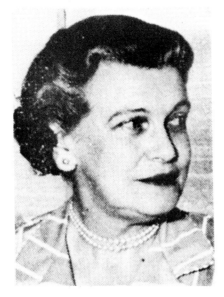

Lady Eunice Oakes, Sir Harry's wife, who was away at the time of his mysterious murder.

Alfred de Marigny while on trial for Harry Oakes's murder; he had taken pains to shave his beard, some said to avoid identification.

his own and prove her husband innocent.

Schindler met with little or no cooperation as he made his rounds of Nassau. He visited Westbourne to find local police scrubbing the place clean, removing fingerprints and traces of blood in Sir Harry's bedroom. His hotel phone was tapped and all those Schindler interviewed were interviewed by local police only hours after he left. Schindler turned up little that could help de Marigny.

At de Marigny's trial police offered a bloody handprint taken from a screen in Sir Harry's bedroom, claiming that this print put him at the scene of the murder. Attorney Higgs, however, brought in experts to prove that it was impossible to lift a print from a screen without taking with it some of the screen's background, which would discount any print. Further, Higgs revealed that the police had brought the son-in-law to the murder scene just after the killing and had made him handle several objects, prints that were later used in attempts to incriminate him. The entire case, Higgs insisted, had been botched by local and Miami detectives who had worked at cross-purposes.

De Marigny had brought suspicion upon himself, however, by shaving off his neatly trimmed Van Dyke beard just before his trial. This, prosecutors claimed, was but a subtle move to confuse any witnesses who saw him near the Oakes mansion at the time of the murder, and to thwart identification of his clean-shaven face. It mattered little. The evidence against de Marigny was so circumstantial that it all but guranteed his acquittal. He was released on November 11, 1943, and went back to his devoted wife.

Meyer Lansky and American organized crime were not brought into de Marigny's trial. Though it was long rumored that the Mafia had sent killers to murder Sir Harry because he refused to back the Lansky gambling scheme, such ideas remained only rumors.

O'Bannion, Charles Dion
GANG MURDER, 1924 U.S.

Chicago bootlegger Dion "Deanie" O'Bannion, whose gang controlled the North Side of Chicago from 1919 through 1930, feuded with Johnny Torrio and Al Capone, successors to Big Jim Colosimo [see entry] over the liquor traffic during the early years of Prohibition. Though he controlled the most opulent area of Chicago, including the Gold Coast, O'Bannion and his minions were constantly encroaching upon Torrio-Capone territory, pushing their homemade beer in near West Side neighborhoods ostensibly under the direction of the Genna brothers, Torrio-Capone satellites.

O'Bannion, a colorful character and a darling of the press—he numbered among his companions such literary lights as Charles MacArthur and Ring Lardner—went out of his way to insult his Italian rivals at every turn, calling them "spaghetti benders," "Sicilian scum," and all the other epithets he could conjure. Further, O'Bannion arranged for the deaths

Dion O'Bannion, Chicago's colorful North Side crime lord, killed by unknown assassins in 1924 in the underworld's first handshake murder. (*UPI*)

Crowds gathering outside Schofield's Flower Shop in Chicago, November 10, 1924, only minutes after three unknown gunmen had shot down Dion O'Bannion.

of Capone lieutenants and hijacked Torrio-Capone booze trucks at every opportunity.

Although he had agreed to operate only on the North Side of Chicago following a gangland meeting in the Sherman Hotel in 1923, where a line was actually drawn on a map making Madison Street the dividing line, O'Bannion had no intention of honoring his commitment (neither did Capone).

Capone raved against O'Bannion, but Torrio held his junior partner in check, reminding him that Mike Merlo, head of the powerful *Unione siciliana*, an ally of the Torrio-Capone faction, was also a personal friend of O'Bannion's. Internecine war would break out among the Italian-Sicilian gangsters, Torrio warned, if Merlo found out that his friend O'Bannion had been murdered by Capone henchmen. Capone nodded agreement and bided his time. Then Mike Merlo died of natural causes, and Capone leaped at the chance to arrange O'Bannion's murder.

The Irish gangleader owned a controlling interest in the Schofield Flower Shop at 738 North State Street. O'Bannion, beyond his reckless bootlegging and gangland operations, loved nothing better than to be among flowers. His shop grew rich, in fact, by providing all the floral wreaths for slain gangsters during the bootleg wars, these numbered in the hundreds. When Mike Merlo died, O'Bannion's flower shop as was expected, received enormous orders for flower arrangements. (Torrio ordered $10,000 worth of flowers, Capone $8,000). One large order for $750 worth of flowers was made on the morning of November 10, 1924. A city sealer named Carmen Vacco ordered the flowers, telling mob leader O'Bannion that "some boys will pick it up later."

Another call some minutes later from an unidentified person asked when the flowers for Mike Merlo's funeral would be ready. The mobster told the caller to send someone at noon to pick them up. A few minutes after the appointed hour, three unknown men walked into O'Bannion's shop. The gangster gave them a wide smile, limping forward on his bad leg which had been injured in childhood. The three men, later described as swarthy but elegantly dressed in expensive suits, warily eyed O'Bannion as he moved slowly toward them. He wore a white smock but underneath were three guns, one in a holster beneath his left armpit, one in his right front pants pocket, and the other in his waistband. He was an ambidextrous killer who had murdered at least twenty-five rival gangsters by his own hand—the most dangerous man in Chicago and the three visitors undoubtedly knew it. But they had planned well.

The shop's porter, William Crutchfield, who was sweeping up in a back room, heard O'Bannion approach the visitors with a cheery: "Hello, boys! You from Mike Merlo's?"

The three men, Crutchfield saw through the opening of a curtain, came forward, walking abreast, in the center a tall man, clean shaven and wearing a fedora and an overcoat, the men flanking him short and stocky. "Yes, for Merlo's flowers,"

End of a gangster—O'Bannion's body being put into a police wagon.

187

New York gangster and Capone ally Frankie Yale, who some claim held O'Bannion's hand while two others shot Deanie to death.

answered the tall man. He reached forward with his right hand, clasping O'Bannion's but not releasing it. He pulled O'Bannion toward him as the other two men stepped on either side of the Irish mobster, pistols drawn. They fired rapidly into O'Bannion, sending bullets into his right breast, larynx, right cheek, and, as the mobster was held in the viselike grip of the tall gangster, a coup de grace through the left cheek.

O'Bannion was dead as he fell backward into a row of geraniums; the tall man had to pry his fingers away from the stiffened fingers of the victim. All three men spun about and raced outside, jumping into a blue Jewett touring car which sped off.

Dion O'Bannion, a choirboy who had turned into Chicago's arch criminal, was dead, the first victim of "the handshake murder," another Chicago invention of the gangland wars, which had already produced such criminal precedents as the "one-way" ride, created by Earl "Hymie" Weiss, an O'Bannion lieutenant, and the use of the submachine gun, first employed by Capone henchman Frankie McErlane.

The killers, police thought, were most likely sent by Al Capone, but no one was ever apprehended for the murder. It was thought that the taller man was Frankie Yale, imported from New York to set up O'Bannion. The others may have been John Scalise and Albert Anselmi, two killers used by the Genna brothers; all of these men were unknown to O'Bannion, but whether or not they were the actual handshake killers is uncertain to this day.

The powerful North Side operation established by O'Bannion did not dissolve with his murder. His erstwhile subalterns, Earl Weiss and George "Bugs" Moran, carried on for years, battling Capone through the 1920s, bringing incredible carnage to the streets of Chicago.

O'Bannion's funeral, following his murder by two days, was the most elaborate such gangster affair on record, setting the style for many gangster funerals to come. More than $50,000 worth of flowers surrounded his casket and were dumped on his grave at Mount Carmel Cemetery.

"We sure gave Deanie a great sendoff," said Earl Weiss, following the ceremonies. He then knocked down a large wreath with a ribbon on it that said simply "From Al." Weiss trampled on these flowers, glaring at Capone across the grave site. (Capone and Torrio were boldly in attendance, feigning innocence, of course.)

As Capone left the cemetery he turned to reporters, who always followed in his wake, and quipped: "Poor Deanie—his head got away from his hat!"

"Old Shakespeare" Case, The
MURDER, 1891 U.S.

For three years Americans had been reading with fascination and long-distance shock about the horrendous fiend that stalked the back streets of Whitechapel in London, the ever frightening Jack the Ripper [see entry]. On April 24, 1891, an event occurred that led the country to believe momentarily that the Ripper had migrated to the United States to continue his grisly preoccupations.

Early in the morning of that day the night clerk of the East River Hotel, one Eddie Harrington, began knocking on the doors of the run-down wreck of a building, rousting the overnight guests who had paid about twenty-five cents each for lodgings. Most of the unsavory denizens of this waterfront dive located at Water Street and Catherine Slip had already departed, but Harrington found the door to Room 31 locked. He opened it with his passkey and, conditioned as he was to all manner of disgusting behavior and repugnant exhibits, Harrington reeled back into the hallway, instantly sick to his stomach. Retching, the clerk recovered his senses and then staggered back down the hallway to summon police.

Officers entered Room 31 some minutes later to find a sixty-year-old woman sprawled on the floor next to a bed. She had been strangled and then carved up, her flesh shredded by a filed-down cooking knife found at the scene. The minute the New York newspapers got hold of the story, they began to blare the news that Jack the Ripper had crossed the Atlantic to vex America. The savage butchery practiced on the victim was similar in modus operandi to that of the notorious Jack. The killer had even carved a cross on the thigh of the woman.

Police soon learned that the haglike prostitute was Carrie Brown, the once-respected widow of a sea captain in Salem, Massachusetts. She had taken to drink following her husband's death, and, to

189

avoid local scandal, moved to New York, where she practiced streetwalking in order to pay for liquor. She was called Jeff Davis by her clients for unknown reasons, but more often customers referred to her as Old Shakespeare, because of the elderly woman's habit of quoting the Immortal Bard while in her cups. (Carrie Brown had been an amateur actress in her early days.) That she was the victim of a migrant Jack the Ripper was highly in doubt, at least in the mind of Inspector Thomas Byrnes of the New York police.

Byrnes and other police officials had sneered at the efforts of Scotland Yard to catch the Ripper, calling their British counterparts bumblers and stating pompously that if the Ripper had attempted the same kind of bold slayings in New York he would "be in jail within thirty-six hours." Now a Ripper-like killer was loose in New York, and Inspector Byrnes vowed that he would shortly be imprisoned. A day after the body was found, police arrested an Algerian named Ameer Ben Ali, who was known along the waterfront simply as Frenchy.

The suspect was dark, short, and stocky, even though witnesses had informed police that Old Shakespeare had returned to her room the night before her corpse was found with a blond-haired sailor. Yes, confirmed the police, the sailor had gone with the old lady and had paid her, too, but he had left the premises of the East River Hotel before dawn. Ali was the culprit, they said. He already had a room in the hotel, number 33. Frenchy had waited until the sailor had gone, then crept out

of his room, went across the hallway to Room 31 and entered, killing and mutilating Old Shakespeare and then stealing her meager earnings before returning to his own room. To prove their point, officers pointed to the trail of blood that could be traced from Room 31 to Room 33. There was also blood on the doorway of Room 33 and inside on the floor. Police claimed that Ali's socks had blood on them, and when they scraped Frenchy's fingernails, they found more blood. One examiner uttered the famous line: "Why, it may be human gore."

According to police it was, and it belonged to Old Shakespeare. Oddly enough, the prosecution insisted that its analysis of the substance scraped from Ameer Ben Ali's fingernails was not only the blood of the victim, but that blood analysis proved that Old Shakespeare's last meal consisted of corned beef, cabbage, and cheese. How examiners were able to deduce this dining fare from the fingernail scrapings was never made public.

Frenchy was put on trial on June 24, 1891. Since the accused could not speak English, an interpreter was used throughout the trial. Two prisoners in the Tombs testified that Frenchy had once owned a knife like the one found by police which had been used in the murder. Ali was put on the witness stand by his defense counsel, but this proved to be a mistake. The excitable Algerian made a poor showing, seeming to pretend to understand English at one moment, appearing to find the language totally incomprehensible the next.

He was asked: "Did you kill Carrie Brown?"

A second after this was interpreted for him, Ali jumped to his feet and began to scream in Algerian French: "I am innocent! I am innocent! Allah is Allah! Allah is great! I am innocent! O, Allah, help me! Allah save me! I implore Allah to help me!" This outburst did nothing but convince jurors, despite the weak evidence against Ali, that he was reacting to the question out of guilt. He was found guilty of second-degree murder and was sent to Sing Sing for life.

Years went by while several New York reporters, notably Jacob A. Riis and Charles E. Russell, began writing inquiries into a case authorities wished to forget. It appeared that the trail of blood leading from Room 31 to Room 33 had not been there when Harrington first discovered Old Shakespeare's body. Then came reports that the bloody trail was merely a faint one of a few drops that led into Ali's room and that the horde of reporters accompanying the coroner to the scene of the crime may have caused the blood to be trailed in the direction of the door. Ali himself, who was in and out of the hallway during the hasty police investigation, may have at the time gotten blood on his clothes and socks.

By the turn of the century shocking facts came out of the small town of Cranford, New Jersey. A man living in that town was known to have visited New York periodically where he picked up prostitutes. He was absent from his work and from home on the night that Old Shakespeare

was murdered and after briefly returning to Cranford, left town forever. Inside his room was found a key with a tag marked with the number 31. This key was sent to New York and put into the lock of the door that once led to Carrie Brown's room in the East River Hotel. It opened the lock. (The killer had locked the door after him when departing the scene of the murder.)

The missing door key taken by a New Jersey man and the fact that there had been no blood in the hallway immediately after Old Shakespeare was found compelled authorities to act. New York Governor Benjamin Barker Odell studied the new findings and then publicly announced: "To refuse relief under such circumstances would be plainly a denial of justice, and after a careful consideration of all the facts I have reached the conclusion that it is clearly my duty to order the prisoner's release."

Unstated was the obvious involvement of Inspector Byrnes, who had undoubtedly acted in a desperate manner to obtain a quick conviction in the case to back up his boasts. The hastily assembled police case certainly made jurors uneasy at Ali's trial in that they returned a verdict of second-degree murder, almost as a way of ameliorating their suspicions that the accused was innocent from the start.

Ameer Ben Ali was released from Sing Sing on April 16, 1902, after serving ten years for a murder he did not commit. He was given a full pardon and hastily sailed to his native Algeria, vowing never to return to the United States, which he considered "a crazy country." Newsmen saw the wronged Frenchy off at dockside and through an interpreter he said before going up the gangplank: "Allah has heard my prayers."

Old Shakespeare's real killer disappeared, though police hunted him for another decade along the Atlantic seaboard. Francis Wellman, who had vigorously prosecuted Ali, building up a case that consisted chiefly of dubious fingernail scrapings, went on to write a best-selling book entitled *The Art of Cross-Examination*.

P

Page, Vera
MURDER, 1931 ENGLAND

Ten-year-old Vera Page of Kensington, in London, was abducted while en route to visit her aunt after school on December 15, 1931. Vera was last seen at 5 PM staring into a chemist's shop window at some soap "dominoes" on display. Her body was found the following morning by a milkman. She had been strangled, sexually abused, and dumped into shrubbery on Addison Road.

Police found soot, coal dust, and candle grease on the child's clothes. In the crook of her arm was found a bandage smelling of ammonia. Vera's red beret was discovered in a basement with an unlocked door a short distance from the chemist's shop. Since the body was dry when found after several days of rain, police concluded that the girl had been dragged into an alley, taken into the basement by her attacker, raped, and then strangled. Her body had been kept overnight in the basement and then taken to Addison Road where it was hidden in the shrubbery.

Detectives soon turned up a likely suspect, one Percy Orlando Rush, who worked in a Kensington laundry where ammonia was used. The bandage found on Vera was slipped onto one of Rush's fingers where he had suffered a cut. It fit perfectly. Moreover, candle grease, coal dust, and soot were found on some of Rush's clothes.

Rush could offer but a weak alibi as to his whereabouts at the time of the girl's disappearance. His wife was away and he had gone shopping on the evening of December 15, he said at an inquest. He had returned home at about eight thirty when his wife joined him. As Rush spoke, a woman in the spectator's section jumped up and shouted: "That man is telling lies!" She would not explain her outburst.

Another woman testified that she had seen a man pushing a wheelbarrow in the direction of Addison Road on the morning when Vera's body was discovered. The wheelbarrow, insisted the woman, contained a bundle wrapped in red cloth. (A red cloth was found in Rush's home.) Unfortunately, the woman could not identify Rush as the man pushing the wheelbarrow. Some cord found in Rush's home was matched to that used to strangle Vera Page. Rush insisted that he had picked up the cord at the laundry where he worked for household uses, pointing out that such cord was of common make.

Despite all of this impressive circumstantial evidence, Rush was not placed on trial and the coroner's verdict, rendered by Ingleby Oddie, stated that Vera Page was murdered by "some person unknown."

Paisley, John
MURDER, 1978 U.S.

A shadowy U.S. Central Intelligence Agency figure, John Paisley, set sail alone in his sloop, *Brillig*, on September 24, 1978, going down Chesapeake Bay. His body— or *a* body, which authorities later claimed was Paisley's—came to the surface on October 1; the corpse was weighted down with thirty-eight pounds of Paisley's own scuba weights and a 9-mm bullet had been fired into the head behind the left ear.

CIA officials, as soon as the body was discovered, hastily announced that Paisley had been retired since 1974 and had long since ceased to have access to sensitive intelligence information. Several newspapers, however, retorted that Paisley, up to the time of his death, was working directly for the White House as an intelligence consultant whose job it was to evaluate Russian military strength. In that capacity Paisley, it was maintained, was privy to top-secret information. (The CIA fear in this instance was undoubtedly that Paisley possessed top secrets which he may or may not have revealed to his murderers, a possibility the Agency understandably refused to admit.)

Paisley apparently had access to a spy satellite program called KH-11, and his authority was far-reaching in that he could order the launching of surveillance satellites. It was also alleged that Paisley had kept sensitive documents aboard his sloop, the *Brillig,* and it was feared that he was murdered so that foreign agents could obtain these files.

At first officials were in doubt that the body found floating in Chesapeake Bay was Paisley's, the corpse being so decomposed that examiners had difficulty in obtaining fingerprints. The problem was solved in a gruesome manner, the hands of the body were severed and sent to the FBI laboratory in Washington, D.C., where prints were removed and matched to the only set of Paisley's prints available, those taken in 1940 in Phoenix, Arizona, where he had been a high school student. (Paisley had been fingerprinted during a war scare when patriotic citizens were asked to volunteer their prints.)

There was still doubt in the mind of Paisley's wife and others who challenged the method of fingerprint identification employed by the Bureau. Some even claimed that prints were supplied to match a corpse substituted for the CIA operative.

The issue is still in doubt to this writing, but John Paisley is considered dead by certain authorities, possibly a murder victim of an espionage plot. His killers, whether they be Russian agents or operatives of another country, have never been identified.

Percy, Valerie
MURDER, 1966   U.S.

In the bedroom of the Percy home in Kenilworth, Illinois, on Chicago's North Shore, in the early morning hours of September 16, 1966, the attractive teenage daughter of Charles Percy was attacked by an intruder, according to most reports. The girl was stabbed and bludgeoned to death by what was thought to be a soldering iron, which, oddly, left a mark on her head similar to the letter A.

Though the family was alerted to the noise made by the intruder—Percy set off a house siren and frantically searched the house—the killer had vanished. Police were completely baffled by the murder, and no one was ever apprehended for the killing, which occurred at the time when Percy was conducting his first campaign for the U.S. Senate. (He was elected in a landslide.)

Investigative reporters Art Petacque and Hugh Hough of the Chicago *Sun-Times* claimed in 1973 to have pinpointed the killer of Valerie Percy, naming Frederick Malchow, a member of a burglar gang that had been preying upon the North Shore residences of the rich. Malchow's name was volunteered to Petacque and Hough by a convicted career burglar, Francis L. Hohimer, who was serving a thirty-year term in the Iowa State Peni-

Valerie Percy, the twenty-one-year-old daughter of Charles Percy, later U.S. senator from Illinois, whose gruesome murder remains a mystery to this day. (*Wide World*)

195

tentiary. Hohimer claimed that Malchow had done the actual killing and that he, Hohimer, had burned the bloody clothes worn by the murderer. Malchow, however, died in a 1967 jailbreak in Pennsylvania.

The *Sun-Times* story was not substantiated by hard evidence and, with Malchow dead, a convenient scapegoat for Hohimer, the newspaper story carried little credence with crime experts. The Valerie Percy slaying is still officially unsolved at this writing.

Piernicke, Dora
MURDER, 1903 ENGLAND

British sleuths have long puzzled over the murder of Dora Piernicke, a Polish prostitute whose throat was cut by a customer on December 31, 1903, in that the killing was almost identical to the Camden Town murder of Emily Dimmock [see entry] three and a half years later.

Piernicke returned to her room on Tottenham Court Road in London with a client in the early morning hours of December 31. A short time later the downstairs lodger heard the breaking of glass and a thumping noise on the floor above. The roomer went up the stairs in his stocking feet, listened at Dora's door and heard heavy breathing, then quiet. Thinking all was well, the roomer went back to his own lodgings.

Piernicke was found by the landlady some hours later, dead, lying on her bed with her throat cut from ear to ear. She had apparently been slashed, fell to the floor, breaking a vase, and had then either somehow climbed into bed to die, or was lifted onto the bed by her killer, who was never found.

R

Redwood, Norman
MURDER, 1937   U.S.

At a little after 6 PM on February 6, 1937, Victoria Redwood received a phone call from her husband, Norman Redwood, a labor union official, who told her that he would be returning to their Teaneck, New Jersey, home within the hour for dinner. A short time later Mrs. Redwood was startled to hear the loud sounds of what she thought were car backfires on Laurelton Parkway. She rushed outside to find her husband at the wheel of the family car, slumped forward on the steering wheel, his body riddled with bullets.

The killing of Norman Redwood, who had recently been elected business manager for the Compressed Air, Subway and Tunnel Workers, Local 102, touched off a nationwide hunt for his killers. The day after the shooting multimillionaire building contractor Samuel Rosoff offered a $5,000 reward for Redwood's killer and then moved to New York City. The move, according to Bergen County Prosecutor John J. Breslin, Jr., was an intentional smokescreen (as was the reward) so that Rosoff could escape New Jersey jurisdiction.

Breslin quickly accused Rosoff of engineering the murder because Redwood had struck his firm and ignored an injunction brought against him by Rosoff. Breslin, on February 28, 1937, publicly stated that Rosoff had acted with Joe Fay, reported overlord of New Jersey's building trades, to rid themselves of a truculent labor leader who refused to make under-the-counter payoff deals for cheap labor and had threatened to bring his union into the CIO.

The prosecutor went on to state that Rosoff had met with Redwood and warned him to cooperate with Fay and himself or he would get "two guns and if I don't use them I will get the men who will use them."

Redwood reportedly laughed at Rosoff and went his own way. Miraculously, two guns were unearthed by dogged police, who by dragging the Hackensack River near the murder scene, found one weapon, the other was located some days later in a park. The serial numbers had been filed off the weapons, but one gun was sent to New Jersey specialists who used a new acid process to raise the serial numbers, and this weapon was subsequently traced to "Luger Moe" Saraga, a New York gun

Labor leader Norman Redwood (*left*) with Sam Rosoff, who was later accused of killing Redwood.

Victoria Redwood, who found her husband shot to death in front of their Teaneck, New Jersey, home on February 6, 1937.

dealer and reported armorer of the Dutch Schultz mob.

Saraga was found in Europe and brought back for questioning. After several days of interrogation, the gunsmith said that he had sold the murder weapon to a man he knew only as "Little Davey." This man was never found. Neither was the owner of the second gun, which had been purchased in Pittsburgh.

Rosoff, who vehemently denied any guilt in the Redwood shooting, had been placed under technical arrest and had been sent a subpoena to testify in the case in New Jersey. The wealthy contractor, however, had other ideas. He had proved that he was not a man who could be manipulated. Rosoff had once carted $1 million in cash before the New York City Board of Estimate when bidding on a single contract. He reacted to Breslin's charges in a similar manner, barging into the Supreme Court of New Jersey and demanding through expensive lawyers that the technical arrest and subpoena be dropped. They were.

Despite Prosecutor Breslin's loud accusations, neither Rosoff nor Fay ever faced trial. Redwood's slayers were never brought to justice.

Reville, Anne
MURDER, 1881 ENGLAND

A classic British murder mystery of the Victorian era, the slaying of Anne Reville, baffled police and courts alike. The thirty-five-year-old Anne was the wife of a well-to-do butcher, Hazekiah Reville, whose shop was in Slough. Reville had two assistants, Philip Glass and Augustus Alfred Payne, a seventeen-year-old who was kept employed through the insistence of Reville's wife as the butcher disliked the youth, stating that he was shiftless and a petty thief.

Reville and Glass were absent from the shop on April 11, 1881, with only Anne Reville and Payne working inside. Payne, according to later statements, finished his work and left for home at closing time. Before the dinner hour passersby stopped before the butcher shop to stare at the strange sight of Anne Reville sitting motionless before the window, staring vacantly ahead. A constable stopped inside to find that she was dead, struck several times from behind with a chopper.

Confronted with the news, Hazekiah Reville immediately incriminated Payne, stating that he had given his wife money before leaving the shop and implying that Payne undoubtedly killed her for these funds. Glass had a concrete alibi and Reville stated that he was outside a tobacco shop waiting for a friend inside to have an order filled at the time his wife was killed. The friend came forward to support this claim. (Some crime experts, however, later insisted that the butcher had run back to his own shop, murdered his wife because she was having an affair with Payne, and then hurriedly returned to the tobacconist's to establish his alibi.)

Augustus Payne was duly arrested and faced trial on April 28, 1881. He proved to be a dull-witted defendant who showed not the slightest emotion over Mrs. Reville's slaying or his own precarious situation. The prosecution, on the other hand, could establish no motive for Payne's killing Anne Reville. The defense pointed out that the wife had shown kindness for the youth, giving him extra money on occasions to buy beer. Payne was acquitted. Though Reville may have had a stronger motive to kill his wife than his apprentice, the butcher was never accused nor brought to trial. The true killer remained nameless.

Reynolds, Emmeline "Dolly"
MURDER, 1898 U.S.

On August 15, 1898, a stylish and beautiful woman approached the desk of New York's Grand Hotel at 31st Street and Broadway. Hotel clerk Paul Rowe responded to her request for a room by pushing forward the hotel register, which she signed "E. Maxwell and wife—Brooklyn." Rowe was enamored of the stunningly attractive woman, taking careful note that she was adorned with expensive jewelry— large, glittering diamond earrings and a diamond and ruby ring. She carried with her a small satchel.

The woman was shown to Room 84 on the fourth floor of the hotel. That afternoon, the woman was seen lunching in the hotel dining room. She left and returned a short time later with a good-looking man, later described as being about thirty years old, having a black mustache,

Dolly Reynolds, the beautiful mistress mysteriously murdered in 1898.

and wearing a dark blue suit and straw hat.

The couple went to Room 84 and, at 6 PM, ordered a bottle of champagne. They were seen leaving the hotel an hour later, the woman wearing more expensive jewelry than when she had arrived—she fairly glittered with diamond earrings, diamond rings and a diamond brooch. The pair returned to the Grand Hotel at 11:30 PM, going to their room.

At about 2:30 AM the woman's companion was seen sneaking down the backstairs of the hotel, but night employees merely shrugged. What guests did in the hotel was their own business.

A hotel chambermaid entered Room 84 at 9:45 AM on August 16 to find the beautiful female guest, fully clothed, lying on the floor, her face down on the carpet, her arms flung outward. The back of the woman's head had been caved in with what was later described as a homemade bludgeon consisting of a lead pipe through which an iron rod had been inserted, a fifteen-inch murder weapon with a crook at one end like that of a shepherd's staff, the straight end wrapped with heavy lineman's tape.

Her earrings and ring had apparently been torn from her and taken. Police found, under the woman's corset, a check in the amount of $13,000, made out to Emma Reynolds and drawn on the Garfield National Bank. It was signed by a Dudley Gideon and endorsed on the back by an S. J. Kennedy. Inside the woman's purse detectives found a slip of paper on which was written an address—370 West 58th Street.

When officers called at this address hours later they were greeted by an elderly black woman named Margaret Adams, who told them that a Mrs. Emmeline Reynolds lived there and that she was Mrs. Reynolds's maid. She was asked to accompany the detectives to the morgue where she identified the body of her mistress. More mystery was added to the case when the maid reported her employer's jewels missing, expensive gems that Mrs. Reynolds kept in a chamois bag in her bedroom. (These were found some weeks later in the house.)

It took little time for police to learn that Mrs. Reynolds was not married at all, that she was plain Dolly Reynolds, the daughter of a successful Mount Vernon, New York, builder, and she had moved to New York to study for a stage career. Other than looking beautiful, Dolly had no talent at all and she failed miserably as an actress. She began selling textbooks to large firms, concentrating on brokers. One of these, Maurice B. Mendham, fell in love with Dolly and offered to set her up in her own house as Mrs. Reynolds. She would pretend to be his wife, he her husband. Dolly, whose fortunes were at low ebb, agreed. A short time later she moved into her handsome West 58th Street lodgings. Mendham was generous to his lovely mistress, giving her expensive jewelry and cash. The wealthy broker also told her that he would have her bad teeth fixed and introduced her to a dentist named Samuel J. Kennedy, the very man who had endorsed the bogus check found on Dolly's body following her murder.

Dolly Reynolds's meeting with Dr.

Dolly Reynolds shown registering at the Grand Hotel in New York, her last residence.

Kennedy apparently blossomed into a clandestine romance, although the dentist later vigorously denied having such an affair. Police went to Dr. Kennedy's office on the morning following her murder and found an older woman and a youth angrily questioning the dentist. The visitors, ironically enough, were Dolly Reynolds's mother and brother, who had traveled from Mount Vernon. Mrs. Reynolds quickly explained to detectives that a week before her daughter was killed, Dolly had returned to Mount Vernon and had told her about Dr. Kennedy and how the dentist had promised to return $4,000 on an impending horserace, one where he possessed an "inside tip," against a bet of $500, Dolly's money, which Kennedy would bet for her. Dolly had stated that she had withdrawn the money from her bank account (really money given to her by her secret sugar daddy, Mendham) and intended to deliver the money to Kennedy on August 16, 1898, the very day her body was found in Room 84 of the Grand Hotel.

Mrs. Reynolds, who had learned of her daughter's death just that morning, tearfully told police how she had given Dolly her best satchel in which to carry the $500 betting money. Now her daughter was dead, and she suspected the dentist of foul play. So did police. Dr. Kennedy was arrested, charged with the murder, and held for trial, which was scheduled for March 3, 1899.

Meanwhile police questioned broker Mendham, who insisted that he was in New Jersey at a party at the time his mistress was murdered. Oddly police accepted Mendham's word, even though another paramour he had maintained had died under mysterious circumstances a few years earlier. His alibi was never checked.

Samuel Kennedy was put into a lineup and identified by Grand Hotel employees as the man who had sneaked down the backstairs early in the morning of Dolly Reynolds's murder. (The coroner fixed the time of her death at 1:30 AM, an hour before the man was seen leaving the hotel.)

The same witnesses testified against Kennedy at his trial. So did a haberdasher who claimed that he had sold a straw hat to a man who told him chattily that he was a dentist named Kennedy the day before the murder. The man seen at the hotel was wearing a straw hat.

Kennedy denied ever buying such a hat and ever being with Dolly Reynolds at the Grand Hotel. Someone, he claimed, had impersonated him. He intimated that Maurice Mendham was behind it all, that perhaps he had sent the impersonator to Dolly for ulterior reasons. It was later theorized that Mendham, tiring of the woman, devised a complicated scheme in which to discard her. He would send a friend to buy off Dolly with a worthless check for $13,000, the man signing it using the bogus name of Dudley Gideon, a person police were never able to locate. Kennedy's name was used to endorse the check, so that Dolly was compromised in accusing Mendham of giving her a phony check. She could not throw it back at the broker unless she wanted to risk his seeing

Kennedy's name and therefore accusing her of being unfaithful. At least that was the theory, such as it was, which attempted to explain the existence of the strange check. It was also felt that Mendham's friend, the man mistaken for Dr. Kennedy, departed about midnight on August 15. Since a robbery had been reported the following morning in the hotel, it was thought that a burglar, seeing Mendham's emissary leave, entered Dolly Reynolds's room and killed her for the expensive jewels she was wearing. In that the gems were missing when the woman was found, this appeared to be a plausible explanation. The iron bar used to kill Reynolds and left behind at the scene of the crime could have been a homemade burglar's tool.

None of these speculations entered into the three trials endured by Samuel Kennedy, who proclaimed his innocence all along, stating that he was in the Staten Island home of his parents with his wife and children at 3 AM on the morning of the murder. His parents supported this claim in court. The dentist was nevertheless convicted and his death sentence was scheduled to be carried out on May 22, 1899.

Kennedy's lawyers, however, were able to unearth witnesses who said he was on the midnight Staten Island ferry on the night of the murder and could therefore not have been the man seen leaving the Grand Hotel at 2:30 AM. A new trial was ordered but ended in a hung jury. A third trial commenced. This time hotel employees were uncertain about Kennedy's

being the man on the back stairs. He was acquitted, after having spent three years in jail.

The true killer of Dolly Reynolds, would-be actress, part-time book seller and full-time mistress, lived namelessly into the twentieth century, quite possibly reading with relish the tens of thousands of words in print speculating about his identity.

Reynolds, Zachary Smith
MURDER, 1932 U.S.

The heir to a $30-million tobacco fortune, Zachary Smith Reynolds had everything to live for. He was handsome, young, and married to one of the world's most beautiful women, famed torch singer Libby Holman, who had made such songs as "Moanin' Low," "Something to Remember You By," and "Body and Soul" famous during her mercurial stage career of the 1920s. Yet, on the morning of July 5, 1932, following a party in his palatial estate at Winston-Salem, North Carolina, Reynolds was found dead with a single bullet fired into his head.

"Skipper," as Reynolds was called by friends, attended the party in his country home on the night of July 4 but seemed preoccupied. "In fact, he had looked as if he were expecting someone," remarked Raymond Kramer, Reynolds's tutor and party guest. At 1 AM the following morning a single shot rang out from the young tycoon's bedroom. His torch singer wife, wearing a silk negligee smeared with

Reynolds, Zachary Smith

Multimillionaire Zachary Smith Reynolds, whose death in 1932 was decreed a suicide, then changed to murder.

blood, ran from the bedroom and through the halls of the great mansion screaming: "Smith's killed himself!"

Servants rushed into the tycoon's bedroom to find him lying on the floor next to his bed, a pool of blood spreading from his head, which had suffered a bullet wound. He was still alive and was rushed to the Baptist Hospital in New Salem, but the wound proved fatal and the tobacco heir died four hours later without regaining consciousness.

A full eight hours after the shooting, police arrived at the Reynolds estate to investigate. They found the .32-caliber Mauser automatic that had killed Reynolds nowhere near the bed where he had fallen, but on a sleeping porch adjacent to the bedroom. Detectives roaming through the house also found Libby Holman's lounging pajamas in a room occupied by Ab Walker and Albert Bailey, the tycoon's close friends, who were visiting at the time. Despite these curious discoveries, W. N. Dalton, coroner for Forsyth County, hastily agreed with Holman decreeing that Reynolds's death was due to suicide. He did not even consider the fact that the tycoon could not have shot himself in the head and then somehow thrown the weapon out French windows so that it sailed around a corner to land on an outside porch.

Others thought the coroner's verdict was strange indeed, and the county sheriff's office launched a separate investigation, the local sheriff defiantly reopening the case and deputizing an army of residents, including the host of Reynolds employees on the estate. The pressure mounting from this renewed investigation caused Coroner Dalton to do a complete turnabout; he stated that a thorough inquest would be held, but that the press would be prohibited from attending. This move all the more sensationalized the shooting with Winston-Salem papers, who clamored against Dalton, stating that the coroner was stifling the freedom of the press.

Dalton, by then a very much muddled coroner who appeared to be inexpertly shielding the Reynolds family, relented and invited the press to the proceedings. His actions had assured the presence of not only the local newsmen but representatives of papers throughout the country.

The highlight of the inquest was the appearance on the stand of the ravishing Libby Holman who tearfully described how she heard her husband call her name before he held a gun to his head and shot himself. She added that Zachary Reynolds was not the happy-go-lucky man of wealth the world thought him to be but a brooding, moody, depressed person who had often threatened to kill himself. The reason? Holman wiped away her tears and confessed the awful family secret—Reynolds was obsessed with being sexually inadequate. This statement confounded reporters and officials alike. Reynolds, through a former marriage, had already sired a girl, Anne Cannon Smith Reynolds, who was two at the time of his death. Though Holman staunchly maintained that her manic-depressive husband was impotent, she admitted, incredibly, in the following breath that

The Reynolds estate outside of Winston-Salem, North Carolina.

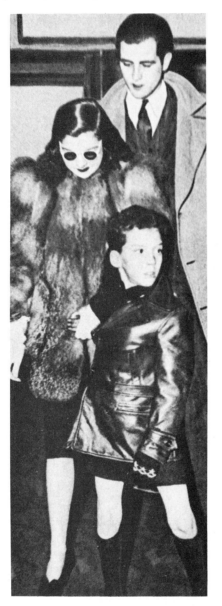

Singer Libby Holman, shown with her son, Christopher, and second husband, actor Ralph Holmes; she claimed Reynolds killed himself but was charged with his murder.

she was three months pregnant with the tycoon's child.

All Mrs. Reynolds's statements produced suspicion in the minds of jurors, who originally felt that the suicide story might have some credence. After listening to the testimony of the sheriff, detectives, and, particularly, Libby Holman Reynolds, the coroner's jury returned a verdict of "death from a bullet wound inflicted by a person or persons unknown." The jurors had opted for murder.

Libby Holman then gave several interviews in which she bluntly stated that she had given up her stellar stage career in 1931 to marry Reynolds. She sounded more like a self-centered prima donna than a bereaved widow, concerned only with her own sacrifice of fame. A short time later Holman and Ab Walker were suddenly charged with murder. In July 1932 Holman was indicted by a grand jury for first-degree murder; this was later reduced to second-degree murder. Walker, charged as an accessory, was allowed to go free after posting a $25,000 bail bond. The press waited for what promised to be one of America's most sensational trials, but it was a legal carnival that never opened its gates.

For reasons never made clear, members of the Reynolds family contacted Prosecutor Carlisle Higgins, requesting that all charges against Libby and Walker be dropped. It was later suggested that the tobacco tycoons wanted to avoid any scandal under any terms. All charges were dropped, and barely two months later Libby Holman gave birth to Zachary Reynolds's child, a boy she named Christopher Smith Reynolds.

The huge Reynolds fortune Holman expected to obtain later came down through negotiations to be $750,000 for the ex-singer and $6 million for her child, who would receive the settlement upon his twenty-first birthday. Then family lawyers, at the last minute, made a legal move to block payment, dredging up an ancient decision by the state's supreme court whereby Nevada divorces were not recognized in North Carolina. Since Reynolds's first wife had been divorced in Nevada, argued the lawyers, she was still the legal spouse of the murdered man and Libby Holman was not legally married to the tobacco tycoon and could therefore not claim any of the Reynolds fortune.

Lawyers for both sides debated the issue hotly for two years until 1934, when Anne, the daughter of Reynolds's first marriage, was awarded by the state court almost $10 million and Libby's son, Christopher, almost $6.5 million.

In 1939 Holman married movie actor Ralph Holmes, the son of character actor Taylor Holmes, but the union soured by 1945 and they separated. Weeks later Holmes, who had served with distinction as a fighter pilot in World War II, committed suicide, swallowing a bottle of sleeping pills.

Tragedy continued to dog the aging Holman. In 1950 when her son was only seventeen, the youth was killed in a California mountain-climbing accident. He was never to see a dime of the fabulous fortune left to him. Holman, however, embarked upon a long legal struggle to obtain the money and was finally awarded $6 million.

Throughout the court battle she periodically returned to the stage, touring the U.S. and Europe in one-woman performances. She enjoyed a popular revival in 1954 when she starred in a Broadway production entitled *Blues, Ballads and Sin Songs*. She later married for the third time, to Louis Schanker, and lived on a 112-acre farm outside of Stamford, Connecticut. The shadow of her first husband's mysterious unsolved murder hovered over the torch singer until the day of her death on June 18, 1971, at age sixty-five.

Ridgley, Elizabeth
MURDER, 1919 ENGLAND

The unsolved murder of Elizabeth Ridgley, a shopkeeper in Hitchin, England, was notable in that the case was completely mismanaged by local police, a display of ineptitude and negligence that infuriated a British court later trying a manufactured case against an innocent man.

Miss Ridgley was found in her shop on January 25, 1919, after an intruder had administered horrible blows to her head. It also appeared that her killer had dragged her about by the hair before murdering her. Beside her body was found the victim's Irish terrier, also killed. Both had been battered to death by a four-pound weight which was found coated with gore on the floor next to Ridgley.

Local police inspected the premises and, incredibly, reported that the victim had suffered death by *accident,* stating that Ridgley had died from "an apparent fall." The ridiculous police conclusions, without openly stating such, presumed that the victim's dog, which had obviously gone to her aid during the attack, had also died accidentally from a fall.

By the time Scotland Yard was called into the case, any possible clues at the murder scene had been obliterated by bumbling constables who had thundered aimlessly about the Ridgley shop. When Yard detectives understandably declared the death a murder, local officials desperately pointed to a laborer, John Healy, as the killer. He was brought to trial on almost nonexistent evidence. Healy had been seen near the shop close to the time of the killing and had a wound on his hand, which police said was a bite from Ridgley's dog. Healy insisted that he had cut himself on a piece of sheet metal.

Healy's trial was brief; he was dismissed for lack of evidence and Justice Darling took the Hitchin police to task for their incompetent handling of the case, calling their so-called investigation "absurd."

Rothstein, Arnold
GANGLAND MURDER, 1928 U.S.

Gambler, financier of all manner of New York rackets, Arnold Rothstein, known as the Big Bankroll, was mysteriously murdered on November 4, 1928, while he sat in a poker game in a room at the Park Central Hotel. At almost 11 o'clock that night an employee saw Rothstein staggering about, clutching his abdomen, near the hotel's servants' entrance. Before he collapsed, the multimillionaire gambler shouted: "I've been shot—call me a taxi!"

Instead, an ambulance was called, and Rothstein was rushed to Polyclinic Hospital. Following an emergency operation, Rothstein lived for two days. He refused to tell police, friends, or relatives who had shot him, observing the underworld code of silence to the last until he died on November 6. To one police acquaintance Rothstein had shouted from his hospital bed: "I won't talk about it! I'll take care of it myself."

Whether or not Mr. Big gave final orders to his minions to eliminate his killer is not known. Oddly enough, after his death, police were unable to find any bank accounts, substantial cash, or other assets Rothstein was known to have possessed. It was later claimed that underworld confederates made off with his fortune, secret caches of enormous amounts of cash Rothstein had hidden. How these Rothstein henchmen came to learn the whereabouts of his secreted treasure is uncertain.

What was certain was that Rothstein had been the most powerful man in the underworld up to 1928. For fifteen years he had dominated New York rackets, and his sphere of influence extended across the country. He had reached, through Abe Attell and others, all the way to Chicago in 1919 to fix the World Series, bribing half the Chicago White Sox team to throw their games. He had made fabulous bets and gleaned millions in winnings on elections and all manner of sports. He had become the greatest loan shark in America, lending out millions and doubling his returns with staggering short-term interest rates.

In his heyday, Rothstein, always carrying no less than $200,000 in cash, would stroll down Broadway, making cash loans of up to $10,000 on the spot to any high roller whose credit was good, recording the transaction only in his head. Mr. Big, from all accounts, possessed a towering IQ, one that would have made him millions in any legitimate pursuit, but, as he said, "I like the fast action." His brain was one giant computer in which he could analyze the most staggering mathematical problems. He was able to compute fantastic odds within seconds and did so when winning at the racetrack, his favorite pastime. (The mental effort resulted in lifelong migraine headaches.)

Rothstein's reputation among underworld associates was solid. He financed gangland operations, backing bootleg gangs run by Waxey Gordon and Dutch Schultz. He financed Larry Fay in his fledgling milk racket and underwrote robberies that required a great deal of "up-front" money. Moreover, Rothstein's word was gold. If he lost a bet or at poker, his second greatest love next to horses, he would write out an IOU if short of pocket cash and pay off within twenty-four hours.

It was therefore a staggering shock to the gambling world that "A.R." had re-

The Big Bankroll, gambler Arnold Rothstein, murdered by persons unknown in New York's Park Central Hotel in 1928.

fused to honor his losses in a big-time poker game, played with a half-dozen plungers between September 8 and 10, 1928. He had apparently lost $320,000. "I'll pay off in a day or two," Mr. Big snorted as he pushed away from the poker table. Later he told friends that he had no intention of paying the big winners, Alvin "Titanic" Thompson and Nate "Nigger Nate" Raymond. "The game was fixed," he sneered.

Less than two months later Arnold Rothstein was dead. Raymond and Thompson were called in for questioning but supplied solid alibis. George "Hump" McManus, a friend of Rothstein's who had set up the marathon poker game in which Mr. Big lost heavily, was reportedly the last man to see Rothstein in Room 349 of the Park Central Hotel, a room registered in McManus's name, on the night of Rothstein's shooting. McManus was put on trial, but no case could be established against him and he was quickly acquitted.

For years "Who shot Arnold Rothstein?" became as popular a line in American households as "Who Killed Cock Robin?" The answer, to this day, has always been silence.

Rouse Case, The
MURDERS, 1980 U.S.

At a little after midnight on June 6, 1980, Bruce and Darlene Rouse were savagely attacked in their suburban Libertyville, Illinois, home. The Rouses were asleep when someone entered their bedroom and mercilessly beat, stabbed, and shotgunned them to death. It was the end of one American dream.

The Rouses had struggled for twenty years to attain the good life—high school graduates who married young in 1959 and embarked upon building financial stability and a family. Bruce started with one Standard service station and reportedly became obsessed with building up a chain, which, over twenty grueling years, he did. At first his wife worked alongside him in the station. Then, as they had children—Kurt, Robin, and Billy—Darlene Rouse took on the chores of housewife and mother.

Bruce Rouse, called a workaholic by his friends, devoted almost every waking hour to his service stations. As his profits soared, he and his wife began to enjoy the good life, buying a thirteen-room home with considerable land in Libertyville at 2057 N. Milwaukee Avenue in 1974, and quickly adding a swimming pool and a stable, where their daughter, Robin, kept two horses. A room upstairs was reserved for expensive electronic games for the children.

Darlene Rouse became active in several social clubs and spent a great deal of her time playing bridge. Some criticized her and her husband for ignoring the children. There was reported strife between the parents and their offspring, and a strained relationship existed between Darlene, who had grown chubby at age thirty-eight, and the work-obsessed husband. The oldest son, Kurt, openly ar-

Kurt Rouse, talking with unidentified friend and brother William (*back to camera*), whose mother and father were mysteriously murdered in 1980.

gued with his parents about drug use, according to reports, and refused to join the army as his mother and father wished. He was periodically thrown out of the house. He retreated to a shack he had built behind the main building, one which boasted a sign reading "Kurt's Place."

Kurt Rouse, twenty, along with his younger brother, Billy, fifteen, and his sister, Robin, seventeen, became prime suspects in their parents' murder. The idea that some stranger entered the Rouse home, not to steal anything (nothing was taken at the time of the murder), but merely to murder the Rouses was the only other prospect left to police.

Police dragging the Des Plaines River four months later recovered a shotgun

211

owned by the Rouses, along with some bloody clothing ostensibly worn by the killer, but no fingerprints could be lifted from the weapon and the clothing was not identifiable.

The Rouse children, to this day, have made no public statements regarding the deaths of their parents. It is known that on the night of the murder Billy, according to his own brief statement, was asleep in an upstairs bedroom. He said he heard nothing. Kurt claimed to have been in his shack behind the main house. He said he heard nothing. Robin, who had been to a dance and returned some time before, during, or after her parents were killed, said she had seen and heard nothing. It is hoped by investigators still working on the case that someone will come forward to tell what has not been told, but as time passes that hope rapidly diminishes.

Rubinstein, Serge
MURDER, 1955 U.S.

An international con man, Serge Rubinstein was an intellectual, born of high-society parents in Czarist Russia in 1908, his father being a financial consultant to Czar Nicholas II. The Rubinstein family barely escaped the Russian Revolution, fleeing to England, where Serge later attended Cambridge and graduated with honors.

Rubinstein gloated over his superior intelligence and thought that only fools stayed within the boundaries of the law

Super hustler Serge Rubinstein, whose faceless killer shut off his wind on January 26, 1955.

when conducting business. At twenty-one, the genius-level con man took a position with a Paris bank. Using deposits, Rubinstein bought up a restaurant chain, then sold it off for a $1-million profit and secretly returned the bank funds.

Using these profits, the entrepreneur manipulated money markets on an international scale, earning many more millions over the years. He had, in the early 1930s, through intricate black market manipulation of the franc, helped to destroy the French economy. In 1935, Rubinstein took over a British firm, the Chosen Corporation, which had large mining operations in Korea. He moved to Japan and secretly sold off the shares of the firm to American investors who paid him close to $70 million in Japanese yen. The investors, thinking themselves shrewd operators who knew that the Japanese had forbidden any of their currency from leaving the country, expected Rubinstein to sell the yen back to them at one-tenth of their value. Inventive as ever, Rubinstein bought up huge amounts of Japanese silk and stuffed the currency into the hollow cardboard tubes around which the silk was wrapped. He then shipped the silk to America. There he unloaded the enormous amount of Japanese yen upon the open market and this caused the yen to be devalued.

To avoid prosecution for his schemes, Rubinstein fled to America, where he lived the high life, dwelling in a Fifth Avenue mansion, giving expensive parties, and acting the playboy. In his spare time the con man managed to gut several companies and realize profits in the millions.

Serge Rubinstein had dozens of enemies, so many, in fact, that he could not remember them all. One of them undoubtedly decided to seek revenge for Rubinstein's blatant transgressions. The millionaire con man was found dead in his bedroom on the night of January 26, 1955, by his butler. Rubinstein was on the floor, his silk pajamas torn to pieces, his hands and feet bound. Bruises and scratches covered his face and neck. A strand of tape covered his mouth. The coroner stated that the con man's death was due to asphyxiation. Police could discover nothing of value missing from Rubinstein's house. Though a massive hunt was made for the killer, police came up empty-handed. The Rubinstein murder ranks with the Rothstein case [see entry] as an utterly baffling New York mystery.

St. Albans, Vermont
BANK ROBBERIES, 1864   U.S.

On October 18, 1864, twenty-two men converged upon the small and prosperous town of St. Albans, Vermont, near the Canadian border. They gathered in the town square at about 3 PM and then half of them ran into the three banks fronting the square while others held startled citizens at bay with drawn guns. In about ten minutes the robbers had gathered up all the cash and gold in the town's three banks and left, thundering out of St. Albans on fast horses. They headed for the Canadian border.

Of the invading force, fourteen men were later captured in Canada. None of them were the leaders of the raid. Though the men admitted they were Confederate soldiers, they refused to name the officers who had led them in the bank robberies. A small amount of money taken in the raid was found on the captured soldiers, but the bulk of the loot, which was intended to replenish the dwindling coffers of the Confederacy in Richmond, was never found, an estimated $114,522.

The St. Albans raid was the first of a series of bank robberies planned in New England by Confederates dressed as civilians. The leaders of the raid were never identified, but the loot was said to have been buried close to Lake Champlain on the Vermont side of the border. A $10,000 reward put up by the St. Albans banks for the recovery of the stolen money and gold went unpaid.

Sands, Gulielma Elmore
MURDER, 1799   U.S.

Twenty-two-year-old Gulielma Elmore Sands, called Elma by her friends and relatives, disappeared on December 22, 1799. Her body was found ten days later at the bottom of a well in Lispenard's Meadow, in Greenwich Village. The Elma Sands case became the first great murder mystery in New York history and has remained a baffling unsolved killing for almost two centuries.

Elma Sands had migrated from New Cornwall, England, to live with her cousins Elias and Catherine Ring, stern Quakers who lived on Greenwich Street not far from the Hudson River. Along with her younger sister Hope, Elma helped the Rings manage their small boardinghouse, cleaning rooms and preparing meals. Two of the paying guests in the house were Levi Weeks, whose uncle was a rich carpenter, and Richard David Croucher, who had just arrived from England.

Croucher made several attempts to woo the pretty Elma, but the young woman spurned his advances. Levi Weeks, the richest young man in the house, first courted another boarder, one Margaret Clark, but she moved away and Weeks turned his attention to Miss Hope Sands. Weeks later lost interest in Hope and began to ask Elma to take walks with him. At first Elma refused, then she seemed to give in quickly to the quiet demands of the dashing Levi Weeks. She went walking with him, and, after Mrs. Ring moved upstate for six weeks to escape a mild outbreak of yellow fever, met with her fellow boarder behind the locked door of her bedroom, quite a scandalous bit of behavior in that strict era.

The clandestine meetings were recorded by most in the Ring household and by fellow roomers like Richard Croucher, whose room was directly across from Elma's, and who placed his bed in the center of his room and left his door open, thereby having a spotlight view of her comings and goings and those of Weeks. Croucher later encountered Elma in the hallway on the second floor near the stairs and murmured some uncomplimentary remark.

Elma let out a loud "Oh!" which brought the chivalrous Weeks racing from his room.

"What's the matter?" he asked his sweetheart.

"Mr. Croucher has insulted me," said Elma Sands, appearing to recover from a mild faint. "And it's not the first time either."

"You had better watch your step," Weeks warned Croucher with a wagging finger.

Croucher gave him his best British sneer before snorting: "You impertinent puppy!" and walking disdainfully into his room, where he closed the door, a rare action on his part in those days.

On the cold and wintry night of December 22, 1799, with George Washington dead six days earlier, Elma Sands left the Ring home and its warm firesides shortly before 8 PM. Several roomers thought they saw Weeks leave with her, but Levi was seen to take a seat in the living room shortly after 8 PM. When Mrs. Ring went upstairs— she had recently returned from upstate New York—she thought she heard someone whispering on the stairs and someone go out the front door. She hurried downstairs and peered out into the night air, sprinkled with lightly falling snow. She recognized no one, especially not Elma Sands and Levi Weeks; it had been rumored that they would run off to be married that night. Mrs. Ring went to the living room. At 10 PM Levi Weeks came in and sat down in silence. He appeared "pale and agitated," according to Mrs. Ring when she later talked to authorities, but this description was undoubtedly clouded with hindsight suspicions.

215

Weeks broke the silence by asking: "Has Hope got home?"

"She has not," answered Mrs. Ring.

"Is Elma gone to bed?"

Mrs. Ring was puzzled at this question, thinking Elma had gone out with Weeks. She finally replied: "She has gone out."

Now Weeks expressed some alarm. "It's strange for her to have stepped out alone at so late an hour."

"I have no reason to think she went alone," answered Mrs. Ring, her implication meaning that she thought Weeks had accompanied her and was now being coy. Weeks then got up and went to bed. Mrs. Ring, slightly amazed by his actions, stayed up past midnight waiting for Elma to return. She finally went to bed after seeing that Elma was not in her bedroom. Mrs. Ring was too tired to send out the alarm, and perhaps too embarrassed. Quaker girls simply did not stay out to such ungodly hours.

Levi Weeks returned home early the following afternoon, interrupting his work to ask if Elma Sands had returned home. He was told she had not returned. At first Mrs. Ring thought the young woman had gone to visit friends, but she dropped this notion after not hearing from Elma for three days. She began to question Levi as to Elma's whereabouts. He could offer no explanation. He insisted that he had not left the Ring house with Elma on Sunday, the twenty-second, but had stepped out briefly to visit his wealthy uncle, who was also his employer, for a short business meeting.

On December 24, some boys playing on Lispenard's Meadow found Elma's muff under some snow. This item was not taken to the Ring household. By January 2, 1800, Elias Ring had alarmed friends and watchmen and was conducting a neighborhood search for the missing Elma. He approached a boarded-up well in Lispenard's Meadow, owned by none other than Aaron Burr, who had sunk the well as part of an abortive scheme to control New York's water supply. The well had failed to yield any water and had been covered up.

Elias Ring uncovered the well and probed the ice-caked waters below with a long pole and hook. He snagged the body of Elma Sands. There were ugly marks about her neck, but physicians later inspecting her could not determine whether she had been strangled or merely drowned.

The frozen body of Elma Sands was placed on display for all those morbidly fascinated with corpses. The city of New York then boasted a population of no more than 50,000, but fully one-quarter of its residents turned out to file past the body of Elma Sands, more than had appeared three weeks earlier in public ceremonies to mark the passing of the father of his country.

Physicians at first suggested that Elma had committed suicide, but the Rings and her friends quickly pointed out that she had been a happy, well-balanced young lady. No, self-destruction was out of the question. Next came the darker supposition—murder. Suspicion immediately fell on Levi Weeks, and he was arrested and held for trial on a charge of murdering the pretty Quaker woman whom he claimed had been the blood of his heart.

Though little evidence could be found to convict Weeks, a bevy of witnesses came forward to implicate him in the murder. On the night Elma Sands disappeared she was reportedly seen by one Margaret Freeman traveling in a sleigh with two men and another woman. This sleigh, said Buthron Anderson, looked like the one owned by the wealthy Ezra Weeks, Levi's uncle. Susanna Bread, a neighbor of the uncle's said that the Weeks sleigh left the stable at 8 PM that night.

Living near the well where Elma was later found, Lawrence and Arnetta Van Norden claimed that, on the snowy night of December 22, 1799, they heard a woman's cry of "Murder!" Van Norden threw open his door to peer into the night, he testified, but saw nothing. One of Van Norden's neighbors, Catherine Lyon, also said she heard the cry, and when she looked outside she saw a woman who looked like Elma near the well.

Beyond the courtroom, the most active gossip was none other than Richard Croucher, the man who had been rejected by Elma for the affections of Levi Weeks. All he talked about was the murder. He had had dreams, said Croucher, in which he had seen ghosts hovering about the well and accusing Levi of murdering lovely Elma. He ordered handbills printed in which he claimed that Weeks was keeping silent on the matter because of his guilt.

Weeks's trial began on March 31, 1800, and it was a sensation, chiefly because of the accused's famous counsels. Rich Uncle Ezra had bought the best legal minds in the country to defend his nephew—Alexander Hamilton and Aaron Burr. Hamilton had recently left the post of secretary of the treasury and was considered one of America's greatest statesmen and patriots. [The two men, ironically, would meet in a duel four years later in Weehawken, both with secret hair triggers on their pistols, and Hamilton would fall with a fatal wound. Burr, the victor, would die in disgrace and exile, his dreams of empire vanquishing him in the end.] The third lawyer to make up the battery defending the accused was Henry Brockholst Livingston, no less a light than Hamilton and Burr. Livingston would later become a member of the U.S. Supreme Court.

Weeks's trial was held in the largest courtroom of City Hall at Nassau and Wall streets to capacitate the overflow crowds. The presiding judge was John Lansing, who was to disappear mysteriously on the evening of December 12, 1829, en route to the Albany night boat from the City Hotel.

Seventy-five witnesses testified in the three-day trial, which twice dragged on late into the night so that candles had to be lit to illuminate the courtroom. Livingston, Hamilton, and Burr took turns questioning the witnesses, breaking down their stories. All of them were a bit confused as to having seen Elma Sands the night she disappeared. A telling witness for the defense was Demas Meed, who ran the stable where Ezra Weeks's sleigh was kept. He emphatically stated that the sleigh did not leave the stable on December 22.

One story later emanating from this dawn-to-dawn trial, a canard really, had Aaron Burr, in one of his stiff addresses to the jury deep in the first night of the trial, suddenly wheel about, grab a candelabrum, and thrust it forward into the first row of spectators so that its candlelight glimmered on the startled face of Richard Croucher, who had so ardently agitated for Weeks's conviction. With a nod to the jury, Burr allegedly stated, "Gentlemen, behold the murderer!" With that, Croucher supposedly jumped up and ran from the courtroom, his hysterical cries echoing after him. There is no truth to this story, other than a courtroom attendant's having held up a candelabrum to Croucher's face, along with others', to identify spectators taking their seats after a brief recess. One of Burr's biographers, James Parton, later incorporated the story to heighten the drama of his prose.

Mrs. Ring's testimony was vital to the defense. The woman, though she continued to suspect Weeks throughout her life, fairly stated that she had never seen Elma and Levi leave her boardinghouse on the night in question. No one had seen them together.

After hearing all that could be said in the case, Judge Lansing firmly addressed the jury, uncompromisingly telling its members that the evidence brought against Weeks was so thin as to be dismissed out of hand. Without leaving the courtroom, the jurors whispered among themselves for about five minutes, then returned a verdict of "not guilty."

The unsolved murder would cause endless debate for years to come. Many felt that the real culprit was Richard Croucher, who had so enthusiastically lobbied for Weeks's conviction. He hated Levi for stealing the attentions of Elma and despised the young woman for spurning his affection for her. But there was no possible way to build a case against him. Croucher was later convicted of raping a young woman named Margaret Miller and sent to prison for life. Paroled, he moved to Virginia, where he was indicted for fraud. Before he could be tried, Croucher slipped aboard a merchant vessel and left for England, where he was reportedly hanged for committing a capital offense.

Weeks, though exonerated, lived with a permanent cloud of suspicion. His life was miserable, and everywhere he went citizens whispered his guilt in the murder of Elma Sands. He finally left New York for the West and disappeared.

Mrs. Ring was one of those firmly convinced until her dying day that Levi Weeks had murdered her pretty cousin. Her anger for the powerful lawyers who had won the defendant's acquittal was seething. She particularly singled out Alexander Hamilton upon whom to vent her wrath. When Hamilton was leaving the courtroom, he passed Mrs. Ring in the foyer of City Hall. He was riveted for a moment by her hate-filled gaze.

"Yes, madam?" he asked of her.

"If thee dies a natural death," hissed Mrs. Ring, "then there is no justice in Heaven."

The visionary Hamilton, who predicted that America would grow to become the world's leading industrial giant, merely smiled at Mrs. Ring's venomous comment, walking out without retorting. Many remembered Mrs. Ring's acid remark four years later when Hamilton died at the hands of his onetime co-counsel, Aaron Burr, a very unnatural death indeed.

Savoy Hotel Slaying
MURDER, 1980 ENGLAND

The mystery of the murder occurring in London's swanky Savoy Hotel on Wednesday, October 1, 1980, continues to stump detectives from Scotland Yard. Piercing screams were heard coming from Room 853 of the five-star hotel on Wednesday evening, and when hotel employees rushed into the room they found a woman half naked and bleeding to death. She never regained consciousness after being stabbed ten times. The woman, never identified, was thought to be a prostitute who had been taken to the room by a man who had checked into the Savoy that day, a man never located.

A man wearing a black leather coat and black trousers was seen running from the hotel shortly after the screams were heard. It was not known whether or not he was the man who had occupied Room 853. He, too, was never found by police.

A knife found in Room 853 was believed to have been the murder weapon, but Scotland Yard never revealed if the knife yielded any identifying fingerprints. To the time of this writing, no suspects in the killing have been arrested.

Staff personnel at the Savoy went unperturbed by the killing, careful to shield the high-paying guests from the crime, these being mostly rich Americans. One stylish American visitor sitting down to breakfast the next morning was told of the killing. Said she, with arched eyebrows of surprise: "I really didn't know anything about this. But then you wouldn't at the Savoy. They are very discreet."

Schuessler, Anton and John, and Robert Peterson
MURDERS, 1955 U.S.

The so-called Chicago Child Murders began with the slaying of John Schuessler, thirteen, his brother Anton, eleven, and their friend Robert Peterson, fourteen, in 1955. The three Northwest-side youths left a bowling alley in the early evening of October 16 and were never seen alive again. Their bodies—naked, beaten, and strangled like the Grimes sisters' after them [see entry]—were found two days later. They had been tossed into a ditch in the Robinson Woods Forest Preserve near Lawrence Avenue and the DesPlaines River.

Chicago was horrified at the brutal slayings, performed undoubtedly by a sex killer

219

Schuessler, Anton and John, and Robert Peterson

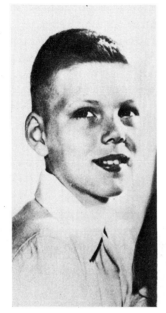

Three Chicago murder victims of the 1955 terror slayings of teenagers (left to right)—Robert Peterson and John Schuessler and his brother Anton. (*Wide World*)

who preyed upon children. Half the detectives in the city spent every waking hour for several months tracking down the slightest clue, and these were all nonexistent, in their search for the killer. More than forty persons confessed to the Schuessler-Peterson murders, but they all proved to be crackpots or publicity seekers.

The bodies of the boys were exhumed and rechecked for wounds some of the phony claimants to the killings described, along with the possibility of unusual sexual assault, but nothing came of this second medical examination. Informants turned in suspects by the scores and many of these leads were checked as far as New York and Los Angeles, but no positive suspects were arrested. As in the Grimes and Judith Anderson [see entries] cases which followed the Schuessler murders, the killer was never apprehended. It has been suggested that the same killer murdered the Schuessler-Peterson boys, Judith Anderson, and the Grimes sisters, but this is mere conjecture by the police and public alike, eager to envision a diabolical mastermind whose intellectual and physical superiority to his pursuers allowed him to escape again and again, much like Jack the Ripper [see entry].

Sheriff, Emma
MURDER, 1908 ENGLAND

In the afternoon of February 19, 1908, John Francis McGuire, a young soldier recently mustered out of service who had become a picture dealer, walked into a police station at Boscombe, England, to report his fiancée missing. The woman, Emma Sheriff, had been a lady's maid and was living in Boscombe in semiretirement. McGuire, only twenty-one, explained that he had been going with Sheriff for three years on and off during his tour of duty. He did not then explain that his fiancée was fifteen years his senior.

McGuire told police that he had sent Sheriff a telegram that morning, informing her that he would arrive that afternoon. She was not at home when he went to her house after coming by train from London, nor had she apparently slept in her bed. Police began an immediate search for the woman.

The following day, February 20, constables spotted a trail of imitation pearls on the cliff path at Southborne. They followed the pearls to a spot down on the cliffs where Emma Sheriff's body lay crumpled. Described as a "frail, nervous little woman," she had been thrown to her death and had hemorrhaged, according to police. They soon found nearby residents who claimed to have seen McGuire walking with the woman near the cliffs. The apprentice picture dealer was arrested and held for trial, which began in May 1909.

McGuire staunchly insisted that he was innocent, that the Southbourne citizens had mistaken him for someone else. He had been in London when his fiancée was killed. Not so, countered the prosecution. McGuire had traveled from London to Boscombe on the eighteenth, not the nineteenth as he claimed, desperate to borrow money from his sweetheart. Prosecutors claimed that when she refused to make a loan as they walked along the cliff path, McGuire attacked her savagely and threw her down the cliff. He then returned to London on the 8:50 PM train from Christchurch. To allay suspicions against himself, he then pretended to visit the woman on the nineteenth, knowing she was already dead. McGuire murdered Emma Sheriff, thundered the prosecutor, in order to rob her of some jewels and cash.

McGuire kept on insisting that witnesses placing him at the murder scene were confusing him with another person. The jury was also confused and could not come to a verdict; its members were dismissed. The accused was kept in prison to await a second trial but the crown, a month later, entered a plea of nolle prosequi, meaning that it was unwilling to prosecute further, undoubtedly due to lack of evidence against McGuire.

The young swain, still sorrowfully telling reporters how much he missed his Emma, was released. The murder of his fiancée was never solved.

Shore, Florence Nightingale
MURDER, 1920 ENGLAND

On the evening of January 12, 1920, some workers boarded the London-Hastings train at Polegate. They noticed a woman, her hat pulled low over her face, who was sitting in an odd position; she seemed as if she was about to slide forward onto the floor. One of the workmen walked to her seat and found the woman's glasses smashed on the floor. He lifted her hat to see that she had suffered horrible head injuries.

Taken from the train unconscious, the victim was identified as Florence Nightingale Shore, a nurse like her namesake, who had been traveling to St. Leonards to visit friends. Within four days, Miss Shore died without uttering a word. Her skull had been crushed, it was speculated, by the butt of a pistol.

No one had been seen with the woman on the train, and her murder remains one of the most mystifying in the annals of British crime.

Siegel, Benjamin "Bugsy"
SYNDICATE KILLING, 1947 U.S.

The most flamboyant and dapper killer of the U.S. crime syndicate in the 1930s–1940s was undoubtedly Benjamin "Bugsy" Siegel, who was sent by board members of the crime cartel, chiefly Meyer Lansky, to the West Coast in 1937 to develop syndicate rackets. The selection of Siegel was an obvious one. Although he had been personally responsible for a dozen murders in New York, where his criminal record began in 1921 for robbery at age fifteen, Siegel was an outgoing gangster who liked to mingle with show business personalities. His early-day partner, Lansky, who headed the Bug and Meyer mob which made millions in bootlegging and smuggling during Prohibition, was a shadowy figure who preferred a low-key profile. Bugsy—so named because of his reckless manner of dispatching gangland rivals—was a limelighter and would fit well into the flashy Hollywood life-style.

Siegel worked with Jack Dragna on the West Coast to develop drug smuggling from Mexico into the U.S. Further, he consolidated California gambling so that the six most western states came under his control. Siegel saw gambling as the greatest source of revenue for the syndicate and, to develop its potential, moved into Las Vegas in 1945, where he began to build the Flamingo Hotel and Casino. At the time Las Vegas was nothing more than a way stop in the desert; Reno was then the capital of Nevada gambling. Siegel, however, realized that Las Vegas's proximity to Los Angeles would make it the greatest center for gambling in the nation, and he single-handedly made the town into exactly that.

The cost of building the Flamingo soared into the millions. Siegel saw the establishment as a monument to his own inventive genius, but those sitting on the crime cartel board in the East, especially Charles "Lucky" Luciano, whose power was vast despite the fact that he had been deported to his native Italy following World War II, felt that Bugsy was squandering syndicate funds. He was warned that if the casino was not a success, he would have to face board punishment.

A hothead, Siegel ignored the warnings and went on lavishly spending to make the Flamingo one of the world's great pleasure spas, with deluxe rooms, pools, and decorations that alone ran into the millions. When he opened the casino, expecting hordes of Hollywood friends and associates to attend, he was met with woefully thin crowds. Most of the Hollywood celebrities had been warned by movie executives not to attend the opening, to deny Siegel the publicity that might be generated by their attendance. Some of the moguls actually threatened their stars with suspension if they dared to "support that hoodlum."

The enterprise was a disaster; Siegel had dumped $6 million of syndicate funds into what appeared to be a white elephant. Though some of his friends, such as George Raft, frequented the Flamingo, the bulk of Hollywood personalities invited to the casino—Siegel had chartered special planes to fly them in from Los Angeles—treated him as if he were a plague victim.

Luciano and others began to pressure Siegel for a return on their enormous investment. Typically, Bugsy not only ignored them but refused to give the syndicate chieftains in New York and Chicago an accounting of his expenditures. Meyer Lansky, Siegel's longtime

Dapper gangster Benjamin "Bugsy" Siegel, who opened up the West Coast for the crime syndicate in the late 1930s.

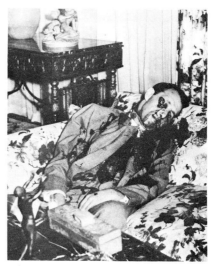

The end of Bugsy Siegel, June 20, 1947, shot by killers unknown.

Bugsy's girl friend Virginia Hill, a bag lady for the mob, who some said knew about his murder in advance.

mentor, called repeatedly to caution Bugsy to treat the matter seriously and to tell him that he was in deep trouble. Siegel's sneering retort was: "Aww, them Sicilians are always carping about their money. They can go to hell!" The remark made its way to Luciano and syndicate sachems in Chicago who resented such ethnic slurs to the point of murder. Such remarks had guaranteed the death of Chicago bootlegger Charles Dion O'Bannion [see entry] in 1924. It was obvious to the crime cartel that Siegel was out of hand and could not be controlled. He had turned maverick and an order, perhaps emanating from Luciano, was sent out to have him eliminated.

Siegel, in the spring of 1947, was then living in both Las Vegas at the Flamingo and in the $500,000 home of his girl friend, Virginia Hill, on Linden Drive in Beverly Hills, commuting every few days between the two cities. Bugsy had been going with Virginia since the late 1930s—she later said they had been secretly married in Mexico—and he adored the fiery redhead from Alabama. He had even named his casino after her, Flamingo being Virginia's nickname.

On the evening of June 20, 1947, Bugsy went to stay in Virginia's lavish Beverly Hills home. His tempestuous sweetheart was then away on a European vacation; her absence later gave rise to the suspicion that she knew her uncontrollable lover was about to be killed on syndicate orders. As he sat reading the newspaper, the glass of a window behind him was shattered and an assassin fired three rounds from a .30-30 rifle into Siegel's body, one of the bullets slamming into his head and ripping out an eye. He died instantly.

Though West Coast police conducted a massive hunt for the killer, no one was ever placed under arrest for the murder. To be sure, someone in the underworld slew the colorful Bugsy in keeping with Siegel's credo, once uttered to Del Webb, the building contractor who built the Flamingo. Webb had been worried about his connection with the notorious gangster, but Bugsy merely patted the builder's shoulder and snorted with a grin: "Don't worry—we only kill each other!"

Bugsy's friend and mentor, Meyer Lansky, who warned him that his Las Vegas ambitions would lead to trouble.

Smith, James
MURDER, 1935 AUSTRALIA

One of Australia's most bizarre, if not downright oddball, murder cases involved one James Smith, a roustabout handyman turned smuggler. Smith, who had worked as an engineer, day laborer, and a poolhall billiard racker in Sydney, Australia, disappeared on April 8, 1935, telling his wife that he was going on a fishing expedition with friends he did not name.

Ten days later spectators at a seaside aquarium in Coogee, a suburb of Sydney, watched fascinated as a vicious looking fourteen-foot tiger shark, recently taken from the ocean, swam beneath their gaze. Toward dusk the shark suddenly began to make frantic movements, wildly churning the waters until it vomited up the foul contents of its stomach. Among the debris floating to the top of the tank was a muscular human arm, the sight of which caused several women in the crowd to faint dead away.

Police physicians later inspecting the arm quickly determined that it belonged to a powerful male, but it had not been chewed off by the shark. The limb had been neatly severed, sliced away by a sharp instrument, which indicated that the arm belonged to a man who had been dismembered and his remains thrown into the ocean. That the man had been a captive was proved by a heavy piece of rope still tied firmly about his wrist.

Shark experts were at first baffled at the human arm being so well preserved but then learned that the shark had not eaten anything since its capture and that its digestive tract had ceased to operate because of shock. [Normally the shark's potent digestive juices would have broken down the arm within thirty-six hours.]

The hand was well-enough preserved so that fingerprints could be taken, and these matched those of James Smith, who had had a prison record. Further adding to the identification of the arm was a wild-looking tattoo of two boxers squaring off in a prize ring. Mrs. Smith identified the tattoo as having been on her husband's arm.

Divers from the Air Force aided police divers in a frantic search for the rest of Smith's body, but it was never found. Police did discover that Mr. Smith had been recently hired to act as a guard or operator of a speedy launch, *Pathfinder*, and that this boat had been running large quantities of opium from liners sailing from China. The *Pathfinder* was notorious in waters off Sydney as a drug smuggler. As the investigation into Smith's death deepened, police began to learn of the vast drug smuggling in the area. In fact, it was revealed that Sydney was the hub of Far East dope smuggling, being the first port of call for ships sailing from the Orient en route to the U.S.

Hundreds, if not thousands, of desperate unemployed men like Smith, suffering in Australia's Great Depression, would do anything to earn money, even smuggle drugs as Smith had been doing. The owner of the *Pathfinder*, Reginald Holmes, could give no explanation for Smith's death. His boat had recently been sunk, he said, and he knew nothing of how Smith, who worked for him, had met his grisly end. Holmes, it was later discovered, was deeply involved in drug smuggling. In fact, the enterprise had made him rich. When investigators returned to question Holmes a second time the wealthy boat builder told them that he and Smith had been blackmailed in the past by another boat builder, one Patrick Brady, a man who obviously knew that the *Pathfinder* was being used for drug smuggling.

Brady, witnesses said, had been seen with Smith on the day of his disappearance. Holmes would not support these statements directly, but privately he told his wife, Inie, that "Brady did it. . . . He put the body in a trunk, took it out in his

226

boat, and dumped it overboard." Inie Holmes later repeated this story to police, but by then her husband was dead and useless as a witness against Brady.

Holmes's theory of how Brady had disposed of Smith's body was supported by forensic specialists Bernard Spilsbury and Sydney Smith, who happened to be attending a scientific convention in Sydney at the time. These two British morgue sleuths conjectured the following: Brady killed Smith for one reason or another, perhaps because he would not pay the blackmail demanded, or as an example of what would happen to Holmes if *he* did not pay the blackmail. A tin trunk and a mattress were missing from Brady's cottage, and three heavy mats and a coil of rope were missing from his boat, according to police who searched both. Brady, said the theorists, took his victim to the boat, placed the body on the mattress and mats, and dismembered the corpse, jamming the remains into the tin trunk. The arm would not fit and was tied to the outside of the trunk, which was then sent over the side. The arm somehow broke loose and was swallowed by the passing shark that later wound up in the Coogee Aquarium.

All of this appeared logical to police, who began to prepare a case against Brady. Three days after the suspect was arrested, a strange report came in from the police boats in Sydney Harbor. A man in a speedboat had been skimming wildly about the harbor. A police launch gave chase, but the boat turned about abruptly and tried to ram the lawmen's boat again and again. A crazy zigzagging chase ensued which lasted for four hours. Finally the speedboat ran out of gas and the police launch came alongside to find the driver passed out on the seat. His entire face was covered with blood from a bullet wound in the forehead. It was Reginald Holmes.

The badly wounded Holmes was rushed to a hospital. He revived to tell officers that he had been shot as he was leaving his home and, to avoid the gunman, had jumped into his boat and sped off across the harbor. He mistook the police boat for one he thought was being operated by his pursuer and that is why he had tried to ram it. Holmes's story, fantastic as it appeared, was accepted, and after he recovered from his wound, he was allowed to return home. He would be the star witness against Brady at an inquest into Smith's death set for June 13, 1935.

Reginald Holmes never testified. He was found shot to death on the morning of the inquest, slumped over the wheel of his car, which had been run off a road leading to Harbor Bridge. The inquest commenced, but without Holmes no case against Brady could be sufficiently established. Those who had said they had seen Brady with Smith on the day of the dead man's disappearance changed their minds; they weren't sure. The visibility that day was poor. They had seen the two men from a great distance. Brady was released.

Two men were later arrested and charged with shooting Holmes, but no case against these would-be killers could be made and they, like Brady, were also released. Leads disappeared, witnesses vanished, and in the end the police were left with two completely unsolved macabre murders, Smith's later being dubbed the Shark Arm Murder by some inventive newspaper reporter in search of a provocative label. It is still called such in Australia today.

Starchfield, William
MURDER, 1914 ENGLAND

The body of eight-year-old Willie Starchfield was found stuffed beneath the seat of the Chalk Farm to Broad Street train at a little after 5 PM on January 8, 1914. A thin cord, still embedded in the boy's flesh, had been used to strangle him to death. When news of this murder was let out, the public became enraged because the boy's father, John Starchfield, had proved himself to be the hero of London fifteen months earlier.

Starchfield, a news vendor whose stand was outside the Horseshoe Hotel on London's Tottenham Court Road, had performed an incredible feat of courage in September 1912, apprehending Stephen Titus, an Armenian tailor who had gone berserk and shot to death Esther May Towers, the assistant manager of the Horseshoe Hotel. As Titus fled the hotel, still clutching the smoking pistol, Starchfield dropped his papers and raced after him, tackling the madman some blocks away. While subduing Titus, Starchfield

was himself shot several times. He managed, however, to hold on to the killer until constables arrived.

For this act of heroism, the British courts awarded Starchfield fifty pounds to compensate him for his wounds. He also received a small pension from the Carnegie Heroes Fund. (Titus, the man he apprehended, was sent to Broadmoor Criminal Lunatic Asylum for life, judged "guilty but insane.")

So it was with great wrath that the public received the news of little Willie Starchfield's brutal and inexplicable murder in 1914. Even more shocking, weeks later, was the announcement that the heroic father had been arrested for killing his own son. A coroner's jury looking into the murder of the Starchfield boy indicted the father on a charge of "willful murder," after hearing several persons testify that they had seen Willie with his father only a few hours before the boy's body was found.

Starchfield's trial was short-lived. It was claimed that he had strangled his son with a rope for arcane reasons and had then stuffed the body into a suitcase and taken it aboard the Broad Street train, where he removed the corpse and put it beneath a seat.

However, no one saw Starchfield on board the train or anywhere near the station. The coroner's jury witnesses, by the time they appeared at the trial, were uncertain as to whether Starchfield had been with his son. Hearing the case in the Old Bailey, Judge Atkin pointed out that there was no real evidence against Starchfield, and he severely criticized the coroner's jury for indicting the accused on mere speculation. Starchfield was released at the judge's order with apologies.

The bereaved father died of his wounds two years later.

Steele, Louisa Maud
MURDER, 1931 ENGLAND

A Lewisham house servant, Louisa Maud Steele, left the home of her employer, Miss Kathleen Andrews, on the night of January 23, 1931, to return a book and purchase some cough syrup at the local pharmacy. When she did not return home by 11 PM Miss Andrews called police. Constables were immediately sent out to search for the young woman but did not find her until the next morning. Her body was discovered in the Blackheath Woods. She was lying on her back with welts and bruises about her face, neck, and body, as if her killer had repeatedly kicked her. There appeared to be bite marks on her neck, which gave rise to wild rumors that the woman had been the victim of a "vampire killer."

The brilliant British forensic pathologist Bernard Spilsbury examined the body and then gave the following report at the inquest: "In my opinion the girl was attacked from behind and the neck of the dress was drawn forcibly backwards, while counterpressure was made on the back of the head and neck. . . . She would probably lose consciousness in a few seconds, so that she could offer no effectual resistance. Probably the pressure was released before death took place. . . . Most of the other injuries were inflicted during life."

The maniac who murdered Louisa Steele was never found.

Stewart, Alexander T.
BODY SNATCHING, 1876 U.S.

One of America's first great business tycoons, Alexander T. Stewart, was laid to rest in 1876. Stewart, who had emigrated from Ireland, opened his first dry goods store in New York in 1825, and before he died he had built colossal department stores at Broadway and Chambers and at Broadway and 9th Street. (These stores were later absorbed into the Wanamaker chain.) A miserly penny-pincher, Stewart spent little on himself, preferring a limited wardrobe and a burgeoning bank account. It was no surprise then when relatives were informed that Stewart had left a gigantic fortune of between $30 million and $40 million.

Stewart's relatives, shortly after the tycoon's death, had been informed that grave robbers might attempt to steal the body. Armed guards were stationed at the St. Mark's-in-the-Bouwerie graveyard where the body was buried, but after a month without incident these men were removed. Three weeks later, on the morning of November 17, 1876, church authorities found that the Stewart tomb

The burial of New York department store tycoon Alexander T. Stewart in 1876; his body was stolen a short time later and held for $20,000 ransom, which was paid to culprits who were never found.

74

had been invaded and the expensive casket containing the remains of the merchant prince had been stolen.

Great publicity attended the theft, one that shocked the public and incensed Stewart's relatives, who immediately offered a $25,000 reward to anyone who would help recover the body. Not until January 1877 was there a response, a letter sent to the Stewart family lawyer. It demanded $200,000 for the return of the body, and it was signed by one "Henry G. Romaine," apparently an alias.

Intermediaries for the family, after exhaustive negotiations, finally met with "Romaine" and others who were wearing masks and exchanged $20,000 for a sack of bones. The body snatchers proved the remains to be Stewart's by also turning over the silver handles made specially for the tycoon's casket.

To ensure the fact that the remains would never again be disturbed, the Stewart family reburied the bones in a special crypt in the Garden City Cathedral, equipped with an intricate alarm system. Over the years it was speculated that the body snatching had been engineered by the king of bank robbers in the nineteenth century, George Leonidas Leslie, but this was never proved. The man calling himself Henry G. Romaine was never identified.

Storrs, George Henry
MURDER, 1909 ENGLAND

One of England's classic mysteries in the Edwardian era, the brutal murder of George Henry Storrs, a prominent and prosperous mill owner, remains as inexplicable today as when it occurred on the night of November 1, 1909. Early in that evening Storrs was playing solitaire as his wife and a niece, Marion Lindley, busied themselves with sewing in the dining room of their home, Gorse Hall, in Cheshire. About nine thirty, Mary Evans, the family cook, was coming up from the cellar when she saw a man lurking behind the kitchen door. He wheeled about and pointed a revolver at her. "If you make a single sound, I'll shoot you," warned the intruder.

The cook ignored the threat and raced into the living room, screaming the alarm. Right behind her rushed the intruder. He spotted Storrs and leaped upon him. The mill owner, a heavyset, towering man of forty-nine who was in excellent physical condition, fought the man to a standstill. Mrs. Storrs grabbed a walking stick and began beating the assailant on the head. The intruder suddenly jumped back and begged: "Please don't strike me again." With that he handed Mrs. Storrs the revolver.

"Go upstairs and ring the alarm bell," Storrs told his wife as he backed the subdued intruder into a corner. Mrs. Storrs went to an upstairs bedroom, shoving the revolver beneath a carpet and ringing the bell to summon police. Marion Lindley, Mary Evans, and a maid, Ellen Cooper, had all dashed from the house when the fight started to find a police constable.

Before Mrs. Storrs returned to the main floor, the intruder—a blond-haired man of slight build with a thin mustache— waited until Storrs turned his back momentarily. At that split second the smaller man quickly produced a long, thin knife and drove it repeatedly into Storr's back. Though mortally wounded, the mill owner grappled with the man and, by sheer brute force, managed to drag the attacker down a hall and shove him into a kitchen pantry, which he locked just before collapsing into a pool of his own blood.

As the niece hurried back to Gorse Hall with a constable and the cook and maid, the crashing of glass could be heard. This was the intruder breaking the pantry window with a wash basin. By the time the constable entered the house the strange attacker had fled. George Storrs lingered for twenty minutes, fully conscious and stating again and again that he did not know who his assailant was; then he died of the multiple stab wounds in his back.

The bold killing shocked the entire north of England, where Storrs was widely known and respected. In fact, he had no known enemies and was well liked by his employees and business associates. Hundreds of men in their mid-twenties, the age of the killer as estimated by members of the Storrs household, were questioned, but no suspects were booked. Then sixteen days after the murder, thirty-one-year-old Cornelius Howard, onetime butcher and a distant cousin to the victim, was arrested and charged with murder. He had, when arrested, been found with a pair of bloodstained socks in his pocket. His coat and pants were spotted with blood and he had a razor-sharp knife.

Howard insisted that he had been severely cut when some glass had fallen on him in his boardinghouse in Huddersfield. Some time later he changed his story, saying that he had cut himself during a burglary he committed in Stalybridge. The suspect was put in a lineup and identified as the killer by the niece, the cook, and the maid. Mrs. Storrs had some difficulty in identifying Howard and was asked to move close to the man. Staring Howard in the face, Mrs. Storrs said to police officers: "I think he is the man. He knows."

Even with such overwhelming identification, Howard was able to convince a jury that he was innocent. He had been playing dominoes, he flatly stated, in the Ring O'Bells public house in Huddersfield at the time of the murder. Many customers from the pub supported Howard's statement, and he was found not guilty.

Six months later another man, Mark Wilde, a onetime army private, was arrested and charged with murdering George Storrs. This man faced trial almost wholly on the testimony of one of his former army friends who had served with him at Malta and had emphatically stated that the revolver Mrs. Storrs took from the intruder belonged to Wilde, identifying the weapon by marks on the butt and a defective safety switch.

Again the Storrs household were brought forward in the new trial and each identified the man as being the true killer of Storrs, but their earlier identification of Howard worked against their statements. Moreover, Wilde had been found covered with blood on the night of the Storrs murder but accredited this to a terrific fistfight he had had with another Stalybridge man. The fight was verified by witnesses. Wilde was acquitted, and the Gorse Hall murder remained a perplexing mystery.

T

Taylor, William Desmond
MURDER, 1922 U.S.

Hollywood's most infamous unsolved murder, barring the results of the investigation into Marilyn Monroe's death at this writing, was certainly the killing of William Desmond Taylor, the urbane, intellectual, and decidedly lecherous film director, on the night of February 1–2, 1922. As the investigation into Taylor's death proceeded, a torrent of scandal was unleashed that collapsed the careers of two of moviedom's greatest silent screen stars and gave the public a gaping view of Hollywood as a roaring real-life Sodom and Gomorrah.

William Desmond Taylor, a tall director with a rugged jaw and piercing eyes, had a crisp British accent and an eye for pulchritudinous stars. In his heyday he was known in Hollywood's inner circles as a man of indefatigable sexual stamina, whose marathon bedroom performances, sometimes with several women each night, were legendary.

Yet the director's past was uncertain even in the minds of his closest intimates. Taylor had mysteriously appeared in Hol-lywood during its embryonic stages, becoming a bit player in the early 1910s. His charming manners and striking face and form soon earned him attention, and he was given large roles, then leading parts. Charles Eyton, general manager of Famous Players–Lasky, a subsidiary studio of Paramount, and Paramount's chief, Adolph Zukor, thought Taylor's directorial abilities were so exceptional that by 1922 he became chief director of Famous Players–Lasky, earning between $40,000 and $50,000 a year, plus bonuses and sweeping expense accounts, a great income for those days when income tax accounted for no more than 4 percent of his annual salary.

The two-story Spanish-style stucco house in which Taylor lived at 404-B South Alvarado Street, now occupied by a business complex, was part of a court consisting of eight houses just east of Hollywood's limits and a stone's throw from Wilshire Boulevard. The other houses were occupied by film people, one of them being Edna Purviance, the leading lady in many Charlie Chaplin films. Unlike most homes owned by Hollywood's stars and moguls, Taylor's house was a model of

William Desmond Taylor as an actor in the early silent era of Hollywood.

cultured tastes, reflecting a well-bred man who appreciated literature and fine art.

Where other homes were decorated with garish and sexually suggestive paintings and tiger and bear skins, the heads of these ferocious animals stuffed, mouths open to bare gleaming fangs, Taylor's home boasted a fine library of thousands of the classics. On his walls hung exquisite prints and a few original paintings by minor masters. The director, by all standards of the day, was a cultivated and refined individual whose life-style, despite his private hedonistic practices, was in sharp contrast to the blatant and gaudy society in which he lived.

Many of Hollywood's greatest female film stars had taken nocturnal tours of Taylor's home—some even bragged of their visits. Though it was known that the great Mack Sennett comedienne Mabel Normand was deeply involved with Taylor, there were others who would be exposed as his lovers following his weird murder, including the fabulous ingenue Mary Miles Minter, who was appearing in films in direct competition with Mary Pickford. Miss Minter, who looked fifteen but who was actually thirty years old in 1922 (though she said she was twenty), had been secretly carrying on an affair with the inexhaustible Taylor, then forty-five.

Mabel Normand received a call from Taylor shortly before 6 PM on February 1, 1922. The director informed the film star that he had two books he wanted her to read and asked her to drop by for them that night. She said she'd pick them up personally within the hour. Normand had her chauffeur, William Davis, drive her to Taylor's home at 6:45 PM.

Henry Peavey, Taylor's butler, a man with a soprano voice and quirkish effeminate habits, answered the door and showed the star inside. She sat in the living room while Taylor talked on the phone to someone. Normand later told police that the director sounded angry during the phone conversation. When he realized that she had arrived, he hung up and joined her, asking Peavey to fix cocktails for them. "You'll stay for dinner, of course," Taylor said.

"No, darling," replied Normand. "I told Davis to keep the motor running. I'm tired and I want to go home."

The director said he understood and retrieved the two books for Normand, one being a biography of Sigmund Freud, the other a work by Nietzsche. He wanted to outline the works briefly for Normand, which had been his routine in their two-year Pygmalion-like association. As she listened attentively for some minutes, cracking peanuts and throwing the shells on the floor, Peavey made the drinks and served them, clucking his tongue disapprovingly at the shells littering the expensive carpet.

"Do you wish me to stay?" Peavey asked his employer.

"No, you may go home," Taylor told him. Peavey first put out a cold dinner for Taylor in the dining room, then left at 7:15 PM. Mabel Normand was still talking to Taylor at that time. The director had stopped discussing the books he had

Mabel Normand, who was one of the most popular comediennes in silent films, found her career a shambles after Taylor's unsolved murder.

235

loaned the star and pointed to his nearby desk, which was littered with bills, receipts, and canceled checks; he explained that he had been working on his income taxes, but that he found the task all but impossible because of the skulduggery committed by a former valet-butler, Edward F. Sands, who had been with Taylor for a number of years before disappearing in late 1921. Sands had run amok after Taylor had gone on a European vacation. The valet had stolen some of the director's jewelry and pawned these gems. He had also driven Taylor's two cars about and had damaged them in accidents. Worse, Sands had run up enormous bills on the director's charge accounts, and forged a number of checks before disappearing with a good portion of Taylor's wardrobe just days before Taylor returned from Europe.

Two burglaries had occurred at Taylor's home after his return, and he suspected the errant valet of being the culprit. More checks forged with the director's signature continued to flow in after being cashed in heavy amounts.

"That contemptible Sands has almost undone me," complained Taylor to Normand, as he pointed to the checks on his desk. "Nearly every one of those checks is forged. He did such a good job that I can't tell which are my signatures and which are his. I've been going over them all day, and it's driving me mad."

"What are you going to do about him?" she asked.

"I'll do plenty if they ever find Sands," Taylor replied in a low voice.

At 7:45 PM Taylor walked Normand to her waiting limousine, the chauffeur Davis jumping out to open the door for her. Through the open car window the director handed Miss Normand the two books. The film star gave him a fond peck on the cheek before she was driven off. Mrs. Faith Cole McLean, who lived in another house at the court with her husband, actor Douglas McLean, watched the leave-taking and saw Taylor return to his house. About a half hour later, at 8:15 PM, Douglas McLean and some of the other residents living in the court heard what sounded like a car backfiring, but they did not investigate; later they said the sound was more like a shot. Faith McLean did look out the window briefly and saw a man leaving Taylor's residence. The description of this individual, later given to the police, heightened the mystery of Taylor's murder, to say the least.

Reported Mrs. McLean: "I wasn't sure then that it was a shot at all, but I distinctly heard an explosion. Then I glanced out of my window and I saw a man leaving the house and going down the walk. I suppose it was a man. It was dressed like a man, but, you know, funny-looking. It was dressed in a heavy coat with a muffler around the chin and a cap pulled down over the eyes. But it walked like a woman—quick little steps and broad hips and short legs."

Some hours after the explosive sound was heard, Edna Purviance, whose house in the court was nearby, saw lights burning in Taylor's home and went to the director's door, knocking. There was no answer and the film star quickly concluded that Taylor was entertaining another female guest; the many ladies, most of them heavily veiled, regularly visiting Taylor, had been noted by the director's neighbors, so it was not unusual that he did not answer his door during evening hours.

Taylor's chauffeur, Howard Fellows, also arrived at the director's home after getting no answer on the phone. He knocked, but Taylor did not come to the door. This, too, was usual procedure for the philandering director. On such occasions Fellows had been instructed merely to leave Taylor's touring car in its parking place and go home, and the chauffeur did so.

At seven thirty the following morning Henry Peavey arrived at Taylor's home; the butler lived out. He collected a milk bottle and, using his key, opened the back door. He began to prepare the director's breakfast. Some minutes later Peavey walked into the living room and saw his employer lying on the floor next to his desk, a chair turned over on his legs. Taylor was fully dressed, his arms by his sides, his legs close together. (Someone later described Taylor in this position as if he were "lying at attention.")

Peavey took a closer look and saw that a small trickle of dark blood had hardened about the director's mouth. Taylor was not breathing. The valet then bolted for the door, running outside and screaming in his soprano voice: "Massa Taylor's dead! Massa Taylor's dead!" (as one Los Angeles newspaper quoted his frantic alarm). Peavey went completely berserk, screeching out the news of Taylor's death as he twitched and leaped along Alvarado Boulevard. His cries brought residents in the court on the run, including Douglas McLean and Edna Purviance.

McLean stopped a doctor he knew who was passing on the street and begged him to examine Taylor. Edna Purviance went inside Taylor's house, spotted him on the floor, and raced back to her telephone, calling Mabel Normand. In turn, Normand called Charles Eyton, Taylor's boss, who next called Paramount chief Adolph Zukor. Purviance, who knew much about Taylor's personal life, also called Mary Minter to break the news. Minter was not available; the call was taken by her very protective mother, Mrs. Charlotte Shelby.

While all these phone conversations were taking place, the doctor called in by McLean went into Taylor's house and knelt beside the director's body. He listened for a heartbeat, felt none, and then took a pulse that did not exist. "This man's dead," the physician informed McLean, who was standing nearby, mouth gaping and eyes popping.

"Of what?" inquired McLean.

The doctor pointed to the rivulet of hardened blood running from Taylor's mouth. "He died of gastric hemorrhage," replied the physician matter-of-factly. With that the doctor went to the telephone and called the coroner's office to report the death. He then walked from the house without further comment.

Within minutes, E. C. Jessurum, owner of the houses in the court, led Charles Eyton into Taylor's house. Following them was Harry Fellows, the dead man's assistant director. The house began to fill up fast. Edna Purviance returned to witness the spectacle of studio chiefs descending upon the scene to eliminate any evidence that might posthumously scandalize their employee and, subsequently, their studio.

Eyton looked about frantically and noticed several liquor bottles in the living room and elsewhere, all in violation of the then enforced Eighteenth Amendment. "Get rid of all this booze quick," Eyton ordered McLean. The actor promptly gathered up the bottles and dashed outside with them to the trash can.

Adolph Zukor, one of the most powerful men in Hollywood, was next to arrive. He took one look at his top director lying dead on the floor and then ordered Eyton, Fellows, and others to "find anything that might damage the studio's reputation and destroy it."

Fellows went into Taylor's bedroom and scooped up piles of love letters and female garments present and returned to the living room, where a fire had been started in the fireplace. Eyton, Zukor, and Fellows took turns feeding the incriminating items into the fire as Edna Purviance and others witnessed the panic. Into this very active house, with most ignoring the corpse on the floor, swept Mabel Norman. She spoke not a word to anyone but moved quickly into the bedroom and desperately began to search for love letters she had sent to the dead man.

Meanwhile Henry Peavey continued his ear-shattering shrieks along Alvarado Drive until neighbors called the police.

238

The valet-butler informed officers that his employer was dead.

A coroner's assistant showed up in response to the doctor's call, which had been placed almost an hour earlier. He stood over Taylor's body, thoughtfully staring at it. "He looks too neat lying there like that," commented the coroner's man.

"Yeah," commented someone else in the room, "like someone had laid him out."

Charles Eyton suddenly exchanged nervous glances with the coroner's assistant and then shouted: "Turn him over! Turn him over!"

Hands reached out and rolled the body over to reveal two bullet holes in the back of William Desmond Taylor. "Murder," whispered the coroner's man, and the word was caught up by those milling about the house, horrifying all. Edna Purviance recovered from the shock, then raced back to her house to call Mrs. Shelby, the mother of Mary Miles Minter, once again. As she was doing this, Mabel Normand slipped out the back door of Taylor's house. She had been unable to locate her love letters.

Mrs. Shelby heard of Taylor's murder from Edna Purviance and drove to the home of her mother, Mrs. Julia Branch Miles, where her daughters Margaret and Mary were staying. Mary Miles Minter had, months earlier, become estranged from her mother and had moved away from her. When she saw her mother approaching the Miles home, Mary locked herself in her room. Mrs. Shelby banged on the door, shouting: "Open this door! I have something to tell you!"

Mary opened the door.

Blurted her mother: "Mr. Taylor was found murdered in his bed this morning!" (Apparently Mrs. Shelby hadn't gotten her facts straight in the hasty call from Edna Purviance.) Then she looked suspiciously at her daughter and asked: "Where were you last night?"

Minter, her face ashen, ignored the question and began a desperate search for her car keys.

Realizing that her daughter was about to go to the Taylor home, Mrs. Shelby shrieked: "You stay in your room and don't you leave until I tell you!"

"Get away from that door!" Minter shouted, and brushed past her mother, racing to the street and a car in which Mrs. Miles sat. The actress and her grandmother drove to Taylor's residence, but police, by then swarming all over the court, refused to allow her inside. The actress began to plead, cry, and become hysterical. But the officers were firm; too many unauthorized people had been walking about the premises already. Mary Miles Minter went to see Mabel Normand, visiting with her for several hours. Whatever these two women had to say to each other about the man they both loved has remained a secret to this day.

Detectives were enraged at the trespassing by the movie people. Any clues that might have been left by the killer had been obliterated. They did find a number of cigarette butts at the back of the house by the kitchen door, which indicated that the murderer might have waited there the previous evening until Peavey and Normand had left the Taylor house.

Investigators were at first perplexed at

Mary Miles Minter, one of Hollywood's most promising young stars, was ruined in the mysterious murder case of William Desmond Taylor.

Taylor, William Desmond

One of the love notes poured from the pen of Mary Miles Minter to the amorous William Desmond Taylor.

the bullet holes in the director's coat and vest since they did not line up, but they then concluded that Taylor had been sitting at his desk, his suitcoat hiked up on his back when he was shot which would cause the discrepancy, and that his body had been laid out later by the killer for unknown reasons. After some searching, police found the letters Mabel Normand had been searching for in one of Taylor's boots. They certainly compromised the comedienne, but they were a lot less torrid than those written by Mary Miles Minter, also found later by police.

On one of her personally printed stationery pads, Mary had written the following note:

Dearest—
I love you . . . I love you . . . I love you . . .
X X X X X X X X X X X X X X X X!
Yours always,
Mary

In another torrid letter, which proved to be a shock to her millions of fans, who thought her to be an adolescent virgin, Minter wrote:

What shall I call you, you wonderful man? You are outstanding on the lot, the idol of an adoring company. You have just come over and put your coat on my chair. I want to go away with you, up in the hills, or anywhere, just so we'd be alone—all alone. In a beautiful woodland lodge you'd be the cook (as I can only make tea) and fetch the water and build the fire. Wouldn't it be glorious to sit in a big, comfy couch by a cozy, warm fire with the wind whistling outside, trying to harmonize with the faint strains of music coming from the Victrola . . . and then you'd have to take off the record.

Of course I don't mean that, dear. Do you really suppose I intended you to take care of me like a baby? Oh, no, for this is my part: I'd sweep and dust (they make the sweetest little dustcaps, you know) and tie fresh ribbons on the snowy white curtains and feed the birds and fix the flowers and—oh, yes—set the table and help you wash the dishes and then in my spare time darn your socks.

I'd go to my room and put on something scant and flowing; then I'd lie on the couch and wait for you. I might fall asleep, for a fire makes me drowsy. Then I'd wake to find two strong arms around me and two dear lips pressed on mine in a long, sweet kiss. . . .

There were other letters, many of them, that found their way into the sensation-hungry tabloids of the day; they turned the Taylor murder into a national scandal, feeding on the delectable details that flowed from the investigation. Beyond hundreds of love letters collected by Taylor, police also found, buried beneath a pile of film scripts, a bundle of pornographic photos showing Taylor with several prominent Hollywood actresses.

No one was safe from the ever-widening scandal, it seemed. Mary Pickford, then Hollywood's top female star, had merely autographed her photo for Taylor. But the fact that the director kept this photo in a frame on his bedstand seemed to intimate that he had relations with America's Sweetheart, or so the gossip mongers of the press suggested. Miss Pickford was asked to comment on Taylor and merely replied: "I will pray."

As scores of detectives worked on the case, the murky past of William Desmond Taylor came to light piece by piece. It was soon learned that the director was not William Desmond Taylor at all—that was merely a stage name. He had been born William Cunningham Deane-Tanner in 1877, the oldest son of a well-to-do Irish family living in Mallow, County Cork. His father had been a colonel in the British army and his grandfather had been a member of the British Parliament. William had been raised to become an officer in the army, following family tradition. He took a degree from Clifton College but broke with his family's wishes in 1895 and joined a theatrical company in Manchester, where he used the stage name of William Desmond Taylor.

Failing at this, he traveled to Canada, where he became an engineer for a brief while, then moved off to join the gold rush in the Klondike. Penniless, Taylor drifted back to New York, and there met his younger brother Dennis. The two of them borrowed money and opened up an antique and art store in Manhattan. Taylor always lived beyond his means, purchasing the best clothes money could buy and dining in the best restaurants. Such expensive habits kept the antique store depleted of funds; Dennis walked about in threadbare clothes most of the time.

Taylor's polished manners and personable style soon ingratiated him to members of New York society. He met Ethel Harrison, a member of the Floradora Sextet, then the Broadway rage. Miss Harrison's uncle was none other than real estate multimillionaire Daniel J. Braker, a fact not lost on the enterprising Taylor. He married Ethel, who knew him as William Deane-Tanner, and the union produced a daughter, Daisy.

The handsome Taylor, still in his early twenties, and sporting a dashing mustache, continued his exorbitant life-style, borrowing heavily from his wife's uncle. He confided to friends that he expected the elderly Braker to leave him a fortune following his death. The real estate magnate died in October 1908, but the reading of Braker's will came as a terrible shock to young Taylor. He sat in the offices of his uncle's attorneys and went white when the following clause was read: "To W.C.D. Tanner, I leave and bequeath the amounts of money owing to me by him."

That was all, not a dime left to Taylor other than what he had borrowed. On October 23, Taylor left his home in Larchmont and went to Manhattan, where he began to drink heavily. He was seen tipsy at the Vanderbilt Cup races on Long Island the following day. Two days after that, October 26, Taylor called an assistant at his antique shop and ordered him to bring him every dime on hand, a little more than $600, which was delivered to Taylor at the Broadway Central Hotel. The assistant noticed that his employer was in a bedraggled state and that he had shaved off his mustache. After the assistant left Taylor pocketed $100 and mailed the remaining $500 to his wife. He then left town, giving no forwarding address.

Dennis Tanner had been left wholly destitute and had to close his shop, this at a time when his wife was about to deliver a baby. She had another within a year. He swore to friends that he would never forgive his brother for ruining him.

It was 1912 before Mrs. Ethel Tanner walked into a New York courtroom to file for divorce, stating that her vanished husband had committed adultery only a month before his disappearance, trysting with a beautiful Broadway showgirl in an Adirondacks retreat under the name of Townsend. She was awarded the uncontested divorce. A short time after this decree was granted, Dennis Tanner, following in his brother's footsteps, also deserted his wife and children.

In 1914, friends of the ex-Mrs. Tanner went to a New York movie house and suddenly bolted upright in their chairs. There on the screen, without his mustache, was none other than William Cunningham Deane-Tanner, only the film credits said that the dashing lead was played by William Desmond Taylor. Also in the same film was Dennis Tanner, playing a minor role. The friends immediately informed Ethel, but she was unconcerned. By then she had remarried, wedding the millionaire owner of one of New York's greatest restaurants, Delmonico's. Taylor's daughter, Daisy, however, wanted to see her father and contacted him in Hollywood. Taylor said he was delighted to hear from her, and when he joined the Royal Canadian Air Force to

William Desmond Taylor, shown in his WWI RCAF officer's uniform, a
photo he liked to inscribe to Hollywood glamour girls after he became one
of Hollywood's top directors.

fight in the First World War in 1915, he stopped off to see his daughter in New York before going to Europe. He cut quite a figure in his captain's uniform and took his daughter to the finest nightspots in Manhattan before departing. He continued to write to her through his palmy days in Hollywood after returning from the service in 1917. (Taylor enjoyed giving female admirers his autographed photo, one in which he wore his officer's uniform, and it delighted him no end to be referred to as "captain" during his Hollywood career.)

The mystery of Taylor's background was then settled, but more unsettling was the revelation that Edward Sands, the corrupt valet-butler who had forged Taylor's checks, wrecked his cars, pawned his jewels, and made off with his wardrobe had been none other than Dennis Tanner, his brother! Many speculated that Sands-Taylor, who had vowed revenge for the financial ruin his brother had brought down upon his head, had killed Taylor. The mysterious younger brother was never found again on either side of the Atlantic.

As all of Taylor's strange past tumbled out of police discoveries, another bombshell exploded in the face of the apprehensive movie moguls. Hard drugs had been involved with some of the Taylor intimates, chiefly the brilliant comedienne Mabel Normand, who was a secret opium addict. She and Taylor had quarreled often over Normand's heavy use of drugs. Though the director was a sexual rake, he condemned drug use as "a filthy, beastly habit." He once caught hold of a man who was blackmailing Normand, threatening to expose her habit unless she paid handsomely. Taylor knocked the man senseless and threatened to shoot him on sight if he ever saw him around Normand again. So incensed was Taylor with the drug dealers working out of Los Angeles's Chinatown, especially those catering to stars like Normand, that Taylor had his chauffeur drive him regularly into the area where he collected information on the drug traffickers which he turned over to the district attorney's office. When this news broke, there was heavy conjecture about drug dealers having killed Taylor for exposing their racket.

Another suspect loomed large before the police. Taylor had been killed with a .38 revolver. It was learned that Charlotte Shelby, the protective mother of Mary Miles Minter, owned a pearl-handled .38-caliber revolver. According to one report, Shelby had been seen practicing her marksmanship with this weapon shortly before the director's murder. Though these facts were known to investigators, Shelby was not brought in for questioning and was allowed to go on an extended European tour. Two years later her daughter Mary told newsmen: "Mother's actions over Mr. Taylor's attentions to me were not inspired by a desire to protect me from him. She was really trying to shove me into the background so that she could try to monopolize his attentions and, if possible, his love. He used to call at our house. But as soon as Mother saw his preference for me, she put a stop to his visits. . . . She cared for him herself."

Many, upon hearing Minter's wrathful statements, remembered Mrs. McLean's description of the man who walked more like a woman, the odd, darkly dressed person she had seen leaving Taylor's house after hearing the explosion on the night of the murder. Could the killer have been Mrs. Shelby dressed as a man, wreaking vengeance upon a Lothario who had spurned her love for that of her daughter? No one ever answered that question.

Motives for the murder abounded. Robbery was quickly ruled out, in that Taylor's lucky diamond ring, which marked his first great film success, *Diamond from the Sky*, was still on his finger when his body was found. He was also wearing his expensive platinum watch, and there were hundreds of dollars in his wallet inside his desk within easy reach.

Even Henry Peavey, the oddball valet-butler was for a time suspected of murdering the enigmatic Taylor. Peavey had been arrested on a morals charge in a Hollywood park a few weeks before the killing. He had screamed his innocence in his soprano voice and had gotten off with some help from Taylor. No one would ever know for sure about Mr. Peavey. He went hopelessly insane and was confined to a Napa mental asylum, where he died of paresis in 1931.

Mary Miles Minter was whispered to know more than she told reporters. Her mother repeatedly harped upon her nights out on the town. Following the death of Taylor, Minter, at first, gave sedate interviews, telling reporters: "I did love William Desmond Taylor. I loved him

deeply and tenderly, with all the admiration a young girl gives to a man with the poise and position of Mr. Taylor." In short, she was saying she had loved him as a father, not as a lover. Yet, the flamboyant Minter was the star attraction at Taylor's circuslike funeral. She entered as hundreds whispered her name, gliding to the bier and leaning over the open casket. Lifting her veil, she kissed the corpse on the lips, then took a seat in the first row.

Somehow inspired by her own performance, Minter suddenly stood up and wheeled about to address the startled throng. "He spoke to me just now," she informed her fans. "He whispered something to me. It sounded like 'I shall love you always, Mary!' " The tabloids went wild with this graveside tale, another garish anecdote in a continuing saga of the macabre. It was just about her last public appearance. The scandals that exploded with Taylor's murder engulfed Minter and finished her career. She was let out of her million-dollar contract and went into premature retirement, stepping into the limelight only when battling her mother in court settlements over her estate. (Mrs. Shelby, by contract, had been receiving 30 percent of Minter's enormous movie salary.) Fortunately, Minter had invested her wages wisely, and her retirement was one of comfort.

Fate was not so kind to Mabel Normand. She had hired a new chauffeur after Taylor's death, Horace A. Greer. He proved to be possessive in a lethal way. On New Year's Eve, 1923, Mabel was getting into her limousine after attending a party at Edna Purviance's only a few doors from where her lover had been murdered. About to join her in the back seat was Denver oil tycoon Courtland S. Dines. The chauffeur, Greer, suddenly yanked the millionaire back to the sidewalk by the arm and shot him in the stomach. (The two men, it was later gossiped, had been waging war with each other over Normand's bedroom favors.) Dines survived and Greer was released from jail, but this added scandal doomed Normand's film career.

Dozens of women's clubs and scores of clergymen mounted a campaign against her, writing thousands of letters to distributors of her films to demand that they be banned. Mack Sennett, who had made her a star and loved her, courageously cast Normand in the lead roles of two more films, *Extra Girl* and *Susanna,* but the films were not released by frightened distributors. "I'm a liability to everyone," Mabel murmured, but she continued to make a few more films in the 1920s, none of them box-office successes.

In 1926 Normand married actor Lew Cody, but her life was full of pain; she was then afflicted with unrelenting tuberculosis, which finally claimed her life on February 22, 1930 when she was thirty-three.

All of the principals in this Jazz Age moviedom drama are now long gone into a mysterious night where the true killer of William Desmond Taylor remains a shadow indistinguishable from the many ghosts moving silently in the dark.

Texas Strangler Slayings
MURDERS, 1968–1971 U.S.

The most murderous sex fiend in modern Texas history was the killer who strangled and mutilated twelve women and abducted two others, who never were seen again, between 1968 and 1971. The first victim was Linda Lee Cougot of Odessa, Texas, who vanished on October 21, 1968, after she had gone to a laundromat. The twenty-four-year-old barmaid's badly decomposed body was found lying in the desert twelve miles northwest of Odessa on December 15, 1968. She had been strangled with one of her own nylon stockings, and the other had been used to tie her hands behind her back. She had been sexually attacked and her clothes ripped to pieces.

Eleven more women, single and married, were murdered in a similar manner near Odessa and Dallas, the last being Mrs. Carolyn Montgomery, a twenty-eight-year-old barmaid. A thirteenth victim sometimes attributed to the strangler was eleven-year-old Johnny Janel Henderson, who was strangled with her own necklace in Odessa, Texas. Her naked body was found in a gravel pit near her home on August 26, 1971.

The killer seemed to swing back and forth between Odessa and Dallas, crossing almost the entire width of Texas and then cutting back, in a pendulumlike movement. In all instances the strangler left no clues to his identity, although, in the case of Mrs. Montgomery, he did leave a crudely scrawled note contemptuously reading: "Got wrong one—sorry."

Texas police searched in vain for the killer, even though many suspects were detained and questioned. On one occasion, a suspect in Amarillo who had a record of attacks on women in laundromats, the site of many of the killer's abductions, was approached in the street by state officers. The twenty-three-year-old man suddenly whipped out a shotgun, placed it to his temple, and, before police could put a single question to him, pulled both triggers, blowing away his head. The killings, however, continued.

The strangler also seemed to pick his victims at random and from all walks of life. Linda Cougot and Carolyn Montgomery were barmaids. Another was a schoolteacher, another a go-go dancer. Most were wives and mothers. Ironically, Mrs. Ruth Maynard, of Odessa, who like Linda Cougot, was strangled with her own stocking, on January 9, 1971, was the wife of a policeman. Mrs. Barbara Moorman of Dallas, murdered on February 9, 1971, was the daughter-in-law of Captain Ben Moorman of the Plainview, Texas, Police Department.

To this date, the maniac the press dubbed the Texas strangler and whose orgy of murder ceased in late summer 1971, has not been apprehended.

Thompson, Lydia
MURDER, 1945 U.S.

The body of forty-seven-year-old Lydia Thompson was found by three mushroom pickers in a marsh twelve miles northwest of Pontiac, Michigan, on October 13, 1945. Mrs. Thompson, the wife of a wealthy Detroit car dealer, had undergone a painful ordeal before death, as investigators later learned. She had been tortured, mutilated, and then decapitated.

Months before her death, Thompson had led a furtive, nerve-wracked existence. She had confided to friends that she was being followed and feared for her life. Her husband had left her and was making plans for a divorce.

Lydia Thompson's last six months on earth were as bizarre as her unsolved murder, a killing that produced a $100,000 investigation that would grind on for several years. Her husband, Victor Louis Thompson, would later be indicted for his wife's murder, an indictment he had been expecting.

The Thompsons had been married for twenty-five years, Louis wedding Lydia following World War I. He was a veteran of the British army and she was a nurse and widow of a Russian soldier. The couple moved to the United States shortly after their marriage, settling in Detroit.

Here, in the hub of the auto industry, Louis opened up a car dealership and flourished. He later established a successful garage and set his wife up in a laundry. He bought a lovely, plush $50,000 home in the Detroit suburb of Orchard Lake. Surrounded by luxury, Lydia lived a Spartan life, insisting that she perform all the housework, even though her husband offered to hire servants.

As Louis's business prospered he poured his profits into his house, build-

Lydia Thompson's hacked-up body was found October 13, 1945, in a lonely marsh outside of Pontiac, Michigan; her brutal killer was never found.

ing an indoor swimming pool, a billiard room, a large sun deck, and an extravagant bar. He gave parties, but Lydia showed no interest in social gatherings. The portly, jovial Louis began to resent his wife's reclusiveness and slowly turned his attentions elsewhere. By early 1945, Lydia had grown suspicious of her husband, paying private detectives to follow him.

The couple reconciled repeatedly in the following months, but inevitable separations followed. In May, Louis went to Miami, staying in a motel. Lydia was told by a detective she had hired that her husband had been joined by one Helen Budnik, his attractive secretary.

Lydia Thompson promptly got on a Florida-bound train, standing most of the way due to crowded wartime conditions. She confronted Helen Budnik, who promised her that she would stop seeing her husband. Louis returned to Detroit on May 30, 1945, but went on seeing Budnik, who had returned home earlier in the month.

By early October Lydia Thompson confided to friends that she had purchased a gun and that she carried it everywhere she went. She stated that men were following her and that her death was imminent. Most thought the woman had become a raving paranoid and humored her. By this time, Louis Thompson had moved permanently from his house to continue his relationship with Helen Budnik.

On the evening of October 11, 1945, an Orchard Lake patrolman saw Lydia standing on the lawn of her house talking to a man and woman, but, being too far off, he could not identify Lydia's visitors. He was the last person to see the woman alive.

When Louis Thompson heard of his wife's killing, he swiveled about in his office chair and stated: "Oh, the poor kid." He went on to tell police that he had given her more than $7,000 in cash in the previous year and did not know what she had done with the funds. She had substantial cash flowing from the successful laundry which Louis had turned over to her, and he therefore was puzzled at his wife's need for more money. It was later speculated that Lydia was paying heavy amounts to detectives to follow her husband. One report even had it that she had given large sums of money to some persons to kill Helen Budnik, but this was never proved.

Police investigating the bizarre murder of Lydia Thompson quickly ruled out robbery. More than $3,000 in diamonds and rubies were found in her Orchard Lake home, along with substantial cash. Toward the end of November, boy scouts uncovered a meat cleaver, the murder weapon, in the marsh where Mrs. Thompson's body had been found, but this was the only clue uncovered in the case. The cleaver bore no fingerprints.

Cash rewards amounting to almost $5,000 were posted for the apprehension of Lydia's killer or killers, with Louis offering a large portion of this money. With no other leads, authorities began to suspect Louis Thompson of murdering his

wife. Four months after Lydia's death, Louis married Helen Budnik, who gave birth to a child in November 1946.

Detectives by the dozen continued to investigate every lead, no matter how preposterous, until Oakland County had spent more than $100,000 in its seemingly futile investigation.

Then, suddenly, on March 23, 1947, Louis and Helen Thompson were indicted for first-degree murder and conspiracy to murder. Circuit Court Judge George B. Murray informed the press that the Thompson slaying was directly linked to labor racketeering in Detroit. Louis Thompson reacted to the indictment in a cavalier fashion, stating: "This ought to clear the air. Judge Murphy had to indict us or clear us, and perhaps this will end the thing."

It was next announced that a door-to-door salesman of pots and pans who had a prison record had killed Lydia Thompson on orders from her husband, receiving $10,000 to commit the murder. The story, as a later hearing revealed, came from the peddler's estranged girl friend. The door-to-door salesman said he was innocent.

"I met this girl a couple of years ago," the peddler testified in court. "She had got some money in an accident case I was witness in, and we began chasing around. She loaned me two hundred dollars. But I'm married and I wanted to break it up. To scare her, I told her I was the guy who killed Mrs. Thompson."

The salesman provided a solid alibi which placed him with friends at the time

Lydia Thompson was murdered. Moreover, the peddler's girl friend admitted that the intimate details she had given police regarding the murder stemmed from a reporter friend who had been covering the investigation. The case against Thompson and his second wife collapsed.

On May 16, 1947, the Thompsons were released for lack of evidence. They immediately left for a vacation in Bermuda. The voluminous records of the Lydia Thompson case were turned over to the state police and still reside in those files, marked open and unsolved.

Many friends of Lydia Thompson have speculated on her gruesome end over the years, but the most feasible conjecture regarding her mysterious end was provided by Mrs. August Gentile, a neighbor: "Mrs. Thompson was so desperate in her efforts to regain her husband's affections that she would have accepted anyone's offer to help her. It would have been an easy way to any persons planning to rob and kill her, after winning her confidence."

"3-X"
BOMBINGS, 1930s U.S.

A maniac bomber plagued New York City in the early 1930s by planting various homemade bombs throughout Manhattan, particularly at the sites of major landmarks—in the Empire State Building, beneath the Brooklyn Bridge—but most of these bombs did not explode. Police were led to them after receiving notes from the madman who constructed them. He always signed his notes "3-X."

None of the bombs killed anyone, although some passersby were injured. The bomber continued his campaign from 1930 to 1933. The bombs and notes then inexplicably stopped appearing. Stranger still was the utter lack of motive on the part of the bomber, who never stated why he was so actively interested in blowing up New York.

Tiffany & Co.
ROBBERY, 1958 U.S.

Though the security of Tiffany & Company was widely boasted to be the best in the world, the posh jewelry firm suffered an enormous loss on August 10, 1958, when two large display windows of their main store on Fifth Avenue in New York City were suddenly smashed by street thieves. In a matter of seconds, between 5:45 and 6:05 AM, $163,300 worth of insured jewels were snatched by the bagmen, who disappeared inside of five minutes before police arrived at the scene.

The windows broken were not connected to an alarm system; the pulverized windows were discovered by a policeman routinely patrolling his beat.

The thieves have never been identified to this writing, nor have the jewels surfaced. It is thought that the gems were smuggled out of the country and, after receiving new settings, were sold in Europe.

Broken windows outside esteemed jewelers Tiffany & Co., at 57th Street and Fifth Avenue in New York, where, hours earlier, thieves made off with $163,000 in jewels. (*Wide World*)

Todd, Thelma
MURDER, 1935 U.S.

Film star Thelma Todd was found dead in her car parked in a Pacific Palisades garage on December 16, 1935, ending a career that included seventy motion pictures made from 1926 to the year of her mysterious death. Though a coroner's jury ruled the actress's death accidental, strong evidence to the contrary indicated that Todd had been murdered.

When the body was discovered, blood was on the actress's face and on the seat of the car and on the running board. Her face was bruised and an autopsy later revealed that the *inside* of her throat was bruised with marks that might have been made by a bottle being jammed down her throat.

Many close to the actress insisted that she had been murdered, and these included her mother and her lawyer. Others suggested that Todd had had difficulties with gangsters, representatives of Lucky Luciano's nationwide gambling network. It was reported that they had demanded Todd turn over the second floor of her popular roadside restaurant on the Palisades for use as a syndicate casino and that she had refused. They threatened to beat her or, worse, kill her.

An anonymous woman in Ogden, Utah, contacted Los Angeles police and stated that she had evidence against a man living in Ogden that would prove that he had murdered Thelma Todd. The L.A.P.D. did nothing, but the Ogden Police Department did conduct its own investiga-

Actress Thelma Todd, who met an inexplicable end in 1935.

tion, and then Ogden's Mayor Harmon Peery and the city's police chief wired their report to Los Angeles, urging that "someone should question the man who has been located." The lead was never followed up. To this day it is believed that certain Hollywood executives, for unexplained reasons, covered up the real facts of this enigmatic case, perhaps with help from some Los Angeles police officials.

U

U.S. Mail

ROBBERY, 1962   U.S.

"The Great Mail Robbery" occurred on a lonely stretch of U.S. Route 3 on August 14, 1962, where the road bypasses Plymouth, Massachusetts. A U.S. mail truck, transferring money from Cape Cod banks to the Boston Federal Reserve Bank, was stopped and looted of a fortune.

Patrick R. Schena was at the wheel of the mail truck, and William Barrett sat beside him in the cab. After the truck passed the Clark Road Cutoff, two cars converged upon the spot, and four or five men quickly placed detour signs so that the mail truck would be the only vehicle on the road.

The two cars then sped down the road, passed the slow-moving mail truck, and, around the next curve, spun about to block the road. The mail truck came to a halt in front of the two cars, and two men dressed as policemen ran to the truck, aiming submachine guns (or shotguns, the drivers were not sure which) at Schena and Barrett, forcing them to lie down in the back of the truck. The men, with the help of two or three others, quickly looted the

truck of its mail bags and then sped off in their autos, taking with them $1,551,277 in small unmarked old bills. It was the largest single robbery in American history to that date.

All Schena and Barrett could later tell investigating officers was that the two men called each other "Buster" and "Tony." Both were described as burly and middle-aged and wore white gloves (which prompted the press to dub them members of the "White Glove Gang"). Just before the robbers departed, Buster shouted to Tony: "I'll see you in Providence!"

This prompted Rhode Island state police to pick up Bernard Domanski, an old bank robber and onetime member of the "Mad Dog Bistany Machine Gun Gang," thinking he might have had something to do with the robbery. He did not, as it was later proved, but Domanski was jailed anyway and charged with violating his parole.

A massive police dragnet extended throughout New England. Outside of West Roxbury, Massachusetts, police found a stolen Oldsmobile which had been splashed with gasoline and set afire. Inside its trunk were the detour signs the thieves had used to seal off Route 3. The car yielded no clues as to the identities of the occupants.

A motorist who had taken the phony detour later stated that he saw a "pimply-faced blond woman whose dark hair was growing out," sitting in a parked car on the other side of the detour. The motorist said that the woman blinked her lights at another car parked down the road in which three men sat, and that this car gave three quick return blinks.

It was speculated that the woman was none other than Jacqueline Rose, who had suffered burn marks on the upper portion of her body. Jackie Rose was the girl friend of bank robber Bobby Wilcoxson, then wanted, along with his partner, Albert Nussbaum, by the FBI for four bank robberies in which a total of $160,000 had been stolen. None of these suspects, however, proved to be the mail truck thieves.

Some claimed that super bank robber Willie "The Actor" Sutton, then serving time in New York's Attica Prison, had masterminded the robbery from his cell. There were other theories that remained nothing more than theories. None of the robbers was ever identified, let alone arrested, and the robbery remains unsolved.

Vancouver Teen Killings
MURDERS, 1981 CANADA

Eight youths from Vancouver, British Columbia area, ages ranging from nine to seventeen, vanished between May 19 and July 30, 1981. Three of the youths were later found dead near Weaver Lake, fifty miles east of Vancouver. These included Raymond King, Jr., fifteen, Daryn Todd, sixteen, and Judy Kozma, fourteen.

The boys had been killed after being struck on the head with a blunt instrument. The Kozma girl had been stabbed nineteen times. All the bodies were found naked; not one piece of clothing belonging to the victims was ever discovered. The bodies were so badly decomposed by the time they were found that medical examiners could not determine whether or not the victims had been sexually molested.

Sex offenders in the Vancouver area were rounded up by the score and questioned, but no strong suspects emerged from the police interrogation. The other five missing youths have not been found to the time of this writing. Police are still searching for the Vancouver teen killer.

Wallace, Julia

MURDER, 1931 ENGLAND

The killing of Julia Wallace in Liverpool, England, on January 19, 1931, is one of the world's greatest murder mysteries, one that moved the writer Raymond Chandler to remark: "It was unbeatable and it will always be unbeatable." The slaying, after exhaustive police work, the shabby trial of Julia's husband, and the voicing of sharp opinions by the world's crime experts, has yielded to this day no murder weapon, no apparent motive, no clues whatsoever, and not a trace of the real murderer.

At 8:45 PM on January 19, 1931, William Herbert Wallace, a fifty-two-year-old Prudential Company insurance agent, returned to his home at 29 Wolverton Street in Liverpool. He was a tall man, six feet two inches, and slim. Wallace was addicted to old-fashioned clothing, habitually wearing a high-crowned bowler hat, a high, rounded detachable white collar called a choker, and a mackintosh which had been out of style for twenty years.

He was a quiet, withdrawn man who worked assiduously at his trade, trudging about Liverpool to sell his insurance and conscientiously collecting weekly payments. His only joys in life, it appeared, were the companionship of his sensitive, charming wife and the game of chess which he played regularly at home and at the Cottle's City Cafe, headquarters for the Central Chess Club, of which he was a member in good standing.

For fifteen minutes Wallace had attempted to enter his house, trying his keys on both the back and front doors without success. He later told police: "I . . . went to the front door. I inserted my key to find I could not open it. I went round to the backyard door; it was closed but not bolted. I went up [through the outside wall door] the backyard and tried the back door, but it would not open. I again went to the front door, but this time found the door to be bolted."

Shortly before 9 PM John and Florence Johnston, who lived next door to the Wallaces, were leaving through the backyard door of their home en route to a musical review when Wallace moved past them, a worried look on his face, keys dangling in his hand.

"Good evening, Mr. Wallace," Florence Johnston said.

Julia Wallace, whose 1931 murder has been labeled the perfect crime.

Wallace turned and said: "Have you heard anything unusual tonight?"

"Why, what's happened?" John Johnston asked.

"I've been out this evening since a quarter to seven," said Wallace, "and when I returned just now I found the front door locked against me. I've been to the front and the back."

Johnston asked: "You've tried the back kitchen door?"

"Yes, but I couldn't open it."

"That's funny. Try it again and we'll wait," Johnston suggested. "If you can't manage to get it open I'll see if my key fits it."

Wallace went again to the back door and slipped the key into the lock, saying over his shoulder to the Johnstons: "She won't be out. She has such a bad cold." He jerked the handle of the door and, with what the Johnstons later described as a look of amazement, Wallace turned toward them, saying, "It opens now."

Johnston told him: "We'll stop here while you have a look around."

The insurance agent nodded and entered his house. The Johnstons heard him call out his wife's name twice. They saw lights go on in several rooms. A few minutes later Wallace came running from the back door, extremely upset. He cried out to the Johnstons: "Come and see! She's been killed!"

The neighbors followed Wallace into the house, going quickly through the kitchen as Johnston asked: "What is it? Has she fallen down stairs?" Wallace made no reply but led them into the small living room. There on the carpet was sprawled the body of fifty-year-old Julia Wallace. Her eyes were wide open. The back of her head had been stove in, skull crushed; a large pool of blood swelled about her head as blood and brains oozed from gaping wounds where she had been repeatedly struck.

Mrs. Johnston knelt beside the dead woman, murmuring: "Oh, you poor darling." Wallace knelt beside her. Both felt for a pulse.

"Is she cold?" Mr. Johnston asked them.

Mrs. Johnston shook her head as if to say no, the body was still warm.

"Don't disturb anything," Mr. Johnston said. "I'm going for the police."

"Yes," encouraged Wallace, "and a doctor, but I don't think it's much use. They've finished her."

As he was about to leave, Johnston noticed a few coins on the floor. Then Wallace looked up to a small cabinet and pointed to a smashed lock. "See—they've broken that off," he said.

"What have they taken?" Johnston asked.

Withdrawing the cash box where he kept his clients' payments before turning them into headquarters, Wallace peered inside. "I can't tell for certain until I've examined my books," he said, "but I think it's about four pounds."

Johnston suggested Wallace check upstairs and elsewhere to see if anything else was missing before he went for the police. Wallace made a quick tour of the house and returned, saying: "Everything's all right up there. There's five pounds in a jar they haven't taken."

Mr. Johnston then ran outside to sum-

The door leading into the Wallace backyard where the mystery began.

mon a constable. Mrs. Johnston felt the victim's hand. "She's colder now," she said.

"They've finished her," Wallace said matter-of-factly. "Look at the brains." Then he added: "Whatever have they used?" He and Mrs. Johnston looked about briefly but could find no murder weapon. The police later reported that a poker from the fireplace was missing and it was assumed that this had been the murder weapon, but that remained only an assumption.

A few minutes later Wallace walked into the kitchen, slumped into his wife's rocking chair, and buried his head in his hands to sob uncontrollably. Mrs. Johnston followed Wallace and tried to console him. She built a fire in the kitchen fireplace and made some tea.

The police arrived within minutes and Wallace told the story of how he had returned home at 8:45 and had found the doors of his house locked, as if to say that the murderer had seen him coming and had bolted the front door, then the back, and, when he had returned to the front door, the killer had somehow managed to slip out the back door, unbolting it so that Wallace's latchkey would open it when he next tried that door.

When the newspapers broke the story, the public was aghast at the murder of the frail, music-loving Julia Wallace, a kindly person who had no known enemies. And with that wave of public shock was a great showering of sympathy for the bereaved husband, William Wallace. This attitude changed on February 2 when it was announced that the police had arrested Wallace and charged him with his wife's murder. Wallace insisted that he was not guilty from the beginning. On the day of his arrest, he had said to officers with an injured expression: "What can I say in answer to such a charge, of which I am absolutely innocent?"

Wallace's trial began on April 22. He was defended by the able Roland Oliver and prosecuted by E. G. Hemmerde. It was at this time that Wallace explained that the killer had lured him from his house on a futile business trip in order to gain entrance to his home, rob his cash box, and murder his wife. The day before his wife's murder, Wallace pointed out, he had a scheduled chess game at Cottle's City Cafe. Someone had called the cafe and asked to speak to him but he had not been present. Samuel Beattie, a fellow member of the Liverpool Central Chess Club, had taken the call for Wallace.

Beattie later verified that he had indeed taken the phone call. It was from Anfield, a borough of Liverpool, and the voice on the other end of the line sounded as if it belonged to an elderly person. Beattie, who knew of Wallace's work, thought that the caller might want to take out some insurance. The conversation, according to Beattie, went like this:

"Beattie speaking."

"Is Mr. Wallace there?" inquired the caller.

"No, I'm afraid not."

"But he will be there?"

"I can't say. He may or may not. If he's coming he'll be here shortly. I suggest you ring up later."

"Oh, no, I can't. I'm too busy. I have my girl's twenty-first birthday on, and I want to do something for her in the way of his business. I want to see him particularly. Will you ask him to call round to my place tomorrow evening at seven thirty?"

Beattie said that he or another friend of Wallace's, James Caird, would give Wallace the message. He asked for the caller's name.

"The name's R. M. Qualtrough."

Beattie then took down the caller's address—25 Menlove Gardens West. He read the name and the address back to the caller to make sure he had got it right. The caller confirmed that he had.

Beattie gave the message to Wallace later that night when he came to the club to play a match. The insurance agent seemed puzzled, telling Beattie that he had never heard of a man named Qualtrough, but he decided to see the man; business was business. It was 6:45 PM the following evening, the evening of his wife's murder, that Wallace set off to see Qualtrough. He wandered about Menlove Gardens, going to West, North, and South, but discovered that there was no Menlove Gardens East. It was a fake address, and there was no R. M. Qualtrough listed anywhere in the vicinity; in fact, there was no such person living in Liverpool. After the discovery of the murder, Wallace told his jurors, he concluded that the murderer had pretended to be Qualtrough and had purposely set up a phony meeting with him more than two miles distant from his home in order to get him out of the house so that he could rob it.

Ridiculous, countered the prosecution. Why would a thief go to such an elaborate

William Herbert Wallace, either a much-abused innocent man or one of the world's most sinister murderers.

plan, murder Mrs. Wallace, and risk detection by such a close shave—knowing Wallace would return to his home after not finding the address—for a mere four pounds?

Wallace's defense counsel retorted that the insurance agent sometimes kept as much as sixty or more pounds in his cash box before turning it over to his firm, and that the intruder had no way of knowing whether the box contained a great deal of money or next to nothing.

This did not impress the prosecutor, who continued to make light of the four-pound theft. In fact, Hemmerde suggested that Wallace, disguising his voice, had called the Chess Club himself, pretending to be Qualtrough to set up his own alibi. He stated that the agent murdered his wife, then went on his empty errand to see the person that he himself had created. Moreover, it was pointed out that Wallace could have easily murdered his wife in the house with the poker, taking this missing implement with him and discarding it somewhere on his journey to Menlove Gardens.

Why then was no blood found on the accused, neither on his clothes nor under his fingernails, which were examined shortly after police arrived? asked defense counsel Oliver.

Then the prosecution, as if lying in wait for this challenge, put forward a bizarre theory. Hemmerde pointed out that a second mackintosh coat belonging to Wallace, partly burned and coated with Mrs. Wallace's blood, had been found beneath the body. Wallace, in his murder frenzy,

said Hemmerde, had stripped completely, donning the mackintosh to shield his body from the blood spurting from his wife's mortal wounds, and had dropped it to the floor just before she fell upon it. In his haste to dress and depart to establish his alibi, he had forgotten the coat. (The prosecutor's sinister image of Wallace stripping naked to murder his wife conjured the vision of the sly valet François Benjamin Courvoisier, who had crept naked to the bed of his master, Lord William Russell, on the night of May 5, 1840, to stab him to death. This was also the same technique some claimed Lizzie Borden [see entry] had employed when slaying her mother and father in 1892.)

Further, the prosecution said that no one had even seen Wallace in the area of Menlove Gardens. Here it was the turn of the defense to shine. Oliver produced four witnesses to whom Wallace had spoken in the Menlove Gardens area as he searched for the elusive Qualtrough's address. Thomas Phillips, a trolley conductor in the area, was approached by Wallace, who asked where 25 Menlove Gardens West might be. He also asked directions from a Mrs. Katie Mather, a clerk named Sidney Green, and constable James Sargent. All of these people appeared in court to testify that they had seen Wallace in the Menlove Gardens area and had told him that there was no Menlove Gardens *West*. This was between seven and eight o'clock on the night of the murder.

No matter, snorted prosecutor Hemmerde, who conceded the fact that Wallace did go on his own self-devised wild goose chase. He had killed his wife *before* leaving the house at 6:45 PM. There had been plenty of time. A forensic expert, Professor John Edward MacFall, stated that he had examined the corpse and his pathology report pinpointed the woman's death at exactly 6:10 PM. This supported the prosecutor's claim that Wallace had murdered his wife before leaving his house.

The defense then countered with a telling blow, presenting fourteen-year-old Alan Close as a witness for Wallace's case. Close, who worked with his father on a milk round staunchly insisted that he had last seen Mrs. Wallace at 6:30 PM and that she had been very much alive. "I remember the time," testified the boy, "because when I passed Holy Trinity Church it was twenty-five minutes past six, and it takes me five minutes to get to Mrs. Wallace's." Nothing could budge the youth from his fixing of the time.

Oliver went on to state that, according to all who knew them, the Wallaces lived in perfect harmony, never arguing and always in each other's company. Mrs. Wallace was devoted to her husband and he to her. Also, Wallace did not stand to gain financially from her death. There simply was no motive for the man to murder his adoring wife. And Wallace, counsel Oliver illustrated, was a man of regularity, of dependability and, above all, sanity.

The pathologist MacFall again took the stand, rendering some opinions on that score. He pointed out how the slayer had repeatedly struck his victim, killing her with uncommon viciousness. "This was not an ordinary case of assault or serious injury," said MacFall. "It was a case of frenzy."His inference was that Wallace had gone momentarily mad and had slain his wife in a wild, uncontrollable fit of rage.

Defense counsel Oliver challenged MacFall with: "The fact that a man has been sane for fifty-two years, and has been sane while in custody for the last three months, would rather tend to prove that he has always been sane, would it not?"

"No, not necessarily," answered MacFall.

"Not necessarily?"

"No," mused the pathologist. "We know very little about the private lives of people or their thoughts."

Oliver then pressed MacFall about the time he had rigidly set for Mrs. Wallace's death, exactly 6:10 PM, pointing out how the milk boy, Alan Close, had seen the woman alive at 6:30 PM. "If she was alive at half past six," said Oliver to MacFall, "then your opinion is wrong."

The pathologist agreed to that proposition, which seemed to be a triumphant point for the defense.

Justice Wright summed up the case for the jury, favoring Wallace's defense, referring to the "loops and doubts" of the circumstantial evidence brought against the defendant. Most believed Wallace would be quickly acquitted, but the jury, after an hour's private deliberation, returned a verdict of guilty.

Wallace was so shocked by the verdict that he actually staggered backward in shock. He had, as he later wrote in a newspaper article, merely been thinking about how he would travel home from the courtroom, entertaining the idea of taking a taxi instead of a bus, a small self-reward for undergoing his terrible ordeal. Instead, he found himself being sentenced to death and then led back to a prison cell.

Wallace appealed his case, which was heard on May 18–19, 1931. The Court of Criminal Appeal overturned the verdict, its members stating that the case against Wallace had not been proved "with that certainty which is necessary to justify a verdict of guilty." The case was quashed and Wallace was set free.

"If only you knew how amazingly thrilling it is to laugh again," Wallace remarked when he stepped from prison. Yet the remaining two years of his life were miserable. In the mind of the public he *had* killed his wife, and everywhere he went he was called a vampire, sex maniac, and mad sadist. He continued to make his rounds, but his regular customers canceled their insurance with him, some even slamming the door in his face. Prudential kept him on, giving him a desk job, but his home life became hellish. Children stood outside his door chanting: "Julia, Julia! What's happened to Julia? She's all chopped up—chop, chop, chop! Killy Willy!"

Unable to bear the taunts anymore, Wallace moved to a small country cottage outside of Bromborough. Here he lived out his days, dying slowly from a kidney disease that finally took his life on February 26, 1933. While living in the cottage,

Wallace cotinued to fill his diary with the memories of his wife of nearly eighteen years before the murder. In one diary entry, entered on March 25, 1929, Wallace had written: "Julia reminds me today it was fifteen years ago yesterday since we were married. Well, I don't think either of us regrets the step. We seem to have pulled well together, and I think we both get as much pleasure and contentment out of life as most people."

Wallace wrote several newspaper articles in which he all but named his wife's killer. He had told police early in the case that he suspected a young man who worked briefly for him, a young man desperate enough to kill for a few pounds, a man who was known to Mrs. Wallace and who would have been admitted to his house by her. The man was never named, but Wallace expected him to pay him a visit at his cottage. In fact, Wallace wrote, he expected the man to make an attempt on his life.

"I know the murderer," Wallace flatly stated. "In the porch of the front door of this lonely house of mine I have fitted an electric switch and lamp. They are not there for the convenience of friendly visitors . . . but to safeguard my life. The position of the switch is known only to myself and before I open my door I touch it, so that the house, outside and inside, and every recess where an assailant may be lurking, are lit up. The figure which one day I fully expect to see crouching and ready to strike will be of Qualtrough, the man who murdered my wife."

But Wallace never saw the mysterious

Qualtrough. He died in his sleep two years later, his last words to a nephew being: "Do good with your life."

Many claimed that the gentle nature exhibited by Wallace was only a pose that he maintained to the bitter end, that he was a most sinister creature who managed to create the perfect murder, a majestic feat in an otherwise dull life that edified Wallace's secret craving for a mastermind's achievement. Others insist that the anonymous Qualtrough did exist and continued to exist long years after the Wallaces were both laid in their graves.

Justice Wright, who had heard the case against Wallace, succinctly summed it up when he remarked: "This murder, I should imagine, must be almost unexampled in the annals of crime . . . murder so devised and arranged that nothing remains which will point to anyone as the murderer."

Wall Street
BOMBING MURDERS, 1920   U.S.

About ten minutes before noon on September 16, 1920, a Thursday, an ancient wagon pulled by an equally ancient horse, a brown bay, some later said, creaked to a stop in front of the U.S. Assay Building at Broad and Wall streets in New York. Its driver was a nondescript fellow by most later accounts, but these witnesses could recall only hazy images, most of them being in shock, their eardrums shattered, cuts covering their bloody faces.

Some said the driver wore a beard, others claimed that he was clean-shaven, still others insisted he wore a dark, flowing mustache. All agreed, including local and federal officers, that he had been some sort of maniacal anarchist. No one was even sure whether the driver had left the wagon or not. Some said he leaped from the seat and ran off through the crowds, others said he calmly sat and waited for his own bloody end.

At precisely 11:59 AM, when the more than 100,000 workers in the Wall Street area were about to break for lunch, there was a tremendous explosion that blew the wagon, the horse, a dozen cars and trucks, and hundreds of people into the air, an earth-shattering roar of explosives that devastated everything within a hundred feet. Not one piece of the wagon was found. Only one hoof from the horse was later discovered in a gigantic pool of blood.

The blast was so powerful that it was heard ten miles distant. First a huge saffron cloud of gas engulfed America's business hub, and then a sheet of flame spread like lightning in all directions and a split second behind the flame came a sideways hailstorm of razor-sharp metal that sliced away everything human in its lethal path. Police later discovered that the maniac who had set off the bomb had packed more than five hundred pounds of window weights, which had all been cut into tiny sharp fragments, into the wagonload of high explosives. It had been one gigantic fragmentary bomb, so elaborately constructed that it had undoubtedly taken the bomber months to create it.

Wall Street

The carnage after the Wall Street bombing of September 16, 1920.

Awnings fifteen stories above had caught fire and were blazing as police, reporters and medical personnel rushed into the area to aid the more than four hundred wounded in the square. (Oddly enough, a statue of George Washington standing with outstretched arms in front of the Subtreasury Building was not scratched.)

One on-the-spot reporter was amazed at the silence engulfing the area just after the blast, finally pierced by the agonizing screams of a badly injured woman. The reporter looked up at the great canyon of buildings surrounding him to see that every window had been smashed by the blast; windows a half-mile distant were later reported blown to pieces. Everywhere was the sound of falling glass. "The gentle sound of tinkling glass falling and slipping from sill to ledge and thence to the pavement came like music," wrote another reporter later.

The exact time of the blast, 11:59 AM, had been fixed by every street clock present which had been smashed by the explosion at that instant. One of the great houses of finance, J. P. Morgan & Company, was devasted. Thomas Joyce, the firm's chief clerk, had been near a window at the time of the explosion, and a shower of flying steel cut him down, killing him instantly. Morgan and his executives were not present at the time.

Scores of physicians and nurses were rushed into the area to aid the stricken hundreds. The bodies of thirty-eight persons, most of them in pieces, were later counted as the official death toll, but the count may have been as high as one hundred or more. The authorities simply weren't sure, since what they found consisted of fragments of bodies—an arm, a leg, a foot in a shoe. . . .

According to the police, the driver of the horse-drawn wagon, still not an uncommon sight in those days, escaped the blast. Authorities vowed to hunt down the mass killer. An artist pieced together,

from the memories of those present who survived, a sketch of the wagon, the horse and driver, and this was shown to hundreds of stable owners. None of them could identify the vehicle.

Some undigested grass which had been inside the horse's stomach, or at least that is where experts said it had been, was found and analyzed. Experts reported with pride that they had determined that the grass had been consumed somewhere in the country, not in any New York stable. This indicated that the driver had driven a great distance with his lethal load, or so it seemed. The report, in the end, proved useless.

More than $100,000 in rewards was posted for the apprehension of the bomber, who was variously claimed to be a mem-

The destroyed offices of J. P. Morgan after the Wall Street explosion.

ber of the Mafia, a Wobblie, a Sinn Fein leader, an anarchist, a Communist, a socialist, an escaped lunatic, an embittered Wall Street broker whose business had failed—the suspects were endless and, in the end, nameless.

Walton, Charles
MURDER, 1945 ENGLAND

Eight miles from Stratford-on-Avon, the body of seventy-four-year-old Charles Walton was found on February 14, 1945. Investigating police realized at first sight of the body that the old man had been murdered in a ritualistic fashion. Walton, a sickly and quirkish old man who had worked as a landscaper, was found beneath an oak tree at the foot of Meon Hill near the village of Lower Quinton. His body had been driven into the earth with a hay fork, which was sticking into it when he was discovered, the prongs driven in at chest level. More ghastly was the sight of Walton's throat, which had been torn away by a sickle blade still in the old man's neck.

Scotland Yard detectives were called into the case, but they could offer no solution, let alone logical clues. They did reluctantly release, however, a statement to the effect that the victim had been slain in the ancient manner of killing witches in the sixteenth century, when in Lower Quinton many a witch had been killed with pitchforks, in the belief that the only way to dissove the evil body and spirit of

the witch was to perform a "stacung," or "sticking" murder.

In checking the history of the area, detectives uncovered the story of James Heywood, a local resident who had denounced Ann Tennant, an eighty-year-old woman of Lower Quinton, as a witch in 1875. Heywood had actually chased the old woman from the village to almost the exact site where Walton's body was found seventy years later and had stabbed her to death with a pitchfork.

Though Yard detectives relentlessly interviewed more than four thousand local residents in their prolonged investigation, not a single clue to the identity of Walton's killer was unearthed.

Welch, Albert
MURDER, 1947 ENGLAND

On November 18, 1947, a railway linesman named Albert Welch, wrote a note to his wife, that read; "Phyllis, I have gone for a walk—shan't be in for tea—Albert." He then took a stroll along a golf course which was near his home in Potters Bar, in Middlesex. Welch utterly vanished.

Six months later some boys playing near the seventh fairway of the golf course found a human arm protruding from some bushes. Police were called and, after several days of digging, the dismembered remains of a man, approximately five feet two inches in height and about forty-five years old were pieced together. The killer, according to a later report, had used a common saw to cut up his victim, performing the grisly job crudely.

After extensive examinations of the dead man's skull and teeth, it was determined that the victim was none other than the missing linesman, Welch. His killer was never found and no motive for the slaying could be established. It was a wonder to police that they were able to fix the man's identity at all and considered that feat a great accomplishment.

Wells Fargo
ARMORED CAR ROBBERY, 1978 U.S.

After picking up shipments of cash at various Staten Island banks for delivery to the Federal Reserve Bank in Manhattan on Tuesday, December 19, 1978, the crew of a Wells Fargo armored car stopped outside Food 'N Things, a Staten Island delicatessen, to buy lunch.

Two of the guards went into the shop to place their order while a third guard stayed inside the locked armored car. The armored car crew had been stopping regularly at the delicatessen to order lunch for more than a year. The two men lined up behind seven other customers waiting to place orders.

Three men dressed like workmen then walked into the delicatessen behind the guards and pulled guns. Within a few minutes, the gunmen had herded the customers, guards, and four employees into the kitchen, forcing them to kneel on the floor where they were handcuffed. "Keep your heads down," ordered one gunman. A customer lifted his head to look at the man and was hit with a gun butt.

The gunmen took the keys to the armored truck from the guards, went outside, and opened the door to the truck, completely surprising the third guard. The guard was forced to drive to a nearby corner, where other members of the gang were waiting. The guard was thrown onto the floor of the truck, handcuffed, blindfolded, and his mouth taped. He managed to see four more men join the original seven, all of whom looted the truck of many white canvas bags containing cash which they transferred to a blue Cadillac with a white top. In a matter of minutes, the truck had been cleaned out and the bandits sped off.

While the robbery was taking place, employees in the delicatessen set off an alarm that brought police within ten minutes. The robbery, according to detectives, was "all very professional." The thieves had certainly noted that the armored car stopped regularly at the sandwich shop and had brought along enough handcuffs not only for the guards inside the delicatessen but for as many customers and employees as might be inside at the time.

On the following day, it was announced that more than $1 million in cash had been taken by the bandits, but two days later reporters talking to law enforcement officials involved in the case put the amount at a staggering $3 million, which topped the similarly enacted U.S. mail truck robbery of 1962 [see entry], and

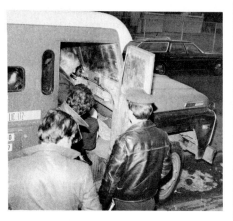

Police inspecting the abandoned Wells Fargo armored car that was commandeered by thieves in Staten Island and looted of up to $3 million in 1978.

approached the enormous haul taken by bandits less than two weeks earlier in the theft of a Lufthansa money shipment [see entry] at Kennedy Airport.

No trace of the bandits or the Wells Fargo money has ever been found.

Welsh, Leila
MURDER, 1941 U.S.

For sheer mystery, few cases approach the murder of twenty-year-old Leila Welsh in Kansas City on March 9, 1941. Miss Welsh's murderer entered her first-floor bedroom window in the early morning hours of that day and crushed her skull with a blunt instrument as she lay sleeping. Next, the intruder, using a sharp-bladed knife, cut the young woman's throat and slashed her body.

Police at work on the case hours later began to turn up many clues left by what appeared to be a very sloppy killer. From a nearby garbage can officers plucked a man's pair of trousers and a shirt, but these led only to a well-to-do Kansas City man who was in no way connected with the victim. Then a butcher knife was found; on it were the fingerprints of another prominent man, who proved similarly not to be involved. A hammer was next found, but this, like the butcher knife, had not been used to kill Welsh.

Detectives began to realize that the killer possessed a Machiavellian mind. He had purposely planted those clues and others—such as a pair of gloves, which had not been used in the murder, that were smeared with the victim's blood; a book of matches with a useless phone number written inside the cover; and, dropped on the bedroom floor, scores of cigarette butts, all of different brands, some coated with lipstick. (It was later concluded that the killer had gone from bar to bar collecting butts from ashtrays for this arcane purpose.)

The many false clues planted by the murderer, of course helped to conceal any real clues that might have been left. The procedure worked exactly as it had been intended. The police were utterly baffled at the murder and the perpetrator—the more so, given the belief that her killer was a male and not a female, since Leila Welsh had no male friends nor known enemies.

The killing of Leila Welsh remains a complete enigma to this day.

Welsh, Richard S.
ASSASSINATION, 1975   GREECE

The chief official of the U.S. Central Intelligence Agency in Athens, Greece, Richard S. Welsh, left a Christmas party on the night of December 23, 1975. As he walked up a street near his home in the wealthy suburb of Paleo Psychio in Athens, three unknown gunmen suddenly opened fire, killing him on the spot.

Welsh, who was attending a party that night given by U.S. Ambassador Jack B. Kubisch, had been identified as the top CIA official in Greece some weeks earlier by Greek and American journalists. This disclosure caused the Central Intelligence Agency to accuse several American newspapers and CIA critics of fingering their agents and thus endangering their lives. In short, intelligence officials maintained, the journalists were instrumental in the murder of Welsh; yet, the critics countered, Welsh's identity had been well-known to hostile intelligence agencies and in Greek political circles.

No clear motive for the killing has ever been established and the responsible parties have not been identified, even though some sources attributed the killing to a terrorist group calling itself November 17, members of which had participated in a bloody abortive uprising on November 17, 1973, against the junta ruling Greece. Others claimed that a rightist group called Eoka, made up of Greek Cypriots, was responsible for the Welsh murder.

The killing spread fear throughout the American community living in Greece at the time, all of its members being labeled potential CIA spies. Hundreds changed their addresses and phone numbers and demanded and got special security guards to watch their homes. The eventual upshot was the enactment in 1982 of a law in the U.S. making it a crime deliberately to reveal the identity of any U.S. undercover intelligence official or agent, even if such could be gleaned or deduced from unclassified sources.

Wilson, Elizabeth

MURDER, 1928   FRANCE

Elizabeth Wilson and her husband, Henry, were members of the expatriate British set living in France during the 1920s, well-to-do socialites who occupied most of their waking hours with leisure and pleasure. In early May 1928, the couple moved to Le Touquet to visit friends and on May 19, 1928, they had tea and cakes at the golf club and then went on to play. Mrs. Wilson stopped playing at 6 PM, telling her husband, who continued to play a round with friends, that she would see him at seven thirty at the American bar in Le Touquet.

Mrs. Wilson then began the long walk toward town, refusing a lift from friends driving by in a car, telling them she would have aperitifs with them in about two hours. Despite her fifty-four years, Elizabeth Wilson looked twenty years younger; she was a dedicated walker and dancer and kept her body in top physical condition. She was seen to enter a small forest bordering the golf course, taking a path toward town that followed the tramline serving the golf course.

Hours passed and Henry Wilson became alarmed when his wife did not appear at the American bar nor for dinner at their hotel in Le Touquet. By midnight he was frantically phoning the police, who immediately began a night search along the roads and byways in and out of the small French town.

Early the next morning the body of Elizabeth Wilson was found in a thicket near the path she had walked down, about halfway between the golf course and the town. Gendarmes found her lying on her back, her arms oustretched, her knees drawn up slightly. Her dress had been pulled upward and her underclothes had been torn away, leaving her naked from the waist down.

Upon close examination police determined that Elizabeth Wilson had been strangled. The killer had also used a short knife to cut her several times; the top of her dress was in shreds. The victim's empty handbag was found on a crossroad down which police thought the killer had escaped.

A post-mortem examination fixed the woman's death at two hours after she had had cakes and tea at the golf course, only a few minutes after she had stepped onto the path. It also revealed that she had been strangled by human hands and that the killer had cut her up *after* murdering her. The slashes were superficial, only one being serious, that which cut the carotid artery. No sexual assault had been made on the woman.

A road mender came forward during the extensive investigation to say that he had seen a man on the crossroad during the time Mrs. Wilson must have met her killer. He identified the man as M. Matras, who turned out to be the music director of the casino orchestra in Le Touquet.

Matras was questioned but denied having seen the British socialite, admitting that he had been walking toward town on the road. He said that he had seen a man, a stranger to the area, sitting near the path that led from the crossroad, with a bicycle lying nearby. The road mender said he had not seen the man mentioned by Matras.

Both of these men were eliminated as suspects in that they were on the crossroad forty minutes before Elizabeth Wilson had been killed. Moreover, her friends told police that the victim had set off with a hurried pace after refusing their offer of a ride, as if she were late for an appointment.

The police then deduced that the woman had a rendezvous with her killer along the pathway and that the killer either intended to rob her of the valuables and cash she was known to have carried in her purse, or to blackmail her for some past indiscretion. Mrs. Wilson, it was firmly thought, knew her killer.

From the bruises on the victim's throat, it was theorized that the killer had attempted to frighten the woman, not murder her, but that he had been carried away and inadvertently strangled her. He had then dragged the body to a thicket and emptied her purse, and fixed her corpse and slashed it superficially so that it would appear that she had been raped and robbed by a stranger, not a person who knew her.

But all the fanciful hypotheses did not alter the fact that the murderer completely escaped. Whoever it was that Elizabeth Wilson went to meet on that sunny path outside of Le Touquet at the tail end of the Jazz Age has remained faceless through the decades.

Wilson, Nathaniel "Buster"
MURDER, 1980 U.S.

Nathaniel "Buster" Wilson, a 1950s rock and roll singer, vanished from his Las Vegas home early April 1980, but no missing person report was ever filed. His body, or what was left of it, was discovered about six weeks later, wrapped in blankets and tied with wire, in an isolated area of Del Puerto Canyon near Modesto, California. The victim had been shot several times in the head; inexplicably his hands and feet had been chopped off. Identification was difficult in that the body was in a state of advanced decomposition.

Police reported that Wilson had been killed elsewhere; then his body was taken to the Del Puerto Canyon area and dumped. They stated further that Wilson, who had been appearing at a Las Vegas lounge at the time of his disappearance, had been the bass singer of the popular group, the Coasters, which had recorded such 1950s hits as "Yakkety Yak" and "Charlie Brown," even though no records officially list Wilson as such.

At the time of his disappearance, Wilson was sharing a home with his group's manager, Patrick Cavanaugh, who was later arrested in San Diego for masterminding a fraud that reportedly bilked businessmen in four states out of a half-million dollars. Cavanaugh insisted that he had no knowledge of Wilson's disappearance nor of his even stranger death.

The case remains a mystery to this writing.

Woodhouse, Joan
MURDER, 1948 ENGLAND

A twenty-seven-year-old librarian for the National Central Library in the Blooms-bury district of London, Joan Woodhouse disappeared over a bank holiday; her body was found in a thicket in Arundel Park in Sussex on July 31, 1948. She had been strangled, but it was never determined whether or not the attractive young woman had been sexually molested. Despite a de-termined effort by Scotland Yard, her killer was never found.

Two of the dead girl's elderly aunts stubbornly refused to admit defeat and continued their own investigation à la Agatha Christie's Miss Marple. Two years later, in July 1950, the dead girl's father ap-peared before magistrates to demand that he be allowed a private warrant to arrest one Thomas Philip George Stillwell, whom Woodhouse charged with the murder.

No application for such a warrant had been granted since 1865, but Woodhouse convinced the magistrates that he had sufficient evidence to justify the arrest. It was granted and, with two officers accompanying him, Woodhouse went to Stillwell's house and arrested him. Stillwell, a day laborer, had been the very man who had discovered Joan Woodhouse's body.

The workman faced a hearing before several magistrates, who were to deter-mine whether or not he should stand trial. Evidence collected by Woodhouse and his sisters proved to be wholly circumstantial and very thin at that. The magistrates dis-missed the charges against Stillwell, and he was released.

The Joan Woodhouse slaying remains unsolved to this day.

Wren, Margery
MURDER, 1930 ENGLAND

At about 6 PM on September 20, 1930, a small girl knocked on the sweet-shop door of Margery Wren in Church Road, Rams-gate. She got no response but persisted in knocking—her mother had sent her on an errand to buy some powdered sugar. She peered into the window of the shop and saw the eighty-year-old Miss Wren sitting in her back parlor. She knocked again, and this time the old woman re-sponded, getting up weakly and almost staggering to the door.

When the child entered she saw that the old woman's face was covered with blood. She seemed in a daze but gave the child what she wanted. The child then raced home to tell her parents, who, in turn, called police. When constables ar-rived at the shop they found the old woman lying on the floor. "I've just had a tumble, that's all," the old woman told them as they helped her to her feet.

A few feet away in a pool of her own blood lay a pair of fire tongs which some-one had used to beat her repeatedly over the head. There were eight wounds on Miss Wren's head, and her head and face were covered with bruises and lacera-tions. Doctors examining her in the hospital some hours later realized that someone had also tried to choke the old lady.

Margery Wren was in a semiconscious state for five days, during which she rambled aimlessly. At first she denied being attacked, saying: "No one hit me—I have no enemies." Next she said a "man with a red face" had assaulted her. Then she said: "There were two of them set about me." She was told that she might not live, and it was best to name her attacker. "You say I am dying," replied Miss Wren, "well, that means I am going home. . . . I do not wish him to suffer. Let him live in his sins. He must bear his sins. I do not wish to make a statement."

Margery Wren died on September 25, 1930, taking the identity of her killer to her grave.

Z

Zodiac Slayings

MURDERS, 1968-69 U.S.

A maniac who suffered from deep feelings of sexual inadequacy, according to psychiatrists studying his case, murdered a half-dozen people in the San Francisco area from Christmas 1968 to late 1969. He called himself Zodiac.

The first victims were seventeen-year-old David Faraday and Bettilou Jansen, who were out on their first date and parked on a lonely stretch of Lake Herman Road between Vallejo and San Francisco. The killer crept up to their car on all fours, it was later determined by police, then jumped up on the driver's side of the car, firing a .22-caliber pistol repeatedly into David Faraday's head, killing him instantly. Terrified, Bettilou Jansen leaped from the car and began to run. The killer stood his ground and calmly fired five more bullets into the fleeing Bettilou's back, killing her.

Not until the following July 4 did the killer strike again, shooting to death a young couple who had been making love in Blue Rock Springs Park. Some hours after these murders a man called the Val-lejo Police Department and droned: "I just shot the two kids in the public park with a nine-millimeter automatic. I also killed those two kids Christmas." He then hung up.

On August 1, 1969, the killer, obviously seeking notoriety through the press, sent notes to newspapers in Vallejo and San Francisco, one of which was a cryptogram. There were many misspellings in the notes and these, authorities believed, had been made intentionally by the killer to cloak his identity. He stated that unless the newspapers published his cryptogram he would begin to kill people at random in a murder orgy the city of San Francisco would never forget. The cryptogram was published, along with a request that the killer give additional proof of his identity.

The berserk killer responded with a note beginning: "This is Zodiac speaking," a name that terrorized the Bay Area for the next two years. He went on to give details of the murders he had committed, describing the position of the bodies as he had left them, how many shell casings should have been found by police, and other information known only to the detectives working on the case and the killer himself.

Two amateur sleuths studying the cryptogram in the newspaper managed to decipher the message where experts had failed. The message, when published, frightened the public to the point of hysteria and revealed that the police were dealing with an absolute lunatic. "I like killing people," the cryptogram stated (its spelling corrected), "because it is more fun than killing wild game in the forest because man is the most dangerus animal of all. To kill something gives me the most thrilling experience. The best part of it is that when I die I will be reborn in paradise and all those I have killed will become my slaves. I will not give you my name because you will try to slow down or stop my collecting of slaves for my afterlife."

Police, however, could do nothing with the decoded cryptogram in tracking down the madman who had written it. All they could do was wait for the killer to strike again. And a short time after sending his last message, Zodiac appeared in a remote picnic area north of San Francisco, approaching Bryan Hartnell and Cecelia Shepard. This was in the afternoon, and the bold killer wore a strange-looking mask with a square hood, like those worn by seventeenth-century executioners. He held the couple captive with a gun and tied them up. Then he put away the gun and drew a long, razor-sharp knife; without a word, he plunged this blade five times into Hartnell's back. He then moved to Shepard's side and stabbed the young woman several times in the back. As she

Police sketches and wanted flyer of Zodiac, the unknown killer who terrorized San Francisco in 1968–69.

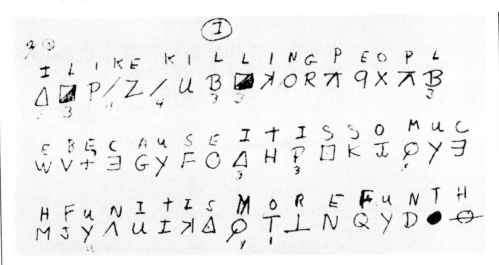

The murder-minded cryptogram Zodiac sent to the San Francisco papers.

tried to jerk free, he rolled her over and methodically stabbed her twenty-three more times.

Leaving the bodies, Zodiac casually strolled to Hartnell's car and scratched out the dates and places of all his killings, including the ones he had just committed. He then strolled away from the picnic site with no more concern for the carnage he had created than someone flipping a cigarette butt into a gutter.

This time, however, he had erred. Hartnell, despite his savage wounds, lived to give a sketchy description of Zodiac. He could not describe the man's face but did state that he was about five feet eight inches in height and overweight. The description was enlarged thirteen days later when Zodiac resurfaced.

The killer got into a San Francisco cab and promptly shot the driver, a part-time college student. He ripped away part of his victim's shirt, no doubt to prove later that he had committed the killing, and raced through a street in Presidio Heights. He was seen fleeing on foot and witnesses later described him as having short reddish hair, perhaps a crew cut, and wearing glasses—an overweight man in his middle twenties.

Police sketches were published in the newspapers and this apparently frightened the killer into inaction. He nevertheless wrote again to the newspapers, threatening to shoot out the tires of some passing school bus on a lonely road and, after thus halting the bus, to shoot the children as they tried to escape. He never kept his gruesome promise. Zodiac did continue to write to the papers—his last letter was received in March 1971—but his murderous activities had ceased. Police felt that he had left the city, had been hospitalized, or was dead. None of these possibilities, given the type of killer Zodiac was, was realistic. Dozens of mass murderers like him in history, from Jack the Ripper to the Texas Strangler [see entries], had struck at random—without reason, without motive. And they had, perhaps like Zodiac, lived beyond the madness that seized their minds and propelled them into murder.

These are the most fearsome kind of killer, seldom caught, the lone slayer who, after satiating himself with murder orgies, somehow snaps back to reality and assumes a normal life-style, unable to think of himself as a dreaded, inhuman monster who has terrorized whole communities.

There is every reason to believe that Zodiac and his horrible predecessors and successors look back upon their own terrible crimes with the strange perspective of manufactured innocence as they make their placid ways through life, maintaining a public posture of common virtue, lying inside respectability, and, at the end, sincerely believing they had nothing whatsoever to do with these hideous deeds reported in the papers those long years ago; *that* was someone else, some strange creature crawling about in the past, their readjusted minds undoubtedly rationalize. And nesting inside this cozy rationalization, the reality of guilt becomes a hazy historical nightmare in which all the lurking slayers are anonymous.

BIBLIOGRAPHY

The research for *Open Files* was done in libraries and archives throughout the United States, in addition to many interviews and lengthy correspondence. Scores of newspapers were used, but these references are too numerous to cite herein. What follows were the most helpful published sources.

BOOKS

Abinger, Edward. *Forty Years at the Bar.* London: Hutchinson, 1930.

Abrahams, Gerald. *According to the Evidence.* London: Cassell, 1958.

Adam, H. L. (ed.). *Trial of George Chapman.* London: William Hodge & Co., 1930.

Adam, Hargrave Lee. *The Police Encyclopedia.* London: Blackfriars Pub. Co., n.d.

———. *C.I.D.* London: Sampson, Low, 1931.

———. *Murder by Persons Unknown.* London: Collins, 1931.

———. *Murder Most Mysterious.* London: Sampson, Low, 1932.

Alexander, Gilchrist. *After Court Hours.* London: Butterworth, 1950.

Alix, Ernest K. *Ransom Kidnapping in America.* Carbondale, Ill.: Southern Illinois Univ. Press, 1978.

Allen, Edward J. *Merchants of Menace—The Mafia.* Springfield, Ill.: Thomas, 1962.

Alverstone, Viscount. *Recollections of Bar and Bench.* London: Arnold, 1914

Anatomy of Murder. London: John Lane, The Bodley Head, 1936.

Anderson, Sir Robert. *The Lighter Side of My Official Life.* London: Hodder and Stoughton, 1910.

Anslinger, Harry J., and Will Oursler. *The Murderers.* New York: Farrar, Straus and Cudahy, 1961.

Archer, Fred. *Ghost Detectives.* London: W. H. Allen, 1970.

Asbury, Herbert. *The Gangs of New York.* New York: Knopf, 1929.

———. *The French Quarter.* New York: Knopf, 1938.

Ashley, F. W. *My Sixty Years in the Law.* London: John Lane, The Bodley Head, 1936.

Ashton-Wolfe, H. *The Underworld.* London: Hurst & Blackett, 1926.

Bibliography

Bancroft, George Pleydell. *Stage and Bar.* London: Faber & Faber, 1939.

Barker, Dudley. *Lord Darling's Famous Cases.* London: Hutchinson, 1936.

Barnard, Allan (ed.). *The Harlot Killer.* New York: Dodd, Mead, 1953.

Bayer, Oliver Weld (ed.). *Cleveland Murders.* New York: Duell, Sloan and Pearce, 1947.

Bell, Edward A. *Those Meddlesome Attorneys.* London: Martin Secker, 1939.

Bell, Quentin. *Virginia Woolf.* London: Hogarth Press, 1972.

Berrett, James. *When I Was at Scotland Yard.* London: Sampson, Low, Marston, 1932.

Besant, Walter. *East London.* Chatto & Windus, 1903.

Bierstadt, Edward Hale. *Enter Murderers!* Garden City, N.Y.: Doubleday, Doran, 1934.

Birkenhead, Lord. *Famous Trials of History.* London: Hutchinson, 1926.

————. *More Famous Trials.* London: Hutchinson, 1928.

Birmingham, George A. [Cannon Hannay]. *Murder Most Foul.* London: Chatto & Windus, 1929.

Bixley, William. *The Guilty and the Innocent.* London: Souvenir Press, 1957.

Bontham, Alan. *Sex Crimes and Sex Criminals.* New York: Wisdom House, 1961.

Borowitz, Albert. *Innocence and Arsenic.* New York: Harper & Row, 1977.

Boswell, Charles, and Lewis Thompson. *The Girl in Lovers Lane.* New York: Fawcett Publications, 1953.

Boucher, Anthony (ed.). *The Quality of Murder.* New York: E. P. Dutton, 1962.

Bowen-Rowlands, Ernest. *In Court and Out of Court.* London: Hutchinson, 1925.

Bowker, A. E. *Behind the Bar.* London: Staples Press, 1947.

Brice, A. H. M. *Look Upon the Prisoner.* London: Hutchinson, 1933.

Brookes, Cannon J. R. *Murder in Fact and Fiction.* London: Hurst & Blackett, 1926.

Browne, Douglas G. *The Rise of Scotland Yard.* New York: G. P. Putnam's Sons.

Browne, Douglas G., and E. V. Tullett. *Bernard Spilsbury: His Life and Cases.* London: Harrap, 1951.

Brynes, Thomas. *Professional Criminals of America.* New York: Cassell, 1886.

Bucknill, Sir Alfred. *The Nature of Evidence.* London: Skeffington, 1953.

Busch, Francis X. *Enemies of the State.* Indianapolis: Bobbs-Merrill, 1954.

Butterfield, Roger. *The American Pest.* New York: Simon and Schuster, 1947.

Canning, John. *50 True Tales of Terror.* New York: Bell, 1972.

Carey, Arthur. *Memoirs of a Murder Man.* Garden City, N.Y.: Doubleday, Doran, 1930.

Carr, John Dickson. *The Life of Sir Arthur Conan Doyle.* New York: Harper & Bros., 1949.

Carr, William H. A. *Hollywood Tragedy.* New York: Fawcett-Crest, 1962.

Casey, Lee (ed.). *Denver Murders.* New York: Duell, Sloan and Pearce, 1947.

Casey, Robert J. *Chicago Medium Rare.* New York: Bobbs-Merrill, 1949.

Caughey, John Walton. *Their Majesties the Mob.* Chicago: Univ. of Chicago Press, 1960.

Childs, Sir Wyndham. *Episodes and Reflections.* London: Cassell, 1930.

Churchill, Allen. *A Pictorial History of American Crime*. New York: Holt, Rinehart & Winston, 1964.

Clarke, Donald Henderson. *In the Reign of Rothstein*. New York: Vanguard Press, 1929.

Clinton, Henry Lauren. *Extraordinary Cases*. New York: Harper & Bros., 1896.

———. *Celebrated Trials*. New York: Harper & Bros., 1897.

Cobb, Belton. *Critical Years at the Yard*. London: Faber & Faber, 1956.

Cohen, Louis H. *Murder, Madness and the Law*. New York: World Publishing Co., 1952.

Cohen, Sam D. *100 True Crime Stories*. New York: World Publishing Co., 1946.

Colby, Robert. *The California Crime Book*. New York: Pyramid Books.

Collins, Frederick L. *Glamorous Sinners*. New York: Long and Smith, 1932.

Collins, Ted (ed.). *New York Murders*. New York: Duell, Sloan and Pearce, 1944.

Corder, Eric (ed.). *Murder My Love*. Chicago: Playboy Press, 1973.

Crane, Milton (ed.). *Sins of New York*. New York: Boni & Gaer, 1947.

Crew, Albert. *The Old Bailey*. London: Ivor Nicholson & Watson, 1933.

Crouse, Russel. *Murder Won't Out*. Garden City, N.Y.: Doubleday, Doran, 1932.

———. *Twelve Unsolved New York Murders*. Garden City, N.Y.: Doubleday, Doran, 1936.

Cullen, Tom. *Autumn of Terror*. London: Bodley Head, 1965.

Curtin, Philip (Marie Belloc-Lowndes). *Noted Murder Mysteries*. London: Simpkin Marshall, Hamilton, Kent, 1914.

Davison, M. H. Armstrong. *The Casket Letters*. Washington, D.C.: Univ. of Washington Press, 1965.

Deans, R. Storry. *Notable Trials: Difficult Cases*. London: Chapman & Hall, 1932.

Dearden, Harold. *The Mind of the Murderer*. London: Geoffrey Bles, 1930.

———. *Some Cases of Sir Bernard Spilsbury and Others*. London: Hutchinson, 1934.

———. *Aspects of Murder*. London: Staples Press, 1951.

de Ford, Miriam Allen. *Murderers Sane and Mad*. New York: Abelard-Schuman, 1965.

De La Torre, Lillian. *Villainy Detected*. New York: Appleton-Century, 1947.

Dilnot, George. *Celebrated Crimes*. London: Stanley Paul & Co. Ltd., 1925.

———. *Triumphs of Detection*. London: Geoffrey Bles, 1929.

Douthwaite, L. C. *Mass Murder*. New York: Holt, 1929.

Duke, Thomas S. *Celebrated Cases of America*. San Francisco: James H. Barry, 1910.

Duke, Winifred. *Six Trials*. London: Gollancz, 1934.

DuRose, John. *Murder Was My Business*. London: W. H. Allen, 1971.

Ensor, David. *I Was a Public Prosecutor*. London: Robert Hale, 1958.

Fabian, Robert. *Fabian of the Yard*. London: Naldrett Press, 1950.

Farson, Dan. *Jack the Ripper*. London: Michael Joseph, 1972.

Bibliography

Fatal Fascination. Boston: Little, Brown, 1964.

Firmin, Stanley. *Scotland Yard: The Inside Story.* London: Hutchinson, 1948.

———. *Murderers in Our Midst.* London: Hutchinson, 1955.

Fordham, Edward Wilfred. *Notable Cross-Examinations.* London: Constable, 1951.

Fosdick, Raymond B. *American Police Systems.* New York: Century, 1920.

Franklin, Charles. *Woman in the Case.* New York: Taplinger, 1963.

Giesler, Jerry, as told to Pete Martin. *The Jerry Giesler Story.* New York: Simon and Schuster, 1960.

Giles, F. T. *The Criminal Law.* London: Penguin Books, 1954.

Godwin, John. *Killers Unknown.* London: Herbert Jenkins, 1960.

Gollomb, J. *Crimes of the Year.* New York: Liveright, 1931.

Gollomb, Joseph. *Master Highwaymen.* New York: Macaulay, 1927.

Goodman, Jonathan. *The Killing of Julia Wallace.* New York: Scribner's, 1969.

———. *The Burning of Evelyn Foster.* New York: Scribner's, 1977.

Goodwin, John G. *Insanity and the Criminal.* London: Hutchinson, 1923.

Graham, Evelyn. *Fifty Years of Famous Judges.* London: John Long, 1930.

Greenwood, William. *Guilty or Not Guilty.* London: Hutchinson, 1931.

Gribble, Leonard. *Famous Manhunts.* London: John Long, 1953.

———. *Adventures in Murder.* London: John Long, 1954.

———. *Famous Judges and Their Trials.* London: John Long, 1957.

———. *Murders Most Strange.* London: John Long, 1959.

Griffiths, Major Arthur. *Mysteries of Police and Crime.* London: Cassell, 1898.

Hammer, Alvin C. (ed.). *Detroit Murders.* New York: Duell, Sloan and Pearce, 1948.

Harlow, Alvin. *Murders Not Quite Solved.* New York: Julian Messner, 1938.

Harrison, Michael. *Clarence.* London: W. H. Allen, 1972.

Harrison, Richard. *Whitehall 1212: The Story of the Police of London.* London: Jarold, 1947.

———. *Criminal Calendar.* London: Jarold, 1951.

Hastings, Sir Patrick. *Cases in Court.* London: Heinemann, 1949.

Higham, Charles. *The Adventures of Conan Doyle.* New York: W. W. Norton, 1976.

Hodge, Harry (ed.). *Penguin Famous Trials* (Vols. I–IV). London: Penguin Books, 1948.

Holyroyd, James Edward. *The Gaslight Murders.* London: Allen & Unwin, 1960.

Hoover, J. Edgar. *Persons in Hiding.* Boston: Little, Brown, 1938.

Hopkins, R. Thurston. *Life and Death at the Old Bailey.* London: Herbert Jenkins, 1935.

Horan, James D. *The Desperate Years.* New York: Crown, 1962.

House, Brant (ed.). *Crimes That Shocked America.* New York: Ace Books, 1961.

Howgrave-Graham, H. M. *Light and Shade at Scotland Yard.* London: John Murray, 1947.

Humphreys, Sir Travers. *Criminal Days.* London: Hodder & Stoughton, 1946.

————. *A Book of Trials*. London: Heinemann, 1953.

Hyde, E. Montgomery. *Cases That Changed the Law*. London: Heinemann, 1951.

Irving, H. B. *A Book of Remarkable Criminals*. New York: Doran, 1918.

Jackson, Joseph Henry (ed.). *San Francisco Murders*. New York: Duell, Sloan and Pearce, 1947.

Jacobs, T. C. H. *Cavalcade of Murder*. London: Stanley Paul, 1955.

————. *Aspects of Murder*. London: Stanley Paul, 1956.

————. *Pageant of Murder*. London: Stanley Paul, 1956.

Jennings, Dean. *We Only Kill Each Other*. Englewood Cliffs, N.J.: Prentice-Hall, 1968.

Jesse, F. Tennyson. *Comments on Cain*. London: Heinemann, 1948.

Jonas, George, and Barbara Amiel. *The Strange Death of Christine Demeter*. Toronto: Macmillan, 1977.

Jones, Gareth Stedman. *Outcast*. London: Clarendon Press, 1971.

Joyce, James Avery. *Justice at Work*. London: Chapman and Hall, 1952.

Katcher, Leo. *The Big Bankroll*. New York: Harper & Bros., 1958.

Kelly, Alexander. *Jack the Ripper*. London: Assoc. of Asst. Librarians, 1973.

Kershaw, Alister. *Murder in France*. London: Constable, 1955.

Kingston, Charles. *Dramatic Days at the Old Bailey*. London: Stanley Paul, 1923.

————. *Famous Judges and Famous Trials*. London: Stanley Paul, 1923.

————. *The Judges and the Judged*. London: John Lane, The Bodley Head, 1926.

Kobler, John. *Some Like It Gory*. New York: Dodd, Mead, 1940.

Kunstler, William. *The Minister and the Choir Singer*. New York: William Morrow, 1964.

Lambert, R. S. *When Justice Faltered*. London: Methuen, 1935.

Lambton, Arthur. *Echoes of Cause Célèbres*. London: Hurst and Blackett, n.d.

Lang, Rev. Gordon. *Mr. Justice Avory*. London: Herbert Jenkins, 1935.

Laurence, John A. *Extraordinary Crimes*. London: Sampson, Low, 1931.

Lawes, L. E. *Meet the Murderer!* New York: Harper & Bros., 1940.

Lawson, John D. *American State Trials*. St. Louis: F. H. Thomas Law Book Co., 1914.

LeAveux, William. *Things I Know About Kings, Celebrities and Crooks*. London: Everleigh, Nash & Grayson, 1923.

LeBrun, George P. *Call Me If It's Murder*. New York: William Morrow, 1962.

Leeson, Benjamin. *Lost London*. London: Stanley Paul, 1934.

Lefebure, Molly. *Evidence for the Crown*. London: Heinemann, 1935.

————. *Murder with a Difference*. London: Heinemann, 1958.

Leighton, Isabel. (ed.). *The Aspirin Age 1919–1941*. New York: Simon and Schuster, 1949.

Bibliography

Lewis, Alfred Henry. *Nation-Famous New York Murders*. New York: G. W. Dillingham, 1914.

Logan, Guy. *Great Murder Mysteries*. London: Stanley Paul, 1931.

Lustgarden, Edgar. *Verdict in Dispute*. London: Wingate, 1949.

———. *Defender's Triumph*. London: Wingate, 1951.

———. *Prisoner at the Bar*. London: Andre Deutsch, 1951.

———. *The Woman in the Case*. London: Andre Deutsch, 1955.

———. *The Murder and the Trial*. New York: Scribner's, 1958.

Macardle, Dorothy. *The Irish Republic*. New York: Farrar, Straus and Giroux, 1965.

McCormick, Donald. *Murder by Witchcraft*. London: John Long, 1968.

———. *The Identity of Jack the Ripper*. London: Arrow Books, 1970.

Machlin, Milt. *Libby*. New York: Tower, 1980.

MacKaye, M. A. *Dramatic Crimes of 1927*. New York: Crime Club, 1928.

MacKenzie, Frederick A. *Twentieth-Century Crimes*. Boston: Little, Brown, 1927.

Macnaghten, Sir Melville. *Days of My Years*. London: Edward Arnold, 1914.

Magnus, Philip. *King Edward the Seventh*. London: John Murray, 1964.

Maine, C. E. *The World's Strangest Crimes*. New York: Hart, 1967.

Marcus, Steven. *The Other Victorians*. London: Weidenfeld and Nicholson, 1966.

Marjoribanks, Edward. *The Life of Sir Edward Marshall Hall*. London: Gollancz, 1926.

Marten, Manuel Edward. *The Doctor Looks at Murder*. Garden City, N.Y.: Doubleday, Doran, 1937.

Martienssen, Anthony. *Crime and the Police*. London: Martin Secker & Warbury, 1951.

Martin, John. *Butcher's Dozen and Other Murders*. New York: Harper & Row, 1950.

Mathew, Theobald. *For Lawyers and Others*. London: William Hodge, 1937.

Matters, Leonard. *The Mystery of Jack the Ripper*. London: W. H. Allen, 1948.

Mellwain, David. *The Bizarre and the Bloody*. London: Hart, 1972.

Minot, G. E. *Murder Will Out*. Boston: Marshall Jones, 1928.

Mitchell, C. Ainsworth. *Science and the Criminal*. London: Pitman, 1911.

Morain, Alfred. *The Underworld of Paris*. New York: Blue Ribbon Books, 1931.

Moreland, Nigel. *Hangman's Clutch*. London: Werner Laurie, 1954.

———. *Background to Murder*. London: Werner Laurie, 1955.

———. *Science in Crime Detection*. London: Robert Hale, 1958.

Nash, Jay Robert. *Bloodletters and Badmen: A Narrative Encyclopedia of American Criminals from the Pilgrims to the Present*. New York: M. Evans, 1973.

———. *Among the Missing*. New York: Simon and Schuster, 1978.

———. *Murder America*. New York: Doubleday, 1981.

———. *Almanac of World Crime*. New York: Doubleday, 1981.

———. *Look for the Woman*. New York: M. Evans, 1981.

O'Brien, Frank M. *Murder Mysteries of New York.* New York: W. F. Payson, 1932.

Oddie, S. Ingleby. *Inquest.* London: Hutchinson, 1941.

Odell, Robin. *Jack the Ripper in Fact and Fiction.* London: Harrap, 1965.

O'Donnell, Bernard. *Great Thames Mysteries.* London: Selwyn and Blount, 1929.

———. *The Trials of Mr. Justice Avory.* London: Rich & Cowan, 1935.

———. *The Old Bailey and Its Trials.* London: Clerke & Cocheran, 1950.

———. *Crimes That Made News.* London: Burke, 1954.

———. *Should Women Hang?* London: W. H. Allen, 1956.

———. *The World's Strangest Murders.* London: Frederick Muller, 1957.

Parminter, Geoffrey de C. *Reasonable Doubt.* London: Arthur Baker, 1938.

Parry, Dr. Leonard. *Some Famous Medical Trials.* London: Churchill, 1927.

Partridge, Ralph. *Broadmoor.* London: Chatto & Windus, 1953.

Pasley, Fred D. *Al Capone.* New York: Washburn, 1930.

Pearce, Charles. *Unsolved Murder Mysteries.* New York: Stokes, 1924.

Pearson, Edmund Lester. *Studies in Murder.* New York: Garden City Publishing Co., 1924.

———. *Five Murders, with a Final Note on the Borden Case.* New York: Crime Club, 1928.

———. *Instigation of the Devil.* New York: Scribner's, 1930.

———. *More Studies in Murder.* New York: Smith & Haas, 1936.

Pinkerton, Matthew Worth. *Murder in All Ages.* Chicago: A. E. Pinkerson & Co., 1898.

Platnick, Kenneth. *Great Mysteries of History.* New York: Stackpole, 1971.

Playfair, Giles, and Derrick Sington. *The Offenders.* London: Secker & Warburg, 1957.

Purvis, James. *Great Unsolved Mysteries.* New York: Grosset & Dunlap, 1978.

Quinby, Ione. *Murder for Love.* New York: Covici, 1931.

Radin, Edward D. *12 Against Crime.* New York: G. P. Putnam's Sons, 1950.

Reid, Ed. *Mafia.* New York: Random House, 1952.

Reik, T. *Myth and Guilt.* New York: Braziller, 1957.

Remarkable Trials of All Countries. New York: Peloubet, 1882.

Reynolds, Ruth. *Murder 'Round the World.* New York: Justice Books, 1953.

Rhodes, Henry T. F. *Clues and Crime.* London: John Murray, 1933.

———. *In the Tracks of Crime.* London: Turnstile Press, 1952.

Roughead, William. *Malice Domestic.* London: Green, 1928.

———. *Rogues Walk Here.* London: Cassell, 1934.

———. *Mainly Murder.* London: Cassell, 1937.

———. *Classic Crimes.* London: Cassell, 1951.

Rowan, David. *Famous American Crimes.* London: Muller, 1957.

Bibliography

Rowan, Richard Wilmer, with Robert G. Deindorfer. *Secret Service: 33 Centuries of Espionage*. New York: Hawthorn Books, 1967.

Rowland, John. *Murder by Persons Unknown*. London: Mellifont Press, 1941.

———. *The Wallace Case*. London: Carroll & Nicholson, 1949.

———. *A Century of Murder*. London: Home & Van Thal, 1950.

———. *Criminal Files*. London: Arco, 1957.

Rumbelow, Donald. *The Complete Jack the Ripper*. England: W. H. Allen, 1975.

Runyon, Damon. *Trials and Other Tribulations*. New York: Lippincott, 1926.

Russell, Donn (ed.). *Best Murder Cases*. London: Faber & Faber, 1958.

———. *Lizzie Borden, The Untold Story*. New York: Simon and Schuster, 1961.

Sandoe, James (ed.). *Murder: Plain and Fanciful*. New York: Sheridan, 1948.

Sann, Paul. *The Lawless Decade*. New York: Crown, 1957.

Sapte, W. *A Century's Sensations*. London: John Barker, n.d.

Scott, Sir Harold. *Scotland Yard*. London: Andre Deutsch, 1954.

Shew, E. Spencer. *A Companion to Murder*. New York: Knopf, 1960.

———. *A Second Companion to Murder*. New York: Knopf, 1961.

Shore, W. T. (ed.). *Trial of Thomas Neill Cream*. London: Hodge, 1923.

Simpson, Helen. *The Anatomy of Murder*. New York: Macmillan, 1934.

Sinclair, Andrew. *Era of Excess*. New York: Harper & Row, 1964.

Singer, Kurt (ed.). *My Strangest Cases*. Garden City, N.Y.: Doubleday, 1958.

Slesser, Sir Henry. *Judgement Reserved*. London: Hutchinson, 1941.

Smith, Edward Henry. *Famous American Poison Mysteries*. New York: Dial Press, 1927.

Smith, Sir Henry. *From Constable to Commissioner*. London: Chatto & Windus, 1910.

Smith-Hughes, Jack. *Unfair Comment*. London: Cassell, 1951.

Sondern, Frederic, Jr. *Brotherhood of Evil: The Mafia*. New York: Farrar, Straus & Cudahy, 1959.

Sparrow, Judge Gerald. *Murder Parade*. London: Robert Hale, 1957.

Spiering, Frank. *Prince Jack*. New York: Doubleday, 1978.

Stevens, C. L. McCluer. *Famous Crimes and Criminals*. London: Stanley Paul, 1924.

Stewart, William. *Jack the Ripper*. London: Quality Press, 1939.

Strange and Mysterious Crimes. New York: MacFadden Publications, 1929.

Sullivan, Edward Dean. *Rattling the Cup on Chicago Crime*. New York: Vanguard, 1929.

Sullivan, Mark. *Our Times* (Vols. I–VI), 1926–32.

Sutton, Charles Warden. *The New York Tombs: Its Secrets and Mysteries*. New York: n.p., 1974.

Symons, Julian. *A Pictorial History of Crime*. New York: Crown, 1966.

Tallant, Robert. *Murder in New Orleans*. London: Kimber, 1952.

Tanner, Louise. *All the Things We Were*. Garden City, N.Y.: Doubleday, 1968.

Templewood, Viscount. *The Shadow of the Gallows*. London: Gollancz, 1951.

Thompson, Sir Basil. *The Criminal*. London: Hodder & Stoughton, 1925.

———. *The Story of Scotland Yard*. London: Grayson & Grayson, 1925.

Thompson, Craig, and Allen Raymond. *Gang Rule in New York*. New York: Dial, 1940.

Thomson, C. J. S. *Poison Mysteries Unsolved*. London: Hutchinson, 1937.

Thorpe, Arthur. *Calling Scotland Yard*. London: Wingate, 1954.

Thurston, Gavin. *Coroner's Practice*. London: Butterworth, 1958.

Triplett, Col. Frank. *History, Romance and Philosophy of Great American Crimes and Criminals*. Hartford, Conn.: Park Publishing Co., 1885.

Van Every, Edward. *Sins of New York*. New York: Stokes, 1930.

Villiers, Elizabeth. *Riddles of Crime*. London: Werner Laurie, 1928.

Walbrook, H. M. *Detective Days*. London: Cassell, 1931.

———. *Murders and Murder Trials, 1812–1912*. London: Constable, 1932.

Walker-Smith, Derek. *The Life of Mr. Justice Darling*. London: Cassell, 1938.

Webb, Duncan. *Crime Is My Business*. London: Muller, 1953.

Wellman, Francis L. *The Art of Cross-Examination*. New York: Macmillan, 1903.

Wellman, Manly Wade. *Dead and Gone*. Chapel Hill: Univ. of North Carolina Press, 1955.

Wensley, Frederick Porter. *Forty Years of Scotland Yard*. New York: Garden City Publishing Co., 1930.

Whitelaw, David. *Corpus Delicti*. London: Geoffrey Bles, 1936.

Williams, Jack K. *Vogues in Villainy*. Columbia: Univ. of South Carolina Press, 1959.

Williams, Watkin W. *The Life of General Sir Charles Warren*. Oxford: Basil Blackwell, 1941.

Wilson, Colin, and Patricia Pitman. *A Casebook of Murder*. New York: Cowles, 1969.

———. *The Encyclopedia of Murder*. New York: G. P. Putnam's Sons, 1961.

Wood, Walter. *Survivor's Tales of Famous Crimes*. London: Cassell, 1916.

Woollcott, Alexander. *While Rome Burns*. New York: Grosset & Dunlap, 1934.

Wright, Selwell Peaslee (ed.). *Chicago Murders*. New York: Duell, Sloan & Pearce, 1945.

Wyndham, Horace. *Famous Trials Re-told*. London: Hutchinson, n.d.

Wyndham-Brown, W. F. *The Trial of Herbert Wallace*. London: Gollancz, 1933.

Young, Hugh. *My Forty Years at the Yard*. London: W. H. Allen, 1956.

PERIODICALS

(Includes Bulletins, Documents, Pamphlets, and Reports)

Anderson, Robert T. "From Mafia to Casa Nostra." *American Journal of Sociology*, November 1965.

Asbury, Herbert. "Days of Wickedness." *American Mercury*, November 1927.

Banay, R. S. "Study in Murder." *Annals of the American Academy of Political Science*, 284, 1951.

Barnhart, K. E. "A Study of Homicide in the United States." *Birmingham-Southern College Bulletin*, 5:25, 1932.

Bell, Daniel. "Crime as an American Way of Life." *Antioch Review*, June 1942.

The Borden Trial (Pamphlet). Boston: H. K. Gratteau. n.d.

Brearley, H. C., and W. Soagle. "How Often We Murder and Why: A Review of Homicide in the U.S." *The Nation*, May 25, 1932.

Brewer, John Francis. *The Curse upon Mitre Square, 1530–1888* (Pamphlet). London: Simkin, Marshall, 1888.

A Brief Narrative of the Trial for the Bloody and Mysterious Murder of the Unfortunate Young Woman in the Famous Manhattan Well (Pamphlet—Sands case). N.p., n.d.

Carpenter, A. "Pattern for Murder." *Science Digest*. June 1947.

Carson, Charles. "One Underworld." *Author and Journalist*, November 1945.

"Chicago's Great Bank Heist." *Time*, November 28, 1977.

Davis, Judge Charles G. *The Conduct of the Law in the Borden Case* (Pamphlet). *Boston Daily Advertiser*, 1894.

"The East End Murders: Detailed Lessons." *British Medical Journal*, October 6, 1888.

Ennis, Phillip. "Crimes, Victims and the Police." *Transaction*, June 1962.

Fox, Richard Kyle. *The History of the Whitechapel Murders: A Full and Authentic Narrative* (Pamphlet). New York: Fox, 1888.

Goldberg, H. "Crimes of Darkness." *Cosmopolitan*, April 1959.

Grinnell, C. E. "Modern Murder Trials and Newspapers." *Atlantic Monthly*, November 1901.

Hardie, James. *An Impartial Account of the Trial of Mr. Levi Weeks for the Supposed Murder of Miss Julianna Elmore Sands* (Pamphlet). New York: M'Farlane, 1800.

Hayne, W. T. *Jack the Ripper, or The Crimes of London* (Pamphlet). Self-pub., 1889.

Hoffman, F. L. "Murder and the Death Penalty." *Current History*, June 1928.

Howe, William F. "Some Notable Murder Cases." *Cosmopolitan*, August 1900.

"Increase of Lawlessness in the United States." *McClure's*, December 1904.

Jarman, Rufus. "The Pinkerton Story" (series). *The Saturday Evening Post*, May 15, 22, 29, and June 5, 1948.

Langberg, R. "Homicide in the United States." *Vital Health Statistics*, 20, 1967.

Lombroso, C. "Why Homicide Has Increased in the United States." *North American Review*, December 1897 and January 1898.

Lundy, Todd. *Mystery Unveiled: The Truth About the Borden Tragedy* (Pamphlet). Providence: J. A. & R. A. Reid, 1893.

"Lust for Blood as an Incentive to Murder." *Current Literature*, August 1909.

Manchester, William. "Murder Tour of New England." *Holiday*, May 1961.

Martin, John Bartlow. "Who Killed Estelle Carey?" *Harper's Magazine*, June 1944.

Maynard, L. M. "Murder in the Making." *American Mercury*, June 1929.

"Millions and Murder." *Literary Digest*, July 31, 1915.

"Murder Mysteries." *The Survey*, May 15, 1932.

The Murder of Sir Harry Oakes. *Nassau Daily Tribune*, 1959.

"Murderous Maniacs at Large." *Literary Digest*, September 15, 1935.

"Murders by Poison." *Harper's Weekly*, November 8, 1902.

"The New Jersey Killings." *Time*, March 22, 1976.

O'Neil, Paul. "The Great Mail Robbery." *Life*, September 8, 1962.

Palmer, G. "Crimes Against Children." *Literary Digest*, October 2, 1937.

Pearson, Edmund. "Perfect Murder." *Scribner's Magazine*, July 1937.

Report of the Trial of Levi Weeks. New York: John Furman, 1800.

"Robbery and Murder." *The Outlook*, November 28, 1923.

Robinson, Archie. "Murder Most Foul." *American Heritage*, August 1964.

Periodicals

"Sentimentality in Murder Trials." *Review of Reviews*, November 1908.

Shaw, George Bernard. "Blood Money for Whitechapel." *The Star*, September 24, 1888.

Shipley, M. "Crimes of Violence in Chicago and in Greater New York." *Review of Reviews*, September 1908.

Sitwell, Osbert. "New York in the Twenties." *Atlantic*, February 1962.

Stearns, A. W. "Homicide in Massachusetts." *American Journal of Psychiatry*, 4:725, 1932.

Teale, E. "Is It Murder?" *Popular Science*, September 1940.

"Unnatural Causes." *Newsweek*, September 1, 1975.

Vallee, Walter, and Robert McNear. "The Night Chief." *Chicago Tribune Magazine*, April 20, 1980.

Wakefield, E. "Brand of Cain in the Great Republic." *Living Age*, January 2, 1892.

Waldron, E. "Murder Tour of the Midwest." *Holiday*, August 1961.

Wigmore, John H. "The Borden Case." *The American Law Review*, November–December 1893.

"Who Is the Real Murderer?" *Literary Digest*, December 15, 1931.

INDEX

293

Index

Index

296

BOOKS BY JAY ROBERT NASH

Fiction
On All Fronts
A Crime Story
The Dark Fountain

Nonfiction
Dillinger: Dead or Alive?
Citizen Hoover: A Critical Study of J. Edgar
    Hoover and His FBI
Bloodletters and Badmen: A Narrative Encyclope-
    dia of American Criminals from the Pilgrims to
    the Present
Hustlers and Con Men: An Anecdotal History of
    the Confidence Man and His Games
Darkest Hours: A Narrative Encyclopedia of
    Worldwide Disasters from Ancient Times to
    the Present
Among the Missing: An Anecdotal History of
    Missing Persons from 1800 to the Present
Murder, America: Homicide in the United States
    from the Revolution to the Present
Almanac of World Crime
Look for the Woman: A Narrative Encyclopedia
    of Female Criminals from Elizabethan Times to
    the Present
People to See: An Anecdotal History of Chicago's
    Makers and Breakers
The True Crime Quiz Book
Zanies: The World's Greatest Eccentrics
The Innovators: Sixteen Portraits of the Famous
    and the Infamous
Murder Among the Mighty: Celebrity Slayings
    That Shocked America
The Crime Movie Quiz Book